SP Pvt. Ltd.

# Panchayati Raj in India
## *Theory and Practice*

*by*
**Rajesh Kumar Sinha**

**2020**

Pvt Ltd

**Studium Press (India) Pvt. Ltd.**

# Panchayati Raj in India
## *Theory and Practice*



ISBN: 978-93-85046-64-3

*Published by*:

**Studium Press (India) Pvt. Ltd.**
*4735/22, 2nd Floor, Prakash Deep Building*
*(Near Delhi Medical Association)*
*Ansari Road, Darya Ganj, New Delhi-110 002*
*Tel.: + 91-11-43240200-15 (15 lines); Fax: 91-11-43240215*
*E-mail: pubdir@studiumpress.in*

*Printed at India*

# About the Editor

**Dr. Rajesh Kumar Sinha** is working as Assistant Professor with the National Institute of Rural Development and Panchayati Raj (NIRDPR) Hyderabad, an apex autonomous institute under the Ministry of Rural Development, Government of India. He is a development professional with more than 19 years of experience in scheme/ project planning, monitoring and implementation in multilateral, government and non-government institutions. He holds a Ph.D. degree from Jawaharlal Nehru University (JNU), New Delhi with UGC Senior Research Fellowship in Public Administration. His research interests lie in rural local governance, rural development, social audit, social accountability, disaster management and capacity building. He has worked with United Nations Development Programme (UNDP), Ministry of Panchayati Raj, Government of India, Society for Participatory Research in Asia (PRIA), India Development and Relief Fund (IDRF) in the past. He has also been volunteering for social causes and is on boards of two reputed social service organisations, AADHAR and ADIG. He has co-authored two books, edited three books and has contributed several articles in books and reputed journals.

# Preface and Acknowledgements

Panchayati Raj system, although a part of Indian history and tradition, has been given a constitutional framework through the $73^{rd}$ Constitutional Amendment Act, 1992 which came into force on $24^{th}$ April 1993. This Amendment was a milestone in Indian democracy in more than one senses. It not only provided a legal status to Gram Sabha as an institution of direct democracy where every member can take part in the decision-making process but also ensured inclusion of marginalized sections of the society such as women, Scheduled Castes (SCs) and Scheduled Tribes (STs) in the leadership positions in Panchayats. Today approximately 46 percent of elected representatives in Panchayats are women.

Twenty-five years have passed since the $73^{rd}$ CAA came into force. Quarter century is good enough a time to take stock of the achievements and challenges Panchayati Raj system in India. It is noticed that although the basic structure of Panchayati Raj system remains same across the country as envisaged by the $73^{rd}$ CAA, there are variations across the country in the size, infrastructure, human resources, power and functions of Panchayats. Varied educational, social and economic status of States also have an impact on the leadership abilities of elected representatives of Panchayats.

Through various articles based on theoretical analysis, empiral study and field experiences written by academicians and practioners, this book tries to understand the journey of rural decentralization in India, the journey full of achievements and challenges. The book also tries to prescribe practical solutions to key challenges being faced by Panchayati Raj system. This book will be useful to policy makers and students of decentralized rural governance in India.

I acknowledge my appreciation to all the chapter contributors, to the Publisher and to to my family members without whose cooperation this volume would not have seen the light of the day. I would also like to extend my acknowledgement to my present and previous colleagues and employers.

September 2019 **Dr. Rajesh Kumar Sinha**

# Table of Contents

# Introduction

Rajesh Kumar Sinha[1]

Panchayats or similar institutions have been part of Indian society since ancient times. There are references of institutions like 'Gana' and 'Sangha' in Mahabharata. In Chola Empire, village assembly was called 'Ur'. During British rule too, such institutions existed. For example through Lord Rippon's resolution in 1882, two tier Rural Boards were created. During movement for freedom struggle, Mahatma Gandhi advocated for self-dependent village republic based 'Gram Swarajya'. Debate continued in the Constituent Assembly. The original Constitution of India included Gram Panchayats in the Article 40 which is part of the Directive Principles of State Policy. The Article says that "State shall take steps to organize village Panchayats and endow them with such powers and authority as may be necessary to enable to function as units of self-government." Schedule 7 of the Constitution placed Panchayats as part of State list. However, post independence thrust on centrally planned development initially ignored Panchayats. However, failure of Community Development Proramme launched in 1952 led to realization of importance of community participation and Panchayats were seen as a platform to facilitate the same. On recommendations of Balwant Rai Mehta Committee in 1959, Panchayats were established first in Rajasthan on October 2, 1959 and later by mid 1960s most of States also set up three-tier Panchayats. However, initial enthusiasm died down and except few, most State governments did not empower these

[1] National Institute of Rural Development and Panchayati Raj, Hyderabad.
*Corresponding author*: E-mail: rajeshksinha@gmail.com

Panchayats. In many States Panchayats got dissolved premature and elections were not held for long time. Since then till 1993, various committees including Ashok Mehta Committee (1978), GVK Rao Committee (1985), LM Singhvi Committee (1986) made recommendations for reviving Panchayats. After a failed attempt through introduction of 64$^{th}$ Constitutional Amendment Bill in 1989, finally in 1993, Part IX was inserted into the Constitution of India through 73$^{rd}$ Constitutional Amendment Act (73$^{rd}$ CAA) which provided a minimum common framework for Panchayats to be adhered by all States. This was a turning point in the history of rural decentralization in India.

The 73$^{rd}$ CAA for the first time accorded constitutional status to three-tier Panchayati Raj system in India. It prescribed to all States, except States having population less than twenty lakhs, to set up Panchyats at district, intermediate (block) and village levels. It also made provision for a Gram Sabha for every Gram Panchayat which is assembly of all registered voters residing in that Gram Panchayat. These three-tier Panchayats were given fix tenure of five years and if dissolved earlier, election would be conducted within six months of dissolution. This way the 73$^{rd}$ CAA provided a certainty of tenure to Panchayats which was missing earlier. Members of all three-tiers of Panchayats are elected directly while chairpersons of district and intermediate Panchayats are to be elected by and from among elected members. It was left upon States to delineate process of election of chairperson of village level panchayats. For conduct and supervision of elections, it provided for setting up of State Election Commission. To study financial status of Panchayts and recommend distribution of revenue between State governments and Panchayats, the 73$^{rd}$ CAA provided for setting up of State Finance Commission every fifth year. Delineating powers and functions of Panchayats, the Act says that State legislatures may empower Panchayats to function as institutions of local self-government so that they prepare plans for and implement schemes for economic development and social justice on 29 matters listed under Eleventh Schedule of the Constitution of India. Another revolutionary feature is the provision of minimum one-third reservation of seats and office of chairpersons for women and provision of similar reservation for Scheduled Castes and Scheduled Tribes according to their proportion the total population. Nineteen States have gone beyond one-third and have increased reservation for women in Panchayats to fifty percent. Reservation for Other Backward Castes has been left to States to decide. In subsequent years, all States have passed their respective State Panchayati Raj Acts in conformity to 73rd CAA. However, nomenclature, powers and functions of Panchayats vary across States. Regular elections of Panchayats, certainty of tenure, entry of large number of women and SCs and STs in position of power, mass political education, and increased people's participation in decision making are among the key achievements of 73rd CAA. Today there are approximately 2.5 lakh Panchayats in India covering all States and UTs except Meghalaya, Mizoram, Nagaland and other Sixth Schedule areas where Part IX does not apply. Sixth schedule areas are governed by Autonomous District Councils and Village Councils. There are approximately 31 lakh elected representatives of Panchayats. Out of these, 46 percent elected representatives are women. Later, in 1996, the provisions of Panchayats (Extension to the Scheduled Areas) Act popularly called PESA Act, was passed for fifth schedule areas of ten states for ensuring self-governance by tribal community as per their traditions and customs. Through this Act Panchayats were extended to fifth schedule areas with certain exemptions and modifications. PESA Act provides for constitution of Gram Sabha for every village and empowers Gram Sabha to preserve tribal identity, protect tribals from exploitation and manage natural resources. Village can be constituted at habitation or group of habitation level and hamlet or group of hamlet level which are smaller than revenue village in case of non-scheduled areas.

Panchayats have key role in attaining rural development through effective planning, implementing, monitoring and social audit. Several flagship central and State schemes have assigned central role to Panchayts. For example, Mahatma Gandhi National Rural Employment Guarantee Act (MGNREGA) has made Panchayats principal authority and provided that minimum fiffty percent of works will be implemented by Gram Panchayats.

Leadership of Panchayats, particularly Gram Panchayats, can make lot of difference in rural areas. We have seen turnaround of Hiware Bazaar, Ralegan Siddhi, Digambarpur, Gangadevipalli and many more Gram Panchayats through positive interventions of elected representatives and functionaries of Panchayats. Realising this, Government of India has been investing in Panchayats through their capacity building under Rashtriya Gram Swaraj Abhiyan (RGSA). Financial devolution to Panchayats have also increased over the years. As per the recommendations of Fourteenth Finance Commission (FFC), Government of India is to provide total Rs. 200,292.20 cr. to Gram Panchayats during five year period between 2015-20, which is a quantum jump from earlier. This grant is being utilized for basic civic services such as drinking water, drainage, streetlights etc. to improve quality of life in rural areas. Nation today is looking towards Panchayats in attainment of sustainable development goals such as no poverty, zero hunger, quality education, good health, gender equality, safe drinking water and sanitation, clean and affordable energy, decent employment, combating climate change, protecting eco-system etc. and national commitments of housing for all, doubling of farmer's income, electricity to every house, all weather connectivity to all habitations, good governance etc. These can only be achieved when Panchayats demonstrate their effective leadership in convergent participatory planning, efficient implementation of schemes/ programmes and regular monitoring of public institutions and functionaries. Recent thrust of the Government of India on convergent Gram Panchayat Development Planning (GPDP) utilizing Mission Antyodaya and Socio-Economic Caste Census (SECC) data, PRI-SHGs convergence, local economic development through Panchayats are right steps in this direction.

Despite such an important role in rural development, Panchayats are facing several bottlenecks. Although most of the State Panchayati Raj Acts have assigned all the 29 subjects listed under Eleventh Schedule to Panchayats, these subjects have not been actually devolved to Panchayats at the appropriate level based on activity mapping. In most of the centrally sponsored schemes, except a few such as MGNREGA, Panchayats have limited role of beneficiary selection and monitoring. These schemes have also created several parallel bodies which undermines the authority of Panchayats. These Panchayats do not have sufficient number of functionaries. In several states one Gram Panchayat Secretary is in-charge of many Gram Panchayats. Most of the Panchayats do not have accounting and technical staff. Line department frontline functionaries are not accountable to and do not report to Panchayats. They are still under the control of departmental officers. Except a few States, Panchayats are still dependent on central and State governments for funds which seriously affects their identity as institutions of local self-government. These central and State funds are mostly tied and do not give freedom to Panchayats to spend according to their felt needs. Panchayats are lacking political will and capacity to collect own tax and non-tax revenue. Inadequate infrastructure such as lack of own office building, poor internet connectivity, inadequate office equipments makes it difficult for them to function. According to one estimate, approximately twenty percent Panchayats do not have their own building and operate from residence of chairpersons. Inadequate capacity, confidence and motivation among elected representatives are other bottlenecks. Panchayats do not receive cooperation of block and district administration, which have so far failed to recognize and respect elected representatives of Panchayats the way members of legislative assemblies and parliament are recognized and respected. Gram Panchayats are chairperson and secretary centric and not functioning collectively. Involvement of members of Panchayts in most of the states is limited to passive attendance of meetings and signing of attendance register. As a result of all these bottlenecks, people do not see Panchayats delivering public goods and services effectively and hence do not participate enthusiastically in Gram Sabha and other processes of Panchayats.

If this is the status of Panchayats today, what needs to be done to empower them and make them more effective? Devolution of functions to Panchayats by State based on activity mapping and principle of subsidiarity followed by devolution of funds and functionaries to carry out devolved functions is the first prerequisite to strengthen Panchayati Raj in India. In case of Panchayats in fifth schedule areas, five state governments which have not yet notified their PESA rules must do so. This cannot be achieved merely by issuing central advisories to States. A forceful demand should come from elected representatives themselves through their State and national level federations. Gram Sabha campaign need to be organized in scheduled and non-scheduled areas to orient and sensitize Gram Sabha members of their rights and duties. Such an empowerment must be followed by effective capacity enhancement through time-bound three-four weeks induction trainings, yearly refresher thematic trainings, mentoring and regular demand-based handholding of elected representatives. Special capacity building drive for women, SC and ST elected representatives is also needed. Development of at least one beacon model Panchayat in every district and conducting exposure visits will go a long way in capacity enhancement as nothing can be more motivating than seeing another Panchayat in the same district and state performing to the fullest of its potential. To enable them to function effectively, adequate infrastructure in terms of office building, broadband connectivity, conventional and solar power, office equipments must be provided to Panchayats, particularly to Gram Panchayats. To promote collective functioning, standing and functional committees of Panchayats need to be activated by training and facilitating their regular meetings. Social capital created by the Self-Help Groups movement across the country be utilized in supporting Panchayats effectively monitor functioning of public institutions such as anganwadi, primary schools, health-sub centres etc. and frontline functionaries such as Auxiliary Nurse Midwife (ANM), agriculture extension workers, Anganwadi Workers, teachers etc. SHGs may also make these Panchayats accountable by participating in Gram Sabha and taking part in social audit.

In the aforementioned background, chaper contributors of this book have looked at various dimentions of Panchayati Raj from theoretical and empirical perspectives. They have not only analysed the constitutional provisions, structure of Panchayati Raj system and various programmes to strengthen panchayats but have also analysed with the help of empirical studies the operational realities.

Twenty years have gone after the introduction of the 73rd Amendment to the Constitutions of India and subsequent passage of confirmative State Legislation in the State Legislatures to create a New Panchayati Raj system for the purpose of establishing a third tier governance permanently in the Indian federal system of governance. Time has come for evaluation of the impact created in the rural communities by the rural government created at the grassroots through the new legislation. Many made attempts to assess the performance and evaluate the impact of the institutions. Prof. Palanithurai, an academic activist involved in the process of decentralization of powers for the past two decades along with many institutions and organizations, in his article titled "Decentralization in India: A Perceptual and Experiential Analysis" looked at the whole process and captured the significant transformation witnessed in the rural society because of the establishment of the new governance mechanism at the grassroots. While mapping out the major achievements, the major weakness and constraints witnessed in the process of decentralization of powers in India have been captured in this write up. It brought to light the potentials of the new mechanism and at the same time it has been indicated that how a fine opportunity has been missed out by the state governments and other stakeholders in strengthening the grassroots governance to ensure the participation of people in the rural areas and more specifically the marginalised in the process of governance and development. It has also indicated a new opportunity created by the Fourteenth Finance Commission to strengthen the New Panchayati Raj System and the new initiative of the central government and National Institute of Rural Development and Panchayati Raj. Basically it is a participatory reflective analysis.

Dr. C.D. Adhikary in his article "Dialectics of Democracy: A Field View from Uttar Pradesh" traces the evolution of Panchayats in India through ancient India, British rule, constitutional debates and later period. Assessing panchayats in practice, Dr. Adhikary argues that Panchayats today are seen more as government organ rather than an institution of self-governance. These panchayats are struggling to ensure participation in Gram Sabha and Ward Sabha. However, the paper also recognizes the achievements of panchayats in empowering women, SC and STs through reservation. On the basis of empirical study in Jalalpur Gram Panchayat in Jamalpur block of Uttar Pradesh, the author found that Opinion on socio-economic development through panchayati raj varies across the community. Some important economic contributions of panchayati raj include fair price shops, work (wage employment) through panchayat, Quarter (Housing schemes like IAY), Immunisation (Through Anganwadi) etc. People do not see any long term impact of panchayati raj on poverty. The study findings offer little to strongly claim evidence of empowerment through panchayati raj. However this has more to do with the narrowness of the concept of empowerment than anything else. Empowerment is not a single process and it manifests in multiple forms. Paper concludes that changes brought by panchayats are small steps towards empowerment of women and backward sections of community.

Dr. Mahipal in his article "Empowerment of Panchayats in India: An Assessment"describes salient features of 73rd Amendment Act and PESA and analyses state-wise status of devolution of functions, funds and functionaries to Panchayats. The paper argues that the core development functions like Agriculture and allied sectors, Animal husbandry and dairying, fisheries, small scale industries, Khadi village and cottage industries, education, health, drinking water, social welfare, women and child development poverty alleviation, public distribution and rural roads and welfare of scheduled castes and scheduled tribes are by and large transferred to Panchayats across the states, but the functions categorized under secondary and tertiary sectors have not been transferred substantially. Limited functional devolution has not been matched by devolution of funds in most of the States. The paper argues that real empowerment of panchayats will take place when they have their own resources at their disposal because such funds would be untied and the Panchayats can use them according to their requirement and priority. But picture is blurred if one sees across the states. Apart from Secretaries and Executive Officers, all other functionaries at all levels of Panchayats are state government employees in most of the states. problem is serious in the sense that at the average manpower at the GP level in States like Uttar Pradesh and Bihar are one- sixth of the national average and need to be addressed immediately. It was also expected that PRIs which would be instrumental in changing attitude of rural elites and enable achieve people's collective aspiration of developing themselves holistically. However, the author says that hopes have been belied because there is no urge for decentralisation at the grassroots. Paper further suggests creating effective demand for empowering Panchayats by forming associations of elected representatives at the local, district, state and national levels in order to enhance bargaining powers and to learn from each other.

Dr. Pradip Parida in his paper "Rural Development and Democratic Decentralization in India: Analyzing the Role of PRIs" tries to explore the possibilities of looking into the future of the participative democracy in India from the point of view of institutions at local level. As all of us admit the fact that 'panchayat' as an institution of governance has tremendous role not only by giving a chance of 'participation' and 'empowerment' to the people at grass root level, but also as an institution of implementation of various programmes, its role and responsibilities are commendable. Nobody can deny the role of 'panachayt' as an institution of 'governance' at local level is highly crucial. In that context, if panachayts plays their role as per the mandate of the constitution, that will bring development and prosperity immensely in the rural sector. In that background this paper is a modest attempt to examine the role of 'panchayat' in rural development, as an institution of democratic decentralization. This paper tries to examine the Public Policy in Indian context today with specific reference to panchayat, working as a catalyst for accelerating the development process. What are the problems encountered by panachayts in implementing the central sponsored/ flagship programmes and how to strengthen their role in the democratic governance is also part of this paper. The paper concludes that in theory PRIs are ought to play great role in ameliorating the poverty in rural areas, but the findings from the field is not much encouraging. The attempt to bring PRIs and CSSs together has not produced any dramatic change. Neither the purpose of improving the programme delivery nor the objective of empowering the PRIs has been realized significantly because of the linkage that exists presently. The author suggests restructuring the CSSs to shed their top-down character and enabling states to appreciate and deepen the decentralization process further.

Dr. Atanu Mohapatra and Dr. Ramkrushna Pradhan in their article "Working of Panchayati Raj Institutions in Odisha: An Overview" traced the history and evolution of panchayati raj system in India right from ancient India to the modern times. Then the paper tries to look at the functioning of panchayats in the context of State of Odisha. The paper argues that under the State laws, wide powers of suspension and dismissal have been vested in the State bureaucracy and places Panchayati Raj Institutions in a position of disadvantage. It also takes away the essential characteristic of PRIs as elected representative bodies and reduces it to a position of subordination *vis-a-vis* Intermediate Panchayats and so on. The present system is, therefore, seen to have actually reinforced dominance and unequal access to power, besides rendering the villagers helpless and alienated. In the prevailing situation in Odisha, the paper suggests that Panchayat must also ensure transparency and accountability of its functioning. Autonomy of the Panchayat is very essential while clearly demarcating the powers and functions of the Panchayat and Panchayat Samiti needs to be specified. The Panchayats should be placed under the control and guidance of the District Collector in order to free it from unwarranted Block level monopoly, financial discrimination and Political subjugation.

Dr. Satyaki Datta and Dr. Rasanand Panda in their paper "State of Panchayati Raj System in India: Inferences from Selected Villages" analyse issues and challenges of panchyati raj system. The paper argues that there nothing to be overwhelmed so much, as panchayats face problems of intervention from political parties, stake groups and bureaucrats. The common basis for this discord is redistribution of power. Based on empirical study of panchayats in border areas of Tamil Nadu, Arunachal Pradesh, West Bengal, Rajasthan, Lakshdweep the paper argues that although separate ministries of the Government of India administer the Panchayat system and defense in India, for the administration of such borderline villages, the Ministry of Defense should also be involved, especially as these villages, blocks or districts have heavy deployment and strategic involvement of the armed forces or the coast guards for the safeguard of the peace and order of the mainland. The Panchayati system has done commendable efforts through out the country and their efforts in the discussed regions are not too bad. However, considering their location and their importance to the defense of the country, a better and special attention should be given to these places.

Dr. Radhika Kumar in her paper “Participation in Development: Decentralised Governance and Development in Andhra Pradesh and Madhya Pradesh” aims at providing a comparative understanding of democratic decentralization in the two states of Madhya Pradesh and Andhra Pradesh during the decade of the 1990s. The case of these two states is interesting as in both, the Panchayati Raj Institutions (PRIs) were pivotal to the welfarist/ populist program pursued by the government in power. Also in both states wide scale institutional changes were effected for purposes of promoting participatory local government. However the method of doing so varied in both. Madhya Pradesh effected decentralisation through the panchayats themselves while in Andhra Pradesh, parallel institutions of decentralisation were established in the form of stake-holder associations for purposes of promoting participation. Given the different institutional paths of decentralisation, the comparison is made meaningful. This is because it will provide the context of distinguishing between the development trajectories of the two states with regard to their efficacy in promoting participation and development. In doing so one will also briefly look at legal, financial and administrative viability of panchayats given that all these factors are crucial in determining the functioning of local level institutions. The paper concludes that the process of institutional decentralisation in both the states has been an evolving process. It identifies two types of shortcomings: first, the legislations for decentralisation are not in place or where legislation has been enacted, in practice funds, functions and functionaries have not been devolved and second, the government has fortified itself with so many caveats in the laws relating to decentralisation that the panchayati raj institutions have no maneuverability to perform their assigned role.

Dr. Archana Kumari in her paper titled "Challenges of Panchayati Raj in Jammu Region: An observation" has examined the provisions of Jammu & Kashmir Panchayati Raj Act and its implementation challenges in Jammu region. On the basis of empirical study of three Gram Panchayats Satriyan (R S Pura), Panjar Kalsote (Udhampur) and Bainglar (Samba) the author observes that the government interventions are hampering the participatory character of local self governance leading to politicisation and controlling of these institutions. Panchayats are not perceived as fair, active and effective institutions. A lot of control is still with government, so the participatory and self governance nature of panchayats is being compromised. The villagers are unaware of many policies related to panchayats like reservation policies, administrative policies and financial policies, due to which they have to remain dependent on local government officers. Paper concludes that in spite of so many acts and amendments, the Panchayati Raj System in Jammu region is still facing these challenges, and suggests that an honest effort is required for implementation of local self governance in this region.

Dr. Rajesh Kumar Sinha in his article "Panchayats in Fifth Schedule Areas: A Review of Implementation of PESA Act" traces evolution of PESA Act, its key provisions and examines the status of its implementation. The paper also describes recent initiatives in States including those in Maharashtra, Rajasthan, Chhattisgarh, Andhra Pradesh. Issues affecting implementation of PESA Act has also been discussed. Paper argues that effective implementation of PESA will not only bring development to tribal majority areas in ten States with Fifth Schedule areas but will also help curb discontent and extremism. Paper concludes that although Government of India and State governments have taken several initiatives towards the implementation of PESA Act, lot more needs to be done. While various line departments of State governments are unwilling to let go their powers, there is also inadequate political will at the central and state level. Some good practices have emerged, particularly in Maharashtra with a push from the Governor office and paper suggests that such good practices need to be scaled up to other States.

Dr. Rajeev Bansal in his article "Social Audit- Community Monitoring for Social Accountability in PRIs" has described the history, concept and process of social audit. Paper argues that Social Audit complements financial audit and presents a true picture. The government or institutional audit may remain the basic auditing practice, but would become far more transparent and inclusive of affected persons and intended beneficiaries by incorporating and integrating the practices of social audits. Social audits may be conducted in addition to government or institutional audits for a sample of activities, especially for those that involve distribution of disaggregated benefits at grassroots level or very large investments e.g. NREGS, ICDS, PDS. The findings of such social audits should be publicly compared to those of the government or institutional audits and correctives be identified and incorporated in both. There should also be a public rendering of action taken. The paper also suggests a model for effective social audit.

Dr. Shabeen Ara in her article "Capacity Building for Strengthening Panchayats: A Review" attempts to study the administrative strengthening and capacity building of panchayats. It furthers examines efforts at empowering, functional mandates, autonomy and self-reliance and self-sufficiency through capacity building. Paper also identifies the availability of formal education for capacity building and challenge of sensitizing the youth, women,

SC, ST in Panchayati Raj to involve them in decision making, to ensure social justice.

Prof. M.A.Ommen in his article "Whatever Happened to Panchayati Raj" examines the empowerment of panchayats in the journey of more than 25 years after passage of 73rd Amendment Act. The paper argues that while the Conformity Acts of States provided all the necessary conditions, other conditions were left to be designed by the State legislatures and governments. With no champions to keep afloat the much-needed social demand for deepening democracy, an agenda for economic reforms, demonetisation, JAM and the like took precedence over this foundational reform. The Ministry of Panchayati Raj since its inception in 2004 made a drive to encourage activity mapping in the States but it slowed down and reached nowhere. The mandate to establish a district planning committee to prepare a draft development plan has been violated and distorted in most States. In all States, parallel bodies encroach on the functional domain of local governments and continue to grow unchecked. Women, adivasis and dalits remain largely excluded. Despite repeated efforts by the Eleventh, Twelfth and Thirteenth Finance Commissions, the continued absence of a reliable and consistent database calls for corrective reforms. Paper concludes that for democracy to succeed there is a need to develop democratic local governance with a sense of urgency.

Dr. Vinay Sahasrabuddhe in his paper titled "Participatory Local Planning/Budgeting: An Experiment with Direct Democracy" has examined the functioning of representative democracy and emergence of direct democracy. The paper argues that over the years, the idea of representative democracy has been facing serious challenges. The toughest of all the challenges is the challenge of trust-deficit. In response to this situation, in regions like the State of California in USA and also at several other democracies what was experimented with, was the idea of direct democracy. However, author argues that direct democracy also presupposes an enlightened, conscious and responsible voter-community. Participatory budgeting leaves elected representatives with less amount of political power and hence reduction in available leverages. Hence, without strong political will and huge resoluteness on the part of elected representatives, this idea cannot be taken further. Participatory citizenship engagement is the prerequisite of Participatory Planning/Budgeting.

# 1

# Decentralization in India: A Perceptual and Experiential Analysis

G. PALANITHURAI[2]

## INTRODUCTION

Being an academic activist working with government's committees both the central government and state governments, civil society organisations, donor agencies, multilateral and bilateral agencies on decentralization over two decades feel that a remarkable opportunity for mobilizing the citizens more specifically the rustic folk and the marginalised in the rural areas for participation in the process of development and governance has been missed. First time in India through the 73rd Amendment to the constitution of India all the segments of the Indian society have been included in the process of governance and development and it was possible only through reservation of seats for the marginalised. It was considered a remarkable opportunity to find solution to many of the critical development issues through a bottom up approach with the active participation of the stakeholders. Totally this opportunity has been missed by the Indian society because of the poor initiatives in strengthening the local governance mechanism created through the historic amendment to the constitution of

[2] Rajiv Gandhi Chair for Panchayati Raj Studies, Department of Political Science and Development Administration, Gandhigram Rural Institute - Deemed University, Gandhigram.
**Corresponding author*: E-mail: gpalanithurai@gmail.com

India. For this lapse many are responsible not only the central and state governments. Creating a vibrant local body governance system is the sole responsibility of the state government. Thus, the state government has the moral and legal responsibility to perform the above task. The organisations, institutions, parties and groups which had been working for emancipation and empowerment of the marginalised in India have also missed this opportunity. There was enough scope to build a mass movement through this opportunity by the civil society and political parties to empower people. Many bilateral and multilateral agencies have turned towards India and evinced keen interest to work with local bodies to bring socio-political and economic transformation in India. Many agencies have expected that Indian society is going to see a behavioural change on the part of the community in the process of deepening of democracy through the local governance practices. But it does take place. This is the saddest part of the story on decentralization. It is a million dollar question as to why this reluctance in strengthening grassroots governance despite the fact that everyone knows that it is good for the people and the country. Is there any danger envisaged by the political parties by devolving powers to grassroots institutions? This is the basic question lingering in the minds of many of the researchers. The scope and potentials of the new rural local governance system is so wide and huge to transform the communities in terms of life and livelihood conditions.

Apart from the above, the new local governance system has the capacity to deepen democracy in the rural communities which is so vital for the establishment of a just society in the rural areas. Democratization of communities embedded in the decentralization framework has opened up a new opportunity to orient the people at the grassroots in democratic practices which will ultimately change the attitude and behaviour of the people. Thus, the potentials of decentralization are huge and vast but used are very limited. The reason for the failure made the researchers to raise a question as to why the system has been made to fail or has it happened inadvertently? It is to be seen in the backdrop of the failures of cooperatives in this country. Everyone knows that cooperative will do well for the poor and yet it is made to fail. Despite inherent systemic weaknesses, the new local governance mechanism has delivered goods in the past two decades substantially both qualitatively and quantitatively. The above conclusion is derived from global and pan Indian studies. Yet, the state governments barring a few are not interested in strengthening the local governments by devolving adequate powers, functions, finance and functionaries. This state of affairs provides scope to look at the design of the state governments in establishing governance at grassroots with suspicion.

Are the state governments committed and sincere in following the objectives of the part IX of the constitution letter and spirit? This does not mean that the state governments are not aware of the potentials of the local governments. This state of affair raises a number of questions among academics, researchers and activists and of them most significant is as to why most of the state governments are reluctant to strengthen local governments to improve quality of governance and service delivery which is always beneficial to the state governments. Is it because the state governments feel that service could be delivered more effectively and efficiently by the bureaucracy than the elected representatives at the grassroots? Will it weaken the state governments if local governments are strengthened? If so why all the state governments have concurred to the 73$^{rd}$ Amendment to the Constitution of Indian and why a few state governments have devolved powers to local bodies and strengthened the local governance system? Are they weakened because of devolution of powers? Having seen the potential, the stand of the many of the state governments on their refusal to devolve powers unequivocally gives an impression that they do not want a powerful institution and leadership at the grassroots as they may be a potential threat to them despite the advantages for the community and the people. The present write up is aimed at mapping up the general trend of decentralization process in India.

## GLOBAL TREND

Decentralization is a global phenomenon not an exclusive Indian phenomenon. It was initiated along with globalization of economy and democratization of society through democracy promotion and deepening of democracy. 80% of the countries in the world are pursuing decentralization seriously to address the issues of the people through establishing governance mechanism at the grassroots (Manor, 2010). Three decades have gone after initiated the decentralization process in a massive way in the world. Devolution of powers has been carried out through different ways. Decentralization process was initiated through (*a*), amending the constitutions of the country; (*b*), amending the provincial constitutions; (*c*), enacting a special legislation to create local governance and (*d*), passing a simple executive order to establish local governance. One should not presume that the outcome of decentralization of powers depends on the mode of implementation of decentralization of powers. The impact of decentralization of powers is determined not on the basis of the mode but it depends on the way in which it is designed and implemented at the ground with the sense of commitment. This can be seen from India and China's decentralization initiatives. India has created the local governance system through amending the constitution. But China has passed only an executive order to create a local governance system. China has given enormous resources to the local bodies with adequate powers to carry out the development activities. But in India despite the amendment to the constitution, devolution is weak and ineffective (Palanithurai *et al.,* 2014, Mohanty *et al.,* 2007). The above initiative of decentralization of powers has produced intended and unintended consequences in governance, administration and society throughout the world.

Research studies have been carried out over a period of three decades globally to map up the consequences of the decentralization process. It has been brought to light that decentralization has created impact in all socio-political, and economic realms (Triesman, 2007). We found global studies, regional studies, national studies, provincial studies and local studies. Variety of theoretical conjecture has been evolved based on the studies and they are being tested around the world. Global studies revealed the different goals and objectives of decentralization of power set out by different countries[4]. They vary from country to country. Intensity of decentralization also varies from country to country depending on their needs and requirements (Meenakshisundaram, 1994; Aziz and Arnold, 1994). Yet, one could find a common pattern in the whole process of decentralization of powers in the world (Shah, 2006). Issues which could not be tackled through the machineries of the nation-state had been given to local governance mechanism to solve them and relieve the governments of the region and the nation from the burden and stress. It was considered as partnership in governance and administration to deliver public goods and services more effectively and efficiently to the public.

Variety of advantages expected out of decentralization of powers. Implications of decentralization in the life and living conditions of the people vary from country to country. They are being studied by an array of academics and researchers from the perspectives of sociology, economics, anthropology, public policy, political science, management, administrative science and a few other disciplines. They are being studied with different perspectives. Of the studies, economic studies received much attention of the policy community. Changes have been effected in the implementation process mostly based on the studies conducted by the economists. Major global trend indicates that majority of the countries looking for decentralization to bring efficiency in service delivery and quality service. Further, it is aimed at achieving downward accountability (Faguet and Carolineposchl, 2015). Hence, economists concentrated in their studies only on the cost of service and quality of service. Major studies on decentralization have been conducted by economists and banking institutions and influenced the policies of the federal governments and regional governments in the world.

## INDIAN CONTEXT

In India, decentralization was conceptualized in the recent decades in the backdrop of the earlier experiences to achieve economic development and social justice through amending the constitution of India. Attempts had been made to create local governments in the past after India got independence as India had the history of local governance. All the attempts met with failures. At the dawn of independence a discourse was initiated for creating a governance system by evolving from below. It was advocated by M.K. Gandhi. But it was powerfully opposed by B.R. Ambedkar by projecting an argument that the existing hierarchical social arrangement will be further strengthened and hence he advocated a strong state system to be created. At that point of time the liberated societies from the colonial yoke reposed faith in nation state not in local governments. The global trend was towards strengthening the state system. As M.K.Gandhi was ahead of time, he was the only person advocating building governance system only from below negating the power of the state system. Yet, due space was created for the establishment of local governance in India but it was left to the will and pleasure of the provincial governments. As a result, barring a few most of the state governments had created local government machinery not with hope and faith. The past experience only made the policy community to follow the path of amending the constitution to ensure its sustainability. Thus, the Seventy Third Amendment to the Constitution of India was enacted and it became part IX of the constitution of India. Given the rich experience in democracy, scope for achieving results through local governance is wider. It gave hope to many that Indian communities' transformation could be achieved fastly through this new initiative. More specifically deepening of democracy could also be achieved through this local governance arrangement. By effective implementation of decentralization in India the very character of the democracy can be changed from representative democracy to representative and participatory democracy. The whole process could be done through mass mobilization. Participation in governance and development is integral part of decentralization (Sivaramakrishnan, 2000). To implement the $73^{rd}$ Amendment to the Constitution of India an array of steps are needed. If really a state government wants to implement the letter and spirit of the constitution, the steps are imperative and essential. It requires a new framework of action.

When decentralization is initiated, both the central and state governments have to agree on the basic goals and objectives without having any suspicion and disagreements. The whole process of decentralization has to be designed in such a way that it should reach the masses through a big bang approach. In India, ever since the idea of Gram Swaraj was conceptualized, it was strongly resisted and that trend continued even during the last quarter of $20^{th}$ and beginning of $21^{st}$ century. No doubt, the middle of $20^{th}$ century arguments and discourses were favorable for strong state formation for development and transformation. It was a global trend. But the experience of the state system brought the new proposition that decentralization will find solution to many of the problems which were unattended and unresolved by the state system. In India, the federal government aligned with the global trend in decentralization but the state governments have looked at the decentralization proposal as a means to weaken the provincial governments as the central government has not initiated the process to devolve powers from the central government to state governments. In India it is designed defectively that powers have to be decentralized from the state governments to local governments and not from central government to state government (Palanithurai, 1999).

Normally decentralization is conceived that power has to be decentralised from the highest decision making bodies to the lowest unit of decision making. It means in India, it is expected that powers have to be devolved from the central government to state governments and state governments to local governments. Further, the local government is in the state list of the constitution. Since, it is a state subject the central government is not able to move beyond establishing local government through the part IX of the constitution of India. Hence, the objectives of the central government have not been realized as the state governments have not agreed with the central government on the decentralization design. The state governments have agreed to create local governments but not the way the central government wants. Further, the central government instead of devolving powers, it takes away the powers of the state governments in the pretext of globalization. Both the state governments and central government are not having adequate clarity on the design of decentralization. Hence, this game for twenty years in India. The state governments have created local governments in order to comply with the provisions of the constitution of India. Barring a few states, the new opportunity was not used fully to deliver goods and services to the people effectively. Scholars with international reputation who have analysed the decentralization process in India have come to the conclusion that the opportunity has been missed in India to get the best results out of decentralization. To make the decentralization more effective and efficient, an array of activities are imperatives which have to be attended to seriously by the state governments (see the steps in the form of a diagram in the Figure-1 given below). It is just like the transfer of power from British to Indians. It is just like a creation of a government. As state governments the local governments have to act independently with their own machineries and resources. To run the machineries of the local governments, they should not look for grants from the state governments. In such a way resource generation powers have to be given to the local bodies. Now the local governments with very little autonomy to generate revenue and thereby local bodies have been shaped as institutions of spending. To implement the 73$^{rd}$ Amendment to the Constitution of India, there are two requirements at the political level in any state. First, there should be a strong commitment and political will on the part of the state leadership. Second, in the absence of political will on the part of the state leadership, there should be a mass movement initiated from below with the initiatives of the civil society and political parties. Apart from the above, there is an yet another possibility and hope we find in local bodies to strengthen the local body system. It is nothing but shaping the leaders and enhancing the capacity of the elected representatives of the local bodies. By doing

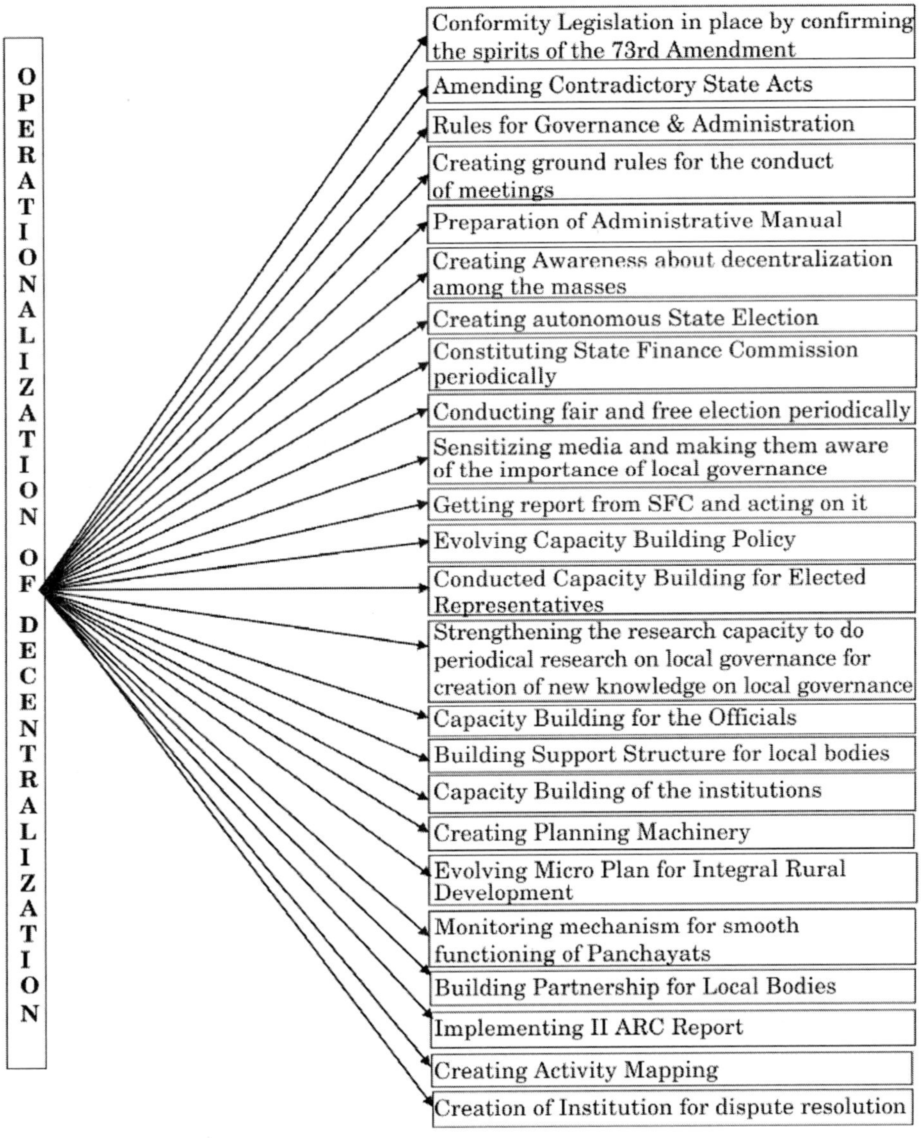


**Fig. 1:** Operationalisation of Decentralization

so, the elected representatives will exhibit their extraordinary talent and vision through their performance in the local bodies. Since local bodies provide enormous scope for the leaders to work on assumed functions, they can work on it and demonstrate their creativity. Extraordinary and visionary leaders have emerged through their performance only by working on the assumed functions (Palanithurai, 2008).

Keeping the above in the backdrop take the devolution reports (TISS, 2015) and the studies (Nagraj *et al.,* 2015) conducted by various agencies for perusal and analysis. On many of the aspects the state governments have not acted firmly and decisively. Only a few states have done the job professionally. Majority of the states are reluctant to take steps to strengthen the institutions. It should be done in a movement mode or campaign mode. In this regard, Kerala has shown the way to other states. To implement the Amendment to the Constitution, a conducive political climate has been created through the expression of a strong will by the leadership. In the same tenor people have been prepared through a strategy of conducting people's campaign. Big Bang approach adopted in Kerala has created a sustainable institutional mechanism for local governance (Isaac and Frank, 2000). Almost it is a model for other state governments to implement the part IX of the Constitution of India. By doing this exercises, the process of politics, governance and development have gone to next higher level compared to the other states. Nearer to Kerala is Tamil Nadu in terms of social development and human development indicators but in decentralization it is different. From the below given Table-1, one can easily gauge the trend of decentralization of powers in Tamil Nadu. Tamil Nadu is a model state for many progressive and transformative activities. But its record achievement in social justice and decentralization is dismal (Palanithurai, 2013; 2012). High on rhetoric and low in performance in both. It worked for achieving state autonomy. It demanded more powers from the centre to the states. In this regard, it is a forerunner state and model state for others. But through the 73$^{rd}$ Amendment to the constitution of India, the state governments have to devolve powers to the local governments without devolving powers to state governments from the central government. It has been repeatedly raised by these two political parties that the centre is not devolving powers but it asks the states to devolve powers. It is not acceptable. That is why J. Jayalalitha, the late Chief Minister of Tamil Nadu vociferously opposed the GST by bringing an argument that the

**Table 1:** Decentralization of Power in Tamil Nadu

| *Sl. No* | *Item* | *State* | | |
|---|---|---|---|---|
| | | *Yes* | *No* | *Partially* |
| 1 | Conformity Legislation | √ | | |
| 2 | Amending Contradictory State Acts | | √ | |
| 3 | Rules for Governance & Administration | | | √ |
| 4 | Preparation of Administrative Manual | | √ | |
| 5 | Awareness about decentralization | | | √ |
| 6 | Creation of autonomous State Election Commission | | | √ |
| 7 | Conducting free and fair elections periodically | | | √ |
| 8 | Sensitizing media and making them aware of the importance of local governance | | | √ |
| 9 | Strengthening the capacity to do periodical research on local governance for creation of new knowledge on local governance | | | √ |
| 10 | Commissioning State Finance Commission periodically | √ | | |
| 11 | Getting report from the State Finance Commission and acting on them | | | √ |
| 12 | Evolving Capacity Building Policy | | √ | |
| 13 | Conducted Capacity Building for Elected Representatives | | | √ |
| 14 | Capacity Building of the officials | | | √ |
| 15 | Evolving micro plan for integrated development | | √ | |
| 16 | Monitoring mechanism for smooth functioning of Panchayats | √ | | |
| 17 | Building support structure | | | √ |
| 18 | Building partnership | | √ | |
| 19 | Implementing II ARC Report | | √ | |
| 20 | Implementing Mani Shankar Aiyar Report | | | √ |
| 21 | Creating Activity Mapping | | √ | |

*Source*: (Computed from the works of the Rajiv Gandhi Chair for Panchayati Raj Studies, Gandhigram Rural Institute – Deemed University, Gandhigram.)

central government is clipping the wings of the state governments. Yet, both the ethnic political parties the DMK and the AIADMK have been consistently evincing keen interest in strengthening the village panchayats and not the other two tiers. It is strange to note that both the DMK and the AIADMK oppose each other on all issues but they concur on one issue namely the devolution of powers. Both never wanted to create a strong local government but wanted a strong gram panchayats to deliver services to the people effectively.

From the above table, one can infer how the state government has created the local governments. In form it exists. In spirit it does not. While evaluating the status of devolution, it would secure high score for its form but in its functioning it cannot secure that much of scores. In order to fulfill the obligations to the constitutions of India, it has created a local body. But the Tamil Nadu government reposed faith only in its bureaucracy and the bureaucracy is not weak as in other north Indian states. The Tamil Nadu bureaucracy is effective and delivers services efficiently. Despite all weaknesses the Tamil Nadu panchayats more specifically the gram panchayats have delivered services more efficiently (Palanithurai, 2005).

## MAJOR ACHIEVEMENTS

Global studies have brought to light the achievements of new local governments (Faguet, 2014). Service delivery was effective through new local governments (Ahmed and Brosio, 2009). Local governments are nearer to the people and responsible and responsive to the people. People can contact the agency for their immediate basic needs at any time. Quality of service provision is high when it is delivered through new local governance mechanism. In India, Dalits have started asserting themselves to claim their entitlements (Mathew and Nayak, 1996). In the same way, women have started asserting themselves and raised their voices on the issues of women and children (Buch, 1999; Kaushik, 1998). Because of the functioning of the local governments, deliberative practice has been improved. Participation has been improved qualitatively and quantitatively in the authoritative bodies of the grassroots governance institutions. Despite barriers women participation in local governance has increased (Palanithurai, 2002; 2014). Time taken to water fetching has been reduced. Women spending more time on other issues instead of spending long hours water fetching. Women started discussing about the quality of water getting from the public taps. People who attended Gram Sabha have started asking questions about the departments of government providing services to the people. Quantum of corruption in development sector has been reduced. New kind of leadership emerged from the panchayats with the active involvement of women as elected representatives. A new way of governance and perspective emerged in the process of governance with the leadership provided by the elected women representatives. These are the major achievements emerged out of the studies conducted by various agencies and individuals. As a result, expectation among various stakeholders from local governance has increased.

There are many problems confronted by the local bodies. They are: lack of adequate powers; inadequate resources; inadequate functionaries; poor capacity of the elected representatives; lack of awareness on the part of the masses about the new local governance system; complicated administrative procedures; absence of administrative manual; absence of simplified procedures for administration; inadequate skilled persons to help the panchayats for the professional activities; poor attention of the mass media towards the local governance issues and a number of other issues. Steps are taken at different levels to improve the conditions of local governance (Mathew and Buch, 2016). Yet, they are inadequate. Theory argues that to get effective outcome from decentralization the society should have: (*a*), high literacy rate in the society; (*b*), Presence of middle class; (*c*), Presence of strong civil society; (*d*), Presence of active media; (*e*), Absence of economic inequality; (*f*), Absence of social inequality; (*g*), Adequate powers, adequate resources; adequate functionaries; adequate awareness among the masses; and presence of capacitated elected representatives in the system. In the absence of the above, decentralization will not deliver intended goods to the people (Pradhan and Mukherjee, 2006).

All the above factors are very essential for the impact making decentralization. In India many of the factors are absent. Yet decentralization delivers (GoI, 2006). The exponents argue that many of the Indian states are losing a very rare opportunity as they have not strengthened the local governance system. As a result, many donor agencies have stopped funding to local governance activities. Many hard core academics who evinced keen interest in doing research in decentralization in the initial state, have moved from the field of decentralization. Yet the central government continues its activities and supports the local governance activities by extending financial support based on the recommendations of 14$^{th}$ Finance Commission report. It is a fact to be recognized that the 14$^{th}$ Finance Commission has taken steps through its recommendations to strengthen the local bodies by awarding unprecedented high amount to Gram panchayats for their effective and efficient service delivery. It is a game changer (Palanithurai, 2017). It is not only the quantum of resources allocated to Gram panchayats but also the activities fixed as mandates to prepare Gram Panchayat Development Plan and conduct social audit. It is a game changer and it is a new opportunity for strengthening the panchayats. Along with the above, a new initiative was undertaken to strengthen the local governance system through building capacity of the interested stakeholders. Now a huge effort is taken at National Institute of Rural Development and Panchayati Raj to build the capacity of stakeholders (Palanithurai, 2017).

## CONCLUSIONS

Since independence, it had been argued that unless a mass movement is being built for decentralization, powers cannot be decentralized. India has produced outstanding visionaries' and they conceptualized decentralization. M.K.Gandhi, Jawaharlal Nehru, Jayaprakash Narayan, Rajiv Gandhi, Sri Aurobindo, Rabindranath Tagore, E.M.S. Nampoodiripad and a few others. We had extensive knowledge base on local governance. We had good history and experience of local governance. Yet, one could not see high commitment on the part of state governments to take it forward at the ground. Everyone expected that after passing the 73$^{rd}$ Amendment to the Constitution of India that at least this time it would reach new heights. While looking at the decentralization process after two decades one would find dismal picture of decentralization of powers in India. Yet, one important theoretical conjuncture emerges out of analysis of pan India studies. Despite all the limitations, the local governance machinery has delivered goods. Thus, it raises hope that it has got scope to deliver goods. But, state governments are missing this opportunity. The State government's faith and hope in state bureaucracy is much more than on Panchayati Raj. The State governments find it difficult to work with local governments as the local governments have got elected representatives. The State governments are comfortable with bureaucracy and not with the elected representatives. In many states even preparatory works for decentralization have not been completed. Even to conduct the local body elections periodically we seek the help of judiciary. In many of the states local body exists but not vibrantly. Secondly, a mass awareness has to be created about the importance of new local governance system. For proper decentralization an array of steps are needed. But those steps had not been taken seriously by the state governments and others stakeholders. Administration needs a manual. But many of the state governments have not prepared administrative manual to run day to day administration. Thirdly, professional leadership training is needed for the elected representatives of the people to build the capacity of the elected representatives. Our training framework and practices are weak and hence we could not create talented transformational leaders. Hence, the whole training programme has to be changed into a leadership training and not mere an administrative training. From the studies, it is inferred that wherever leaders had been shaped, there we find remarkable transformation of communities. Fourthly, a transparent resource flow system has to be created. The Fourteenth Finance Commission recommendations have to be used letter and spirit to strengthen the local governments.

## REFERENCES

Ahmed E. and Brosio G. (*eds*). (2009). Does Decentralization Enhance Service Delivery and Poverty Reduction? Cheltenham: Edward Elgar.

Aziz A. and Arnold D. (*eds*). (1996). Decentralized Governance in Asian Countries. New Delhi: Sage Publications.

Buch N. (1999), From Oppression to Assertion: A Study of Panchayats and Women in M.P, Rajasthan and UP. New Delhi: Centre for Women Development Studies.

Faguet J.P. (*ed*). (2014). Decentralization and Governance, Special Issue of World Bank. Washington D.C. World Bank, No.53.

Faguet J.P. and Carolineposchl (*eds*). (2015). Is Decentralization Good for Development: Perspectives from Academics of Policy Makers. London: Oxford University Press.

GoI. (2008). Study on Elected Women Representatives in Panchayati Raj Institutions. New Delhi: Ministry of Panchayati Raj.

Isaac T.M.T. and Frank R.W. (2000). Local Democracy and Development: People's Campaign for Decentralized Planning in Kerala New Delhi: Left World.

Kaushik S. (1998). Participation of Women in Panchayati Raj in India: A stock taking. New Delhi: National Commission for Women.

Manor J. (1999). The Political Economy of Democratic Decentralization Washington D.C: The World Bank.

Manor J. (2010). 'Local Governance' in Jayal N. G.and Mehta P.B. (*eds*) The Oxford Companion to Politics in India. New Delhi: Oxford University Press.

Mathew G. and Buch N. (2016). Status of Panchayati Raj in the States and Union Territories of India. New Delhi: Concept Publishing Company.

Mathew G. and Nayak R.C. (1996) "Panchayats at Work: What it Means for the Oppressed" in Economic and Political Weekly, XXXI: 27.

Meenakshisundaram S.S. (1994), Decentralization in Developing Countries. New Delhi: Concept Publishing Company.

Mohanty M. *et al.* (*eds*). (2007). Grassroots Democracy in India and China: The Right to Participate New Delhi: Sage Publications.

Nagaraj H.K. *et al.* (2015). Decentralization and Empowerment for Rural Development. New Delhi: Foundation Books.

Palanithurai G and Sathish K. (2012). Status of Rural Local Bodies Finance in Tamil Nadu New Delhi: Concept Publishing Company.

Palanithurai G. (1999), New Panchayati Raj System at Work: An Evaluation New Delhi: Concept Publishing Company.

Palanithurai G. (2002). "Impediments to Empowerment of Women: Experiences of Elected women representatives in panchayats in Tamil Nadu." Indian Journal of Political Science 63:1.

Palanithurai G. (2003). Dalits and Dalit Representatives in Rural Local Governance New Delhi: Concept Publishing Company.

Palanithurai G. (2017). "Fourteenth Finance Commission: A Game Changer for Gram Panchayats in India" Local Government Quarterly Vol. LXXXVIII: No.1, January- March.

Palanithurai G. (2017). Interview on Transforming India through Strengthening Panchayati Raj Institutions by Constant Training and E-enablement, Pragati News Letter of NIRD&PR No.263, April.

Palanithurai G. (*ed*), (2014). Federating Elected Women Representatives of Local Bodies in India New Delhi: Concept Publishing Company.
Palanithurai G. *et al.* (2008), Change Makers at Grassroots: Local Governance in Action New Delhi: Concept Publishing Company.
Palanithurai G. *et al.* (2014). Governance at Community Level in China and India: A comparative Anaylsis New Delhi: Concept Publishing Company.
Palanithurai P. (2005). Process and Performance of Gram Panchayat Women and Dalit Presidents New Delhi: concept Publishing Company.
Pradhan P. and Mukherjee D. (*eds*). (2006). Decentralization and Local Governance in Developing Countries: A Comparative Perspective. Cambridge Mass: MIT Press.
Shah A. (*ed*). (2006) Local Governance in Developing Countries Washington D.C; The World Bank.
Shah A. (*ed*). (2006) Local Governance in Industrial Countries Washington DC: The World Bank.
Sivaramakrishnan K.C. (2000). Power to the People? The Politics and Progress of Decentralization. New Delhi: Konark.
TISSS. (2015). Devolution Report 2014-15. New Delhi: Government of India.
Triesman D. (2007). The Architecture of Government: Rethinking Political Decentralization. New York: Cambridge University Press.

---

***Prof. G. Palanithurai*** Rajiv Gandhi Chair for Panchayati Raj Studies has been an academic activist working for strengthening the governance institutions at the grassroots. He has published 76 books, 126 research articles in refereed journals, 187 popular articles in leading Newspapers and 83 monographs in the field of rural local governance and decentralization of powers. He was a visiting professor in Cologne University, Germany. He was a Dean, Faculty of Social Sciences, Dean, Students Welfare in the Gandhigram Rural Institute (Deemed University managed by Ministry of Human Resource Development, Government of India).

# 2

# Dialectics of Democracy: A Field View from Uttar Pradesh

C D Adhikary[3]

## INTRODUCTION

Concept of Panchayats has evolved during the ancient India, British rule, constitutional debates and later period. Panchayats today are seen more as government organ rather than an institution of self-governance. These panchayats are struggling to ensure participation in Gram Sabha and Ward Sabha. However, the achievements of panchayats in empowering women, SC and STs through reservation are well recognised. Empirical study in Jalalpur Gram Panchayat in Jamalpur block of Uttar Pradesh, found that opinion on socio-economic development through panchayati raj varies across the community. Some important economic contributions of panchayati raj include fair price shops, work (wage employment) through panchayat, quarter (housing schemes like IAY) and immunisation (through Anganwadi) etc. People do not see any long term impact of panchayati raj on poverty. The study findings offer little to strongly claim evidence of empowerment through panchayati raj. However this has more to do with the narrowness of the concept of empowerment than anything else. Empowerment is not a single process and it manifests in multiple forms.

[3] Department of Sociology, Banaras Hindu University, Varanasi.
**Corresponding author*: E-mail: cdadhikary@gmail.com

## DECENTRALISATION

Decentralisation is basically a process of downward shift of power, authority and responsibility from higher levels of government to the lowest one. It concerns with the processes of public governance and affairs of the State. It denotes the range of power distribution between different tiers of government in favour of the tier at the bottom. There are a variety of terms that decentralisation has come to be associated with. The terms like deconcentration, delegation and more particularly devolution, the last being closest to the meaning of decentralization, are liberally used in the discussion of decentralisation. Devolution involves a process in which lower level units of government are created and/or strengthened in terms of political, administrative and fiscal powers (Crook and Manor, 1998; Jha and Mathur, 1999). Decentralisation or devolution of power involves a composite concept of power, a package that includes the power to decide, power to execute and power to mobilize money.

It is more than a accident that there is a great deal interest in the decentralisation process, particularly the democratic one, which nearly coincides with the beginning of modern development. Decentralisation has been increasingly posed as an imperative to meet demands of equity and economic growth. Development and decentralisation has come to be seen as different sides of the same process. Advocates as well as Adversaries of decentralization today (their number swelling everyday) find themselves tied to the development discourse, to the extent of risking a blurring of distinction (at least a heuristic one) between the two. Decentralised governance today has come to occupy a pride of place in the development discourse. The links between development and decentralization are not far to seek. As centralized planning has failed to reach the poor at the bottom, development practitioners have pinned there hope in people centric government through decentralisation to deliver development. Decentralisation affords judicious resource allocation, make development delivery more need based because of more accurate time and place knowledge, can create pluralist pressure within and between decentralized units to include marginal voices in society, increase counter balancing and accountability by all stake holders of government and development (Lal, 2001). Thus no wonder, decentralization of governance, no matter democratic or undemocratic and more particularly democratic decentralization has become a universal panacea for centralized stagnation and economic disparity world wide and an institutional miracle for national development and progress. The idea of development and progress, in this paper has little to do with the deservedly discredited $18^{th}$ century progress theory of Ferguson, Condrorcet and Voltaire that had its basis in philosophy of history. The notion of progress implied here is limited by modern development imperatives which is democratic at the same time.

Push for decentralisation in contemporary democratic India today is founded on a long drawn dialectical tension between centralisation and decentralization, especially since independence. Prior to independence and before the British came to India, it had a long tradition of self-sufficient village administration system famously eulogized by Charles Metcalfe as *Village republics.* Early precursor of decentralization during British rule is to be found in Rippon Resolution as early as in 1882 which aimed at involving the 'intelligent class of public spirited men' in the management of rural areas under British rule and led to the formation of Distinct Boards and Taluk Boards with nominated members. This was to be followed by the constitution of Royal Commission on decentralisation in 1907 which extended the ambit of decentralized governance down to the village level. Mention must be made of Montague- Chelmsford reforms making local self-government a transferred subject under the scheme of diarchy. However these developments were of peripheral interest in the extent to which they bear upon the dialectical development of decentralisation push in India and were mostly auxiliary to the interests of a centralized to colonial state (Maddick, 1970; Morris-Jones, 1971). While the pre-British Village republics represented an extension of the periphery to the centre, where the later is dependent on the former, the British effort at decentralisation reversed the process where the centre extended to the periphery and became a part of dependent development.

In post-independent India, The dialectical development of centralization *vis-à-vis* decentralization is embodied in two alternative choices: one is the choice of Westminster style representative democracy advocated by Nehru and other liberal democratic national elites; the other is the choice of indigenously evolved long tradition of participatory democracy posed by Gandhiji, M N Roy, Chittaranjan Das, Rajgopalchari and others. Gandhiji drawing on the long tradition of village panchayats (A troubled tradition due to invasions and British distortion not withstanding) argued for a political system having its base in Indian villages and its superstructure at the centre. The choice of centralized representative democracy at the time of independence was dictated among other things by the conditions following bloody partition, the urgency of integrating princely states, the need to cover the distance through rapid rural and industrial development which thought to be possible only through central planning and probably an imagined parallelism between parliamentary democracy and industrial revolution both of which had their origin in Britain (Mukherji, 2008). This is, however, not an end to the push for Gram swaraj and participatory democracy as an alternative the traces of which are to be found in subsequent national efforts at building of different development institutions. Most of these institutions and development strategies they followed (however symbolic they might be) pretend to have a Gandhian flavour (Consider for example the first launching of community development programme on Oct 2,1952, Gandhi's birth anniversary, first committee to recommend for panchayati raj system was headed by Balwant Rai Mehta, a noted Gandhian). Also the weight of Gandhian charishma behind the idea of Gram Swaraj could manage, at the time of framing of our Constituition, a face saving insertion of art. 40 which enjoined upon the *States to organize village panchayats and endow them with such power and authority as may be necessary to enable them top function as units of self-government*. Art 40 in the Directive principles of state policy, as was expected and being non-justifiable, was not taken seriously by any of the states. Indian political system continued to remain a federation at two levels- Union and States. As Mukharji has said 'The Constitution of India declares India as a union of states. .. The union- states duality runs through the entire content of the Constitution... the framers of the constitution opted for a federation with a strong centre. Subsequently the logic of the strong centre concept shaped congress politics and policies of central planning in such a way as to make the centre much stronger'. There is no fundamental change in the political structure even after the passing of 73rd and $74^{th}$ Constitution amendment. A third stratum of government below the states continues to be seen with speculation by ruling dispensations at the centre as well as the states. The political structure created during independence combined with political development unfolding in the 70s and 80s have created a political environment in India that remains hostile to the deepening of panchayati raj system (Johnson, 2003).

Our passage towards panchayati raj system as we have it today owes much to the way in which Nehruvian Community development project shaped up in the decades of 50s.The community development programmes launched in 1952 by the centre with generous support from Ford Foundation of United States of America for all round development of villages were loosing steam towards the end of 50s. The Balwant Rai Mehta committee (1957) was constituted, in this back drop, by the government on the request of the National Development Council to asses the working of community development programme. The Committee recommended, among other things, for creation of representative and democratic institutions in the village to evoke local interest and excite local initiative in the field of community development. This is how a three tier decentralised panchayati raj system came to be established in several states starting with Rajasthan in Oct 2, 1959. However the initial enthusiasm fizzled out during second five year plan following the death of Nehru, the political confusion in the backdrop of Indo-Pak war, the aggressive centralization by Indira Gandhi during 1966-77, the proliferation of targeted anti-poverty programmes during the 70s and last but not the least, the consequent creation of DRDA. The revival of interest in the panchayats had to wait till December 1977 after Janata party came to power and setting up of Ashok Mehta committee. The recommendation of Ashok Mehta committee marked a real shift in the concept of panchayati raj from an implementing agency to a political institution (Mohanty, 1995; Mathews, 1995). It held that 'Panchayati raj like democracy at the national and state level, is both an end and a means. As an end it is an inevitable extension of democracy...' Some other important recommendations of Ashok Mehta Committee were a two tier model of decentralization, party basis election and reservation for women and weaker sections. The recommendations of the committee were not implemented as the Janata government collapsed in 1980. Two more committee appointed by new congress government was G V K Rao committee in 1985 and L M Singhvi committee in 1986. Two important recommendations given by Rao committee were the district as the basic unit of policy planning and programme implementation and holding of regular election to the panchayats. L M Singhvi committee recommended that local government should be *constitutionally* enshrined and that Gram Sabha (the village assembly) should be the base of decentralized democracy in India. It was Rajiv Gandhi who took the mantle of giving Constitutional status to panchayati raj institutions through $64^{th}$ amendment introduced in 1989 which was defeated in Rajya Sabha. The immediate provocation was of course a concern for fixing leakages and administrative efficiency to deliver development to the poor. The same bill was introduced as $73^{rd}$ and $74^{th}$ Constitutional amendment bill in 1992 and came in to force from April 24, 1993. Thus Panchayati Raj Institutions in India is not a consequence of a quest for participatory village self-government but was a tentative response to the failure of community development as well as targeted anti-poverty programmes.

The $73^{rd}$ amendment holds out many promises of taking the national political system closer to the ideals of Gandhian village self-rule. The significance of $73^{rd}$ amendment lies in, among other things, giving a Constitutional status to panchayati raj institutions. This might fall short of institutionalization of a third stratagem of government *vis-à-vis* the union of the states. Still nonetheless the new Constitutional status saved these underprivileged institutions from oblivion by providing a fixed five year term and mandatory election within six months of dissolution. Another important thing that stands out is the recognition of gram sabha constituted by all the voters at the panchayat level as a deliberative body which is expected to prepare plans of economic development and social justice and implement the development schemes. This is where the panchayati raj system come closet to the idea of direct participatory democracy. Ambedkar had been a counter voice to the Gandhian aspiration of village as the basis of Indian polity, for legitimate fears of oppressive village system and caste atrocities. $73^{rd}$ amendment marks a much needed correction by making provision of reservation to women (which is going to be 50% of total seats soon), SCs, STs, OBCs, and other marginalized groups. 'Had Ambedkar been alive today, he would have been more than pleased...Had Gandhi been alive today, perhaps he would have smiled and said- I told you, that is why I got you the article 40...' (Mohanty, 1995).

## PANCHAYAT AND PEOPLE- THE CONNECT

The present section focuses on the question of how has nearly 50 years of Panchayati raj Institutions fared in India. To say the least there is no consensus on this. There are positives from the panchayati raj experience only to be outweighed by criticisms by many. The hype surrounding this third tier of government called panchayati raj system seems to have no strong grounding as autonomous village government. The very idea, since the time of Balwant Rai Mehta committee, of panchayati raj system is evidently one of a supplement to development effort from above couched in western political idioms (Sirsikar, 1996). The resurrection of interest in the theme by late Prime Minister Rajiv Gandhi was marked by a characteristic search for efficient administrative delivery of development whereby each paise spent on development reaches the target poor. This is also borne by the topsy-turvy journey of panchayati raj system since India embarked on the path of planned development. Local government idea has always been fraught with suspicion and state leaders always see political rivals in panchayat leaders. Therefore it is natural for these institutions to see waves of ascendancy and decadence in its evolution, depending on the climate and political dispensation above it (Avasti, 2006). There are many who debate the essence of 73$^{rd}$ amendment itself as an exercise at decentralization. The task force on devolution of powers and functions upon panchayati raj institutions (2001) found that most of the states have satisfied only the basic requirements relating to the transfer of functions, functionaries and funds to the panchayats. World bank's three volume study of Indian decentralization also echoes the same unwillingness on the part of states to vest the panchayats with administrative and fiscal autonomy. The states have on the other hand tried to remote control these grass root institutions through instruments like 1) Application of Law 2) Removal, Dismissal and assessment of Panchayat Functionaries 3) Right to override panchayat decisions 4) Review and Inspection of Panchayat Record 5) through control of fiscal powers and resources.

Panchayats have no tax powers of their own unless assigned by the States. The tax bases of panchayati raj institutions are often narrow and not remunerative. Panchayats are also unwilling to raise tax for fear of loosing the local support base. There exists an uneasy relationship between the bureaucracy and panchayat functionaries in the absence of administrative devolution. There has been a pool of research findings to suggest the uneasy relationship between bureaucracy and panchayat functionaries. While the administrative machinery, being accountable to their respective line departments, tends to maintain a *paper-mentality*, the panchayat functionaries tend to press on deliverables which is a necessity for them to face people. The chasm between the administration and people has widened over the years in the absence of meaningful transfer of administrative power to panchayats. The kind of decentralisation we have today has 'created two opposing bureaucracies- the politicians and the officials. The official resent their subordination to local leaders who in turn has very little capacity to extract compliance from the officials while the Sarpanches and Pradhans tend to be arrogant because of their power over the officials...in the process the panchayat functionaries (particularly at the Samiti level) assume executive rather than deliberative functions and start interfering with administration. There are instances of cordial relation between officials and panchayat functionaries but this may be a result of either subservience of the official to the non-officials or due to their joining hands for a mutual sharing of spoils' (Bhalerao, 1964). Robert Wade in his study of Andhra Pradesh also points to the rent seeking behaviour of officials associated with rural development and panchayati raj. His arguments make for an even stronger case as he asserts that corruption in the system of local government takes place within a larger framework of a 'market for public office, popular democracy and limited economic opportunity' (Wade, 1985).

Many argue that despite free competitive politics at the grass root level, panchayats continue to be controlled by a handful of powerful elements. Gram sabha as a general assembly practically works as an instrument of different sectional interest. There is evidence of breaking down of community consensus. This becomes particularly problematic when there is a generalized public apathy towards these institutions and the consequent non-participation by women and other sections of society (Deshpande and Murthy, 2002). Many studies have pointed out that woman panchayat functionaries in larger part of India participate in gram sabha through their males. Weaker sections are yet to overcome the limits of elite patronage and loyalties in the prevailing agrarian structure. As far as the customary structure of domination, caste, class differences (land) etc. prevails, the progressive provisions in the panchayati raj system to include marginal groups in society will fail to bear any fruit.

Panchayati raj system in India has a dual character. It uses the strength of traditional village panchayat system to deliver on modern development goals. This, however, does not mean that our traditional value system is always in harmony with the objectives of planned development. People fail to reconcile with these modern institutions due to this duality involved in our panchayati raj system and makes them apathetic towards it. Panchayats come to be seen not as village institutions but a typically *Sarakari* (government) office. There has been a plethora of panchayat studies to show that participation in panchayats by people is very poor. Many a times gram sabha and palli Sabha (as in Orissa) struggle for mere quorum (Bandopadhyay *et al.,* 2003). The panchayat functionaries especially women and weaker section lack leadership capacity. The SIRDs, as in most states, are not enough to train the panchayat functionaries in the nuances of panchayati raj system. Eleventh schedule of the Constitution lists 29 items to be transferred to panchayats. All the states are yet to do this. Those who have transferred the subjects to panchayat have held back the grant of adequate power, staff and fund to discharge the functions.

These depressing nationwide scenarios also have bright spots. There are few studies to draw our attention to the change taking place in the working of the panchayati raj. Crook and Manor in their study of panchayati raj in Karnataka, 1998 point to impressive women participation despite the handicaps of education. When seen within the context of an expanded participation (Crook and Manor, 1998), SC/STs are found to be more likely to be part of election campaign. However the relative insignificance of campaigning in comparison to contesting election and other forms of participation and the high stake SCs/STs, as beneficiary participants (Hiraway, 1998), have in panchayats through welfare programmes has to be taken into account for understanding participation. Studies also point out that rural class structure is declining as a determinant of panchayat participation and participants in panchayati raj institutions are drawn from the poor than the non-poor (Gahatak and Ghatak, 2002). Similarly the traditional rural depressors like bondage, caste are gradually disappearing or at least on their way out from the village. Our villages are benefiting from green revolution, High Yield Variety seeds, non-farm work opportunity (due to both industrial as well as welfare density), development of rural labour market, land redistribution in favour of landless and small framers and anti-poverty programmes. This holds promises for the health of panchayati raj system. Traditional male dominance in our society is also bending towards more gender equality. Women and dalits by virtue of their panchayat membership are now part of public gaze. They are now coming to terms with their new espouser and thereby growing in confidence and collective strength. Old leaders are replaced by the young. There is evidence of a challenge to Upper caste dominance by middle castes and OBCs. Landless and small farmers have become panchayat members, which is politically very significant given our long history of social exclusion (Joshi, 2008). The social standing of SCs and STs has also improved by their grafting into panchayat bodies. At least they are not maltreated today by the upper caste to the point that they will retaliate by mistreating. Also a New class of rural leaders, a new generation 'sons of the soil', have emerged today in our villages.

## JALALPUR GRAM PANCHAYAT

Gram panchayats in Uttar Pradesh were established by Uttar Pradesh Panchayati Raj Act,1947. Two other tiers of local government, namely Block or *khand* panchayat and District panchayat was established in 1961. After the 73rd Constitution amendment the state act was suitably amended in April 1994 and a uniform three tier structure of panchayats came to be established. It was provided that a village or a group of village with 1000 or more population will constitute a gram panchayat. Along with conforming to different provisions of 73rd amendment, Uttar Pradesh panchayati raj act makes provision of allowances for panchayat functionaries and monthly sitting of Gram Sabha.

Jalalpur Gram Panchayat in Jamalpur block of Uttar Pradesh is one of the very backward gram panchayats (see Table 1 below) located in the backward Mirzapur district. Jamalpur is located near national highway 07 towards east of Mirzapur. Jamalpur block has total of 93 Gram panchayats with a population of 20, 6,693. Livelihood activities are mostly based on agriculture. Majority population belongs to other backward castes (OBCs) with a scheduled caste population of 31,404 (see Table 2 below). Socio-

**Table 1:** Poverty in the Panchayat

| | *Beneficiary Cards* | | | | | | |
|---|---|---|---|---|---|---|---|
| ***Year*** | ***2002*** | ***2003*** | ***2004*** | ***2005*** | ***2006*** | ***2007*** | ***2008*** |
| BPL Cards | – | – | – | – | – | 92 | 92 |
| APL Cards | – | – | – | – | – | | 1500 |
| Antodaya Cards | – | – | – | 54 | 54 | 62 | 62 |
| NREGA (Job) Cards | – | – | – | – | – | – | 242 |

*Source:* (PRA Exercises. NB: Total Population is 3200. BPL and APL Survey was conducted in 2005-06.Total APL surveyed was 2947 and BPL was 253 out of which only 1500 (APL) & 92 (BPL) have got cards as on 2008).

**Table 2:** Social Composition of the Gram Panchayat

| *Caste Groups* | *Number of HH* | *Location* | *Total Population* |
|---|---|---|---|
| Scheduled Caste | | | |
| Gond | 2 | Middle | 15 |
| Chammar | 20 | South | 150 |
| Dussath | 8 | East | 25 |
| Dharkar | 10 | North | 35 |
| Kahar | 2 | East | 10 |
| OBC | | | |
| Patels (Kurmi) | 50 | North, West | 500 |
| Athriyas (Kurmi) | 60 | North, East | 700 |
| Biars | 150 | North, East, South | 1450 |
| Ahirs (Yadavs) | 25 | North | 175 |
| Noniya (Chauhans) | 03 | Middle | 18 |
| Kumbhar | 03 | Middle | 07 |
| Lohar | 04 | West, Middle | 22 |
| Nao | 10 | Middle, West | 42 |
| Gupta (Teli) | 15 | North, Middle | 35 |
| GENERAL | | | |
| Brahmins | 15 | North | 100 |

*Source*: (*PRA Exercises*)

economic profile (see Table 3 below) of Jalalpur gram panchayat in Jamalpur block is no different.

The present enquiry into the working of local government institutions is based on a backward panchayat in Mirzapur district known as Jalalpur panchayat. The materials used in the study are

**Table 3:** Economic Changes

| *Land* | *2009* | *2007* | *2005* | *2003* |
|---|---|---|---|---|
| 0-5 Acre | 700 HH | 600HH | 545HH | 500HH |
| 5-10 Acre | 35HH | 50HH | 60HH | 60HH |
| 10 Acre and Above | 6HH | 7HH | 7HH | 7HH |
| Pucca House (Number) | 350HH | 315HH | 300HH | 275HH |
| Factory/Govt Job. (Numbers) | 700/150 | 600/100 | 520/90 | 500/95 |
| Farm Labourers (Number) | 1500 | 1550 | 1700 | 1800 |
| Business/Trade | 20HH | 10HH | 07HH | 05HH |

*Source*: (PRA Exercises. N.B: HH stands for household. Land Fragmentation is on the increase due to breaking down of joint family. People sell their land mainly to construct pucca house and marriage. More people are now going to work in factories due to drought condition since last three years).

collected through focused group discussion and PRA (Participatory Rural Appraisal) exercises. Presentation of the study findings follows a narrative style.

Jalalpur panchayat in Mirzapur consist of two villages namely, Jalalpur and Bishnupur, Bishnupur being the smaller one. The gram panchayat has a population of 3250 out of which 1925 are voters. As per available record (2002) there were 245 BPL families. Now there are 92 BPL cards, 64 Antodaya cards and 400 APL cards. There are also 217 job cards under NREGA programme.

K*urmis*, a backward caste, are the dominant group in the panchayat with respect to number, land ownership and political support base. There are two sub groups among the kurmis, namely *Patels* and *Athriyas*. Another sizable population is that of *Biars* who are mostly agricultural labourers and work on patels land. On an average, the patels own 5-10 acres of land. These castes have been tenant cultivators earlier and have come to acquire ownership from erstwhile absentee land lords. The biars are mostly landless. There are also other caste communities like Yadavs (OBCs), Chammars (SCs) and 3-4 Brahmin households. The Yadavs are traditionally milkmen. They also own some land as small and marginal farmers. The Chammars, who traditionally, took up leather works, now, depend on agriculture as labourers for livelihood. They are on the southern side of the village as always.

Jalalpur Gram Panchayat is now headed by a kurmi Barun Singh. He belongs to the dominant Patel community and is a graduate. His political clout is high as he also happens to be the president of all panchayat pradhans in the block. The panchayat being OBC dominated the pradhan reflects, 'we always have reserved candidates even in unreserved seats. Earlier a septuagenarian, Rambriskha Singh, used to be the face of panchayat (he had won twice before, including the one his wife won). Now a day the contest is getting thicker. Old horses are giving way to new blood, albeit unwillingly (Rambrishka is determined to win back power this time in 2010)'. There are 11 panchayat members belonging to Biar and Patel community out of which six are women. All the members are below 40 years. 'Little education also helps in winning election'- opines the grampradhan who himself is a graduate. There are Brahmins (3-4 family) in the village who remain outside panchayat politics for lack of number. Traditionally the kurmis and biar are in a patron client relationship- the former being land owners and the later farm labourers on their farm. However this traditionally dependent relationship has less determinant influence on political behaviour of the caste communities as has been made out to be by many. Biar support in election is little less than assured. Last election, the gram pradhan position being reserved for women, a biar women Zeera Devi had to be accepted as unanimous choice. All the contestants withdrew their candidature and reached his home to garland Zeera Devi, recalls Kalpu, the ex-*pradhan pati*. Winning and loosing in election depend on the blocks supporting the candidate. Political support is always in groups. There is also widespread buying of votes by distributing money, liquor to husbands or saree to wives. A veteran village politician has already declared about Vijaya Dashmi Utsav inviting all for a feast to mobilize support in view of election next year.

Gram Panchayat sittings are held once in a week in the Pradhan's house- informs Ashok Kumar, the Gram Rozgar Sevak. Women members do not turn up always but necessary papers are sent for their signature. Decisions are always taken through consensus of all panchayat members. Final decision, of course, rests with the pradhan. People see panchayat pradhan as very powerful. He gets all development work done, distribute job cards and select beneficiaries of different development schemes. People frequent pradhan's house to solve different collective or personal problems- development or otherwise. Disputes in the panchayat are considered first by gram pradhan. Women come to panchayat for immunization programmes run by Anganwadi. The poor come to panchayat for want of work. Mostly the biars and kurmis participate in panchayat activities or remain in touch. Panchayat pradhan and other members in that order seem to have taken the place traditional village elites. People frequently petition the gram pradhan for different urgent community work (*e.g.* Renovation of a village Pond in recent past). However 'good contact with panchayat members, especially gram pradhan is a must' for getting any benefit from panchayat- informs Lalmani.

Has the reservation made any difference? There is no unanimity on the issue. As the power positions in the panchayat are shared by backward castes majority in Jalal Pur, they do not fully appreciate the significance of reservation. However some opine that reservation has bestowed public importance and esteem on people (Women in particular) who would have never seen it otherwise. A case in point is that of Guddi (A Chammar scheduled caste), a panchayat member and a first timer. Guddi feels grateful for her election into the present panchayat. She thinks that her life is more worth living now. Though she is not very politically empowered and lacks an awareness of her responsibility as a panchayat member still the excitement in the air is clearly evident. All other women panchayat members also feel very important in their community.

Opinion on socio-economic development through panchayati raj varies across the community. Some important economic contributions of panchayati raj include fair price shops, work (wage employment) through panchayat, Quarter (Housing schemes like IAY), Immunisation (Through Anganwadi) etc. People do not see any long term impact of panchayati raj on poverty. Some senior people inform that rich villagers have become richer. However those who were poor they are still poor for generations now. There is no discernible change in land distribution system in the panchayat. Major part of land is owned by kurmis, especially patels among the kurmis. 'If one wants to be rich one must be a gram pradhan at least for one term. All who have been gram pradhans have at least a *pucca* (concrete) house today'- jokes an elder. This brings out the importance of 'gram panchayat market' for the villagers. Many openly acknowledges the existence of spoils from the implementation of development schemes.

## DISCUSSION AND CONCLUSION

It will be an exaggeration to completely rule out the impact of panchayati raj system on the life of people. Panchayat is being seen as an instrument of power- the power of money supply (including the spoils from the system), power of being in office, power of being known to government officers etc.There has been an increase in people's political consciousness based on recognition of the rationality of village politics. People know whom to vote, what to expect and how to bargain for benefits. There has emerged clear voting blocks which almost consistent with the traditional caste affinity groups. Biars and Kurmis in Jalal Pur see common political cause despite being in unequal relationship. Caste consciousness being high in the area it helps in political mobilization along caste lines. When it comes to politics all backward castes freeze into one block. There is also an increasing tendency towards consensus choices. Buying out candidates to prevent division of vote base is very often part of strategic game plan. However this is not to argue for any backward caste consolidation. Recently there have been cases of caste conflicts between Kurmis and biars on the issue of management of a village temple.

There is evidently a process of what Harold A Gould called political revitalization (Gould, 1971). A new breed of leaders has emerged in the village who are perceived qualitatively better, young and aggressive. The new leaders are looked at with hope and are thought to be smart. The degree of contestation and opposition has also undergone change. Politics in the villages are now more intense as compared to our traditional monolithic society.

It is commonly believed that panchayati raj institutions have largely remained implementing agencies of development schemes designed from above. Materials collected from the field do suggest that people perceive panchayats as a body that offers benefits for the poor. However it is found that panchayat functionaries especially gram pradhans, by the sheer weight of prestige he enjoys, has critical role to play in non-development issues like family quarrels, caste conflict and village peace. The leaders, As Barun Singh, the gram pradhan would recount, swiftly switch between the modern and the traditional world. Is it the beginning of a 'new traditionalism' (Gupta, 1976)?

The study findings offer little to strongly claim evidence of empowerment through panchayati raj. However this has more to do with the narrowness of the concept of empowerment than anything else. Empowerment is not a single process and it manifests in multiple forms. Baviskar in a useful elaboration of the concept has identified five types of empowerment (Baviskar, 2008). Empowerment can come through (*a*) opening up (*b*) acquiring symbolic features (*c*) using power for self (*d*) using power for own community (*e*) using power for larger society. Women in Jamalpur panchayat stand somewhere between the first and second type of empowerment. Women panchayat members were aware of their special position in signing papers. Of course these powers come to them even if they do not come out and this is not usually the cases. There is also the case of a woman, Zeera Devi, who has been contesting elections unsuccessfully for last two times before she was elected pradhan in the last panchayat term. Probably these are small steps before a big leap in women empowerment. As to the empowerment of other sections is concerned there is evidently a new boldness among the backward castes which is at least rational given the fact they are in control of a public institution.

## REFERENCES

Bandopadhyay *et al.* (2003). 'Dependency versus Autonomy: Identity Crisis in India's Panchayats'. Economic and Political Weekly, XXXVIII (38), September.

Baviskar B.S. (2008). Including the excluded, Empowering the Powerless-Case Studies of Panchyati Raj in Maharashtra. *In* Barik B.C. & Sahoo U.C. (*Ed*). Op. cit.

Bhalerao C.N. (1964). Some Social, Political and Administrative consequences of Panchayati Raj, Asian Survey, Vol. 4, April.

Crook R.C. and Manor J. (1999). Democracy and Decentralisation in South Asia and West Africa. Cambridge University Press.

Deshpande S.V. and Murthy G.BV. (2002). 'Pressures from Below: Decentralised Governance in Karnataka, Economic and Political Weekly, 4th May.

Gahatak M. and Ghatak M. (2002). 'Recent Reforms in Panchayat System in West Bengal: Towards a greater Participatory Governance'. Economic and Political Weekly. January.

Gould H.A. (1971). A Review of People's Image of Community Development and Panchayati Raj, by Lalit K Sen, V R Gaikwad and G L Verma, National Institute Of Community Development, Hyderabad, 1967 in Journal of Asian studies, Vol. 31, No. 1, November.

Gupta G. (*Ed.*). (1976). 'Family and Social change in Modern India'. California Academic Press.

Hiraway I. (1989). Panchayati Raj at Crossroads. Economic and Political Weekly, Vol. 24, No. 29, 22 July.

Jha S.N. and Mathur P.C. (*Ed*). (1999). Decentralisation and Local Politics: Readings in Indian Government and Politics, Sage.

Johnson C. (2003). Working Paper 199 on Decentralisation in India: Poverty, Politics and Panchyati Raj, Overseas Development Institute, United Kingdom.

Joshi S. (2008). 'Panchayat Leadership in Gujrat', cited in Barik B.C. & Sahoo U.C. (*Ed*), op. cit.

Kumar G. (2006). Local democracy in India: Interpreting Decentralisation. Sage, New Delhi.

Lal D. (2001). The Poverty of Development Economics. OUP, Delhi;

Maddick H. (1970). Panchayati Raj: A Study of Rural Local Government. Orient Longman, New Delhi.

Mathew G. (1995) Status of Panchayati Raj in India. Concept. New Delhi.

Mohanty B. (1995), 'Panchayati Raj, 73rd Constitution Amendment and Women', Economic and Political Weekly, Vol. 30, No. 52,

Morris-Jones W.H. (1971). The Government and Politics of India. Hutchinson University Library. London.

Mukherji P.N. (2008). 'Representative and Participatory Democracy-Indigenisation of Indian Democracy' in Barik B.C. & Sahoo U.C. (*Ed*), Panchayati Raj Institutions & Rural Development, Rawat, Jaipur.

Oommen M.A. (1999). Panchayat finance and Issues related to Inter-governmental Transfer. In Jha S.N. and Mathur P.C. (*Ed*) op.cit;

Sirsikar V.M. (1966). 'Political Role of Panchayati Raj'. Economic and Political Weekly, Vol. 1, No. 14, Nov. 19.

Wade R. (1985). The market for Public Office: Why the Indian State is not better in Development, as cited in Craig Johnson, op. cit.

---

***Dr. C D Adhikary*** is Associate Professor in the Department of Sociology, Banaras Hindu University, Varanasi. In past, he has worked with Centre for Youth and Social Development. There are a number of journal articles and book chapters to his credit.

3

# Empowerment of Panchayats in India: An Assessment

MAHIPAL[4]

## INTRODUCTION

In order to address the problem of poverty, hunger, illiteracy and unemployment Government of India had launched various developmental and welfare- oriented programmes/schemes through Five Year Plans to enable the people to lead a life with dignity. The Community Development Programme and the National Extension Scheme were introduced for the all-round development of rural society. The Balvantray Mehta Team was constituted in 1957 to bring about people's participation in rural development. This Team suggested democratic decentralization for enlisting people's participation in developmental activities and, towards this end, suggested the creation of Panchayati Raj Institutions (PRIs) at district and sub district levels. But after an initial phase of ascendancy and growth of Panchayats, these institutions became a victim of the lack of political will, hostility of bureaucracy and apathy of people. The Report of the Asoka Mehta Committee (1977) pointed out that the PRIs had failed in their objectives on account of unfavorable political environment. Later on, the G.V.K. Rao Committee (1985) and the Singhvi Committee (1986) were constituted to suggest ways and means to

[4] Director in the Ministry of Rural Development, Govt. of India.
**Corresponding author*: E-mail: mpal1661@gmail.com

strengthen the PRIs. But despite all this, the viability, sustainability and empowerment of these institutions remained at the mercy of the State Governments.

The enactment of the 73rd Amendment (Govt. of India, 1992) to the Constitution (hereafter referred to as the Central Act) was a watershed in the field of decentralization as it, inter alia, provided certainty, continuity and strength to the Panchayati Raj System (PRS) in the country. Later on, PRS was also extended to the Scheduled Areas by PESA (the Provisions of the Panchayats (Extension to Scheduled areas) Act, 1996) hereafter referred to as the Extension Act. Panchayats have been in existence in India in one form or other even before independence and more than two decade has elapsed after the enactment of the 73rd Amendment to the Constitution and more than one decade has elapsed after the enactment of the Provisions of Panchayats (Extension to Scheduled Areas) Act 1996 (Govt. of India, 1996).

In this backdrop, it appears appropriate to review the functioning of the Panchayats from the point of view of ascertaining as to what extent have these institutions enabled the people to participate in delivering good governance at local levels and in the light of experiences, suggest ways and means for further strengthening the PRS in the country. Hence, the present paper endeavours to assess the empowerment and entitlement of the PRIs. Although, the term 'institution of self-government' (ISG) has not been defined in the Act, the percept and the connotation are well understood. In order to function as ISG, the Panchayats transferred functions and availability of requisite manpower to handle devolved functions. In other words, Panchayats should have functional, financial and administrative autonomy at their levels.

## SALIENT FEATURES OF THE CENTRAL AND THE EXTENSION ACT

The main features of the Central Act and brief comments on these are being given in this section. The Central Act has both mandatory and enabling provisions for Panchayats. Following are the salient features of this Act: (i) Formation of Gram Sabha at the village level; (ii) Uniform three-tier system at the village, block and district levels with exemption for intermediate level in States with population of less than two million; (iii) Direct elections to all seats for all members at all levels; (iv) Indirect elections of the chairpersons at the intermediate and apex levels, the mode of election for the lowest level has been left to the State; (v) Reservation on rotational basis for the Scheduled Castes (SCs) and Scheduled Tribes (STs) in proportion to their population both for the membership as well as chairpersonships of the Panchayats at all levels; (vi) Reservation of not less than one-third of the seats and offices for women; (vii) Five year term; (viii) Fresh elections within six months in case of suppressions or dissolution; (ix) Devolution of powers and responsibilities by the State in the matters preparation and implementation of plans for economic development and social justice including implementation of schemes relating to the subjects listed in the Eleventh Schedule of the Act; (x) Setting up the State Finance Commission after every five years to review the financial position of these institutions and to make suitable recommendations to the State on the distribution of funds among the Panchayat; (xi) Setting up the State Election Commission for holding Panchayat elections under its superintendence, direction and control; (xii) The 74$^{th}$ Amendment to the Constitution provides for constitution of District Planning Committee to prepare a draft plan for the whole district comprising Panchayats and municipalities. Although, this provision is a part of the 74$^{th}$ Amendment Act, the States have agreed to extend it to the 73$^{rd}$ Amendment Act. Hence, for all practical purposes, it is also assumed to be a part of the Central Act (Mahipal, 2001; 2004).

The Central Act gave birth to the third generation of the Panchayati Raj in India. The main lacuna of this Act, however, is that, instead of clearly specifying the functions and powers of Panchayats, it has left it to the discretion of the State governments. The Article 243 G of the Constitution clearly says: the legislature of a State may, by law, endow the Panchayats with such powers and authority as may be necessary to enable them to function as institutions of self-government and such law may contain provisions for the devolution of powers and responsibilities upon Panchayats at the appropriate level subject to such conditions as may be specified therein, with respect to (a) the preparation of plans for economic development and social justice and (b) the implementation of schemes for economic development and social justice as may be entrusted to them including those in relation to the matters listed in the Eleventh Schedule.

This Article is the corner- stone of the entire thrust on democratic decentralisation as visualised in the Act. It is, however, not mandatory on the part of the State Government to implement this because the word "may" is used five times in this Article. Thus, it is at the discretion of the State Government to give or "not give" powers to the Panchayats. It implies that the power sharing with the Panchayats depends on the political leadership at the State level. We have the example of West Bengal where Panchayats elections were being held since the seventies *i.e.*, even before the Amendment because the political party in power has political will for strengthening the grassroots democracy.

## EMPOWERMENT AND ENTITLEMENT OF THE PANCHAYATI RAJ INSTITUTIONS

The state governments were supposed to transfer the functions, finance and functionaries pertaining to 29 subjects listed in the Eleventh Schedule of the Constitution to the PRIs to enable these bodies as institutions of self government. The connotation ISG has been defined in terms of enjoying functional, financial and administrative autonomy in their functioning at different levels. Let us discuss these aspects of Panchayats on the basis of the findings of the Devolution Report 2015-16, Ministry of Panchayati Raj, Government of India.

## DEVOLUTION OF FUNCTIONS

The basic principle (that is, what can be done at a particular level should be done at that level only) has not been adhered to by the states while allocating functions among the three tiers of Panchayats. As mentioned earlier, the state governments were supposed to transfer to panchayats functions pertaining to 29 subjects listed in the Eleventh Schedule of the Constitution. The core of decentralisation is to carve out functional domain of the Panchayats in such a way that these institutions function as local governments in the state and prepare plans for economic development with social justice at their levels.

The devolution Report, in addition to 29 functional areas for PRIs listed in the Constitution, 11 additional items included in various State Acts were also added to this list and the list was circulated to States to assess the status of devolution of functions to Panchayats. The functions were classified into primary, secondary and tertiary for convenience of analysis of extent of devolution to Panchayats. Out of total functions, 7 functions are kept in the primary sector, 5 in the secondary sector and 28 in the tertiary sector. Three aspects of devolution have been enumerated under functional devolution namely, the progress in empowerment of PRIs by the State legislatures, functions in which executive orders regarding devolution have been issued and operationalised by the State departments, and amending various allied laws which are inconsistent with the Constitutional provisions under the Amendment.

Table 1 presents the progress in transfer of functions in the Primary Sector by State across type of interventions. It may be seen from the table that states of Kerala, Karnataka, Tamil Nadu Chattishgarh, Himachal Pradesh, J & K and West Bengal have delegated functions by Legislature, executive orders issued and operationalised. But all have not been changed in the allied acts. Karnataka, Kerala, Tamil Nadu are the three States which have also carried out changes in the allied acts. Chhattisgarh has reportedly covered 7 functions and 6 allied acts. Arunachal Pradesh has recorded that 6 allied acts have been amended, while Gujarat has covered (TISS and MoPR, 2016).

Allied acts in 5 functions Sikkim, Rajasthan and Telangana have covered the seven functions but have amended 3, 2 and 1 allied

**Table 1:** Progress in Transfer of functions in the Primary Sector by State across type of interventions

| ***Name of State/UT*** | ***Primary*** | | | |
|---|---|---|---|---|
| | ***Number of Functions delegated by legislature*** | ***Number of Executive Orders issued*** | ***Number of Executive orders Operationalised*** | ***Number of Changes in allied acts*** |
| Andaman and Nicobar Islands | 0 | 7 | 7 | 0 |
| Andhra Pradesh | 7 | 5 | 3 | 0 |
| Arunachal Pradesh | 0 | 6 | 6 | 6 |
| Assam | 0 | 7 | 0 | 0 |
| Bihar | 0 | 6 | 0 | 0 |
| Chandigarh | | | | |
| Chhatisgarh | 7 | 7 | 7 | 6 |
| Dadra and Nagar Haveli | | | | |
| Daman and Diu | 7 | 7 | 4 | 0 |
| Goa | 00 | 0 | 0 | 0 |
| Gujarat | 6 | 0 | 6 | 5 |
| Haryana | 7 | 3 | 3 | 0 |
| Himachal Pradesh | 7 | 7 | 7 | 0 |
| Jammu and Kashmir | 7 | 7 | 7 | 0 |
| Jharkhand | 7 | 5 | 5 | 0 |
| Karnataka | 7 | 7 | 7 | 7 |
| Kerala | 7 | 7 | 7 | 7 |
| Lakshadweep | 3 | 3 | 3 | 0 |
| Madhya Pradesh | 5 | 5 | 5 | 5 |
| Maharashtra | 6 | 4 | 4 | 1 |
| Manipur | 3 | 3 | 1 | 0 |
| Punducherry | 0 | 6 | 6 | 0 |
| Odisha | 1 | 0 | 0 | 0 |
| Punjab | 7 | 1 | 1 | 0 |
| Rajasthan | 7 | 7 | 5 | 1 |
| Sikkim | 7 | 7 | 6 | 3 |
| Tamil Nadu | 7 | 7 | 7 | 7 |
| Telagana | 7 | 3 | 3 | 2 |
| Tripura | 4 | 4 | 4 | 0 |
| Uttar Pradesh | 6 | 3 | 0 | 0 |
| Uttarakhand | 5 | 3 | 2 | 0 |
| West Bengal | 7 | 7 | 7 | 0 |

*Source*: (Devolution Report 2015-16 , Ministry of Panchayati Raj, Government of India)

act respectively. Maharashtra has covered 6 functions and amended 1 allied act whereas Madhya Pradesh has covered 5 functions and also amended 5 allied acts. Rest of the States are in between as the table indicates. For example, in Arunachal Pradesh instead of delegating functions by legislatures delegated by executive orders. Bihar is another case where executive orders with regard to 6 functions have been issued but not operationalised.

Table 2 presents the progress in transfer of functions in the Secondary Sector by State across type of interventions. Here also Kerala, Karnataka and Tamil Nadu have again done the best possible, covering (TISS and MoPR, 2016) all the requisite steps under these functions. Rest of the States are in between as the table shows. Most of the states have not devolved functions of this category to the Panchayats.

Table 3 presents the progress in transfer of functions in the Tertiary Sector by State across type of interventions In this sector, Karnataka, Sikkim and Himachal Pradesh have covered 28 functions each (TISS and MoPR, 2016). Kerala has covered 27 functions out of the possible 28 and has amended 27 allied acts. Karnataka has recorded that 28 allied acts have been amended. Tamil Nadu has amended 24 and Gujarat 22 allied acts. Arunachal Pradesh has amended 12 acts, Chhattisgarh 11, Rajasthan 6, Maharashtra and Madhya Pradesh 5, Manipur 2 and Tripura 1.

The particulars of amendment of allied acts in all the three sectors by Karnataka, Tamil Nadu and Sikkim seem to be strikingly higher than what was reported during the previous years. More details of nature of devolutions is needed to be studied in future. If we see sector wise mapping of the functions devolved on Panchayats indicate we found that under Primary Sector 26 states have transferred Animal husbandry, dairying and poultry. Fisheries sector is transferred on Panchayats in 25 States and the sector Agriculture including extension transferred to Panchayats in 24 states.

In the secondary sector 26 states have transferred small-scale industries and khadi village and cottage industries to the

**Table 2:** Progress in Transfer of functions in the Secondary Sector by State across type of interventions

| ***Name of State/UT*** | ***Secondary*** | | | |
|---|---|---|---|---|
| | ***Number of Functions delegated by legislature*** | ***Number of Executive Orders issued*** | ***Number of Executive orders Operationalised*** | ***Number of Changes in allied acts*** |
| Andaman and Nicobar Islands | 0 | 5 | 5 | 0 |
| Andhra Pradesh | 5 | 3 | 3 | 0 |
| Arunachal Pradesh | 0 | 5 | 5 | 4 |
| Assam | 0 | 4 | 0 | 0 |
| Bihar | 0 | 3 | 0 | 0 |
| Chandigarh | | | | |
| Chhatisgarh | 4 | 4 | 4 | 4 |
| Dadra and Nagar Haveli | | | | |
| Daman and Diu | 5 | 5 | 2 | 0 |
| Goa | 0 | 0 | 0 | 0 |
| Gujarat | 1 | 0 | 1 | 1 |
| Haryana | 5 | 1 | 1 | 0 |
| Himachal Pradesh | 5 | 5 | 5 | 0 |
| Jammu and Kashmir | 2 | 2 | 2 | 0 |
| Jharkhand | 1 | 1 | 0 | 0 |
| Karnataka | 5 | 5 | 5 | 5 |
| Kerala | 5 | 5 | 5 | 5 |
| Lakshadweep | 0 | 0 | 0 | 0 |
| Madhya Pradesh | 2 | 2 | 2 | 2 |
| Maharashtra | 2 | 1 | 1 | 0 |
| Manipur | 2 | 2 | 2 | 2 |
| Punducherry | 0 | 0 | 0 | 0 |
| Odisha | 1 | 1 | 1 | 0 |
| Punjab | 3 | 3 | 3 | 3 |
| Rajasthan | 5 | 5 | 5 | 0 |
| Sikkim | 5 | 5 | 5 | 0 |
| Tamil Nadu | 5 | 5 | 5 | 5 |
| Telagana | 0 | 0 | 0 | 0 |
| Tripura | 1 | 1 | 1 | 0 |
| Uttar Pradesh | 5 | 0 | 0 | 0 |
| Uttarakhand | 0 | 0 | 0 | 0 |
| West Bengal | 5 | 5 | 5 | 0 |

*Source*: Devolution Report 2015-16, Ministry of Panchayati Raj, Government of India

**Table 3:** Progress in Transfer of functions in the Tertiary Sector by State across type of interventions

| ***Name of State/UT*** | ***Tertiary*** | | | |
|---|---|---|---|---|
| | ***Number of Functions delegated by legislature*** | ***Number of Executive Orders issued*** | ***Number of Executive orders Operationalised*** | ***Number of Changes in allied acts*** |
| Andaman and Nicobar Islands | 0 | 14 | 13 | 0 |
| Andhra Pradesh | 13 | 8 | 8 | 0 |
| Arunachal Pradesh | 0 | 12 | 12 | 12 |
| Assam | 0 | 10 | 0 | 0 |
| Bihar | 0 | 3 | 0 | 0 |
| Chandigarh | | | | |
| Chhatisgarh | 11 | 11 | 11 | 11 |
| Dadra and Nagar Haveli | | | | |
| Daman and Diu | 18 | 16 | 13 | 0 |
| Goa | 3 | 0 | 0 | 0 |
| Gujarat | 22 | 0 | 22 | 22 |
| Haryana | 17 | 7 | 6 | 1 |
| Himachal Pradesh | 28 | 28 | 28 | 2 |
| Jammu and Kashmir | 23 | 23 | 23 | 0 |
| Jharkhand | 13 | 10 | 01 | 0 |
| Karnataka | 28 | 28 | 28 | 28 |
| Kerala | 27 | 27 | 27 | 27 |
| Lakshadweep | 7 | 8 | 8 | 0 |
| Madhya Pradesh | 7 | 9 | 7 | 5 |
| Maharashtra | 25 | 25 | 24 | 2 |
| Manipur | 2 | 2 | 2 | 0 |
| Odisha | 14 | 14 | 14 | 0 |
| Punducherry | 0 | 0 | 0 | 0 |
| Punjab | 8 | 8 | 8 | 0 |
| Rajasthan | 13 | 13 | 13 | 6 |
| Sikkim | 28 | 28 | 28 | 0 |
| Tamil Nadu | 24 | 24 | 24 | 24 |
| Telangana | 8 | 15 | 15 | 1 |
| Tripura | 7 | 7 | 7 | 0 |
| Uttar Pradesh | 15 | 1 | 0 | 0 |
| Uttarakhand | 2 | 10 | 4 | 0 |
| West Bengal | 24 | 24 | 24 | 0 |

*Source*: Devolution Report 2015-16, Ministry of Panchayati Raj, Government of India

Panchayats. Non-conventional source of energy is transferred only in 24 states and rural electrification in 23 states. Fuel and fodder is transferred only in 22 states. This follows almost the same pattern as in minor forest produce and social forestry and farm forestry in the primary sector.

Under tertiary sector the most popular function transferred to Panchayats is education in 29 states followed by health in 27 states, drinking water in 26 states, social welfare including welfare of handicapped and mentally retarded in 26 states, women and child development in 24 states, family welfare and rural housing in 24 states, poverty alleviation programmes in 23 states, public distribution systems in 22 states. Construction of roads, culverts etc. function is transferred only in 23 states. Urban functions like fire services, slum improvement and upgradation, cattle pound and prevention of cruelty to animals, provision of amenities and facilities like parks, garden and play grounds are transferred to Panchayats in few S. Public amenities including street lighting, parking lots, bus stops and public States. Functions like burials and burial grounds, cremation and cremation grounds, regulation of land use and construction of buildings, solid waste management are covered only in few states. Interestingly planning and social development have not assigned to local governments in a majority of states is a serious matter of concern because the panchayats are expected to prepare plan for economic development and social justice including 29 subjects listed in the $11^{th}$ Schedule of the Constitution.

Broadly , the core development functions like Agriculture and allied sectors, Animal husbandry and dairying, fisheries, small scale industries, Khadi village and cottage industries, education, health, drinking water, social welfare, women and child development poverty alleviation, public distribution and rural roads and welfare of scheduled castes and scheduled tribes are by and large transferred to Panchayats across the states. But the functions categorized under secondary and tertiary sectors have not been transferred substantially.

## DEVOLUTION OF FINANCE

Functional devolution to Panchayats without matching funds is a delusion. This is in fact what has happened in most of the States. Before listing the functions to be performed by the Panchayats, a number of states have introduced certain qualifying clauses. For example, in Andhra Pradesh, Haryana and Tamil Nadu, it is 'within the limit of its funds'. In Punjab, it is 'to the extent its funds allow to perform'. In Himachal Pradesh and Madhya Pradesh, the clause is 'as far as the Gram Panchayat funds at its disposal'. This makes the picture about finances dimension of the Panchayats empowerment hazy because it is the resources at their disposal that determine their role in performing developmental activities in their respective areas of operation. Gujarat and Karnataka do, however, have Panchayat-friendly provisions in this regard. In Gujarat, as per Section 204 of the Panchayat Act, if the income of a Gram Panchayat is not commensurate with its functions, the Taluka Panchayat shall take necessary steps to provide resources to enable it to perform its functions effectively. The Karnataka Panchayat Act provides for grant arrangements for the Gram Panchayat under which a grant is to be given to it by the state government (Section 208).

On the issue of the role of the State Finance Commissions (SFCs) in financially empowering the Panchayats, the Mid-Term Appraisal of the $9^{th}$ Plan observed that: "More buoyant taxes like sales tax and excise are kept out of the purview of PRIs. All SFCs have put great emphasis on internal revenue mobilization but none has suggested any effective mechanism for PRIs to generate their own revenue. The SFCs reports have paid less attention to the issue of autonomy, financial management and auditing procedures. The main deficiency of the reports lies in the fact that the recommendations are not based on clear statement of the spending responsibilities of local bodies. Indeed, the absence of attention to the elementary principle, that the expenditure assignment must precede any tax or revenue assignment, has made most of the SFCs recommendations suspect" (Planning Commission, 2000).

The Working Group on the State Resources in year 2002 also commented in the same manner: "The suggestions of the first generation SFCs if fully implemented will go a long way in improving the revenue generation capacity of the local bodies. However, the SFCs have failed to take a comprehensive view and the resource sharing between the state and local bodies still remains limited and unsettled. The state governments have also been slow and hesitant in accepting the recommendations of the SFCs."

As Table 4 depicts one of the unique features of India's fiscal decentralisation is the high level of asymmetry of the relative shares of expenditure and revenue assignments between the federal, provincial and local governments (TISS and MoPR, 2016).

In above table which contains expenditure and revenue assignments of different governments from 1998-99 to 2007-08 indicates that expenditure assignment has been less than 8 per cent and revenue assignment has been less than 4 per cent for Panchayats. It shows a very minimal role of the local government in local development whereas as per Article 243 G of the Constitution, these institutions are expected to prepare plans for economic development and social justice at their levels.

**Table 4:** Expenditure and revenue assignment-relative shares of central, state and local governments

| ***Expenditure assignment*** | ***1998-99*** | ***2002-03*** | ***2003-04*** | ***2004-05*** | ***2005-06*** | ***2006-07*** | ***2007-08*** |
|---|---|---|---|---|---|---|---|
| Centre | 47.47 | 47.25 | 42.67 | 43.30 | 45.51 | 44.40 | 47.70 |
| State | 46.97 | 46.57 | 50.99 | 50.02 | 47.87 | 48.68 | 45.19 |
| Local Government | 5.74 | 6.18 | 6.34 | 6.68 | 6.62 | 6.92 | 7.11 |
| ***Revenue Assignment*** | ***1998-99*** | ***2002-03*** | ***2003-04*** | ***2004-05*** | ***2005-06*** | ***2006-07*** | ***2007-08*** |
| Centre | 55.89 | 55.40 | 56.08 | 55.21 | 55.33 | 56.13 | 58.11 |
| State | 41.10 | 41.00 | 40.47 | 41.43 | 41.38 | 40.83 | 39.07 |
| Local Government | 3.01 | 3.6 | 3.50 | 3.37 | 3.29 | 3.04 | 2.82 |

*Source*: Devolution Report 2015-16, Ministry of Panchayati Raj, Government of India

The insult to injury was added on this account by the finding of the Report of the Task Force of Devolution of Powers and Functions to the PRIs brought out by the Ministry of Rural Development which pointed out that the mandatory provisions of the 73rd Amendment Act have not been implemented in letter and spirit by most of the states/ union territories even about a decade after the coming into force of the said Act (Ministry of Rural Development, 2001).

## OWN RESOURCES OF PANCHAYATS

The real empowerment of panchayats will take place when they have their own resources at their disposal because such funds would be untied and the Panchayats can use them according to their requirement and priority. But picture is blurred if one sees across the states. Generally, Property tax, cess on land revenue, surcharge on additional stamp duty, tolls, tax on profession, tax on advertisement and octroi are likely to be the major contributors in the own source revenue. These together contribute to around 8 per cent of the overall receipts in PRIs across all states. But the issue is that a large number of sources of revenue for which powers are assigned to local government are not collected. And even if collections are organised, collection efficiencies are poor. The poor performance of Panchayats in generating own revenue have been attributed by recommendations of different State Finance Commissions to expand the own source domain of PRIs have not been implemented by some State governments, the rates of own sources are not periodically reviewed and revised, quite often there is no floor rate and only an upper limit is prescribed which effects revenue mobilization, reluctance of Panchayats to levy taxes, poor administrative capability , non-assignment of productive local assets to panchayat and enabling routes for leasing and lending of common resources, inadequacies or non-existence of systems for sharing income from mining of minor minerals, inadequate mechanisms for levying service charges / user charges on properties of State Government and Union Government.

The relative importance of own sources of revenue by Panchayats varies from state to state. However, GPs in a number of states have been given substantive powers for collecting own revenue whereas Panchayat Samitis and District Panchayats have much lower revenue collection powers.

Table 5 presents the estimates of own tax revenues across the states. It may be seen from the Table that at G P level, per capita tax collection is the highest in Maharashtra followed by Kerala, Karnataka, Tamil Nadu. Assam, Odisha, Sikkim and West Bengal have very meager contribution. In rest of the States, GPs have no tax collection at their levels. At intermediate level , Maharashtra, Telangana and Gujarat and at apex level Maharashtra, Uttarkhand, Haryana and Telangana are having greater share of own tax revenue (TISS and MoPR, 2016).

## DEVOLUTION OF FUNCTIONARIES

Control over the personnel of the Panchayats pertaining to the 29 subjects of the 11th Schedule by Panchayats is no less important than transferring the functions and finances to them. The State Panchayat Acts provide powers for inspection, inquiring into their affairs, suspension of Panchayat' resolutions, issuing directions, etc., to the state governments. Besides, the key functionaries, namely, Secretaries and Executive Officers, at all levels of Panchayats are state government employees in most of the states. For ensuring administrative autonomy, the Panchayats should have their own service cadre. In Tripura, for recalling a state government employee, a resolution to that effect has to be passed by a majority of the members of the Panchayat.

Now, let us discuss the status of this dimension of the empowerment of Panchayats. The Devolution Report 2015-16 has evaluated the strength of this dimension of devolution to Panchayats on the basis of (a) sanctioned own functionaries and functionaries in local institutions, per thousand population (b) availability of functionaries as a proportion of sanctioned positions.

**Table 5:** Distribution of per capita own tax collection in Rupees by state across tier of Panchayat 2015

| ***Name of State/UT*** | ***Per capita own tax Collection in Rupees 2015*** | | |
|---|---|---|---|
| | ***Gram Panchayat*** | ***Block Panchayat*** | ***District Panchayat*** |
| Andaman and Nicobar Islands | 0.00 | 0.00 | 0.00 |
| Andhra Pradesh | 56.93 | 0.00 | 0.00 |
| Arunachal Pradesh | | | |
| Assam | 4.52 | 0.50 | 0.53 |
| Bihar | | | |
| Chandigarh | | | |
| Chhatisgarh | 0.00 | 0.00 | 0.00 |
| Dadra and Nagar Haveli | | NA | |
| Daman and Diu | 0.00 | NA | 0.00 |
| Goa | 0.00 | NA | 0.00 |
| Gujarat | 65.95 | 13.21 | 10.77 |
| Haryana | 32.37 | 6.02 | 4.01 |
| Himachal Pradesh | | | |
| Jammu and Kashmir | 0.00 | NA | NA |
| Jharkhand | | | |
| Karnataka | 93.84 | 0.00 | 0.00 |
| Kerala | 178.09 | 0.00 | 0.00 |
| Lakshadweep | 0.00 | NA | 0.50 |
| Madhya Pradesh | | | |
| Maharashtra | 209.36 | 28.34 | 51.19 |
| Manipur | | NA | |
| Odisha | 7.35 | 0.00 | 0.00 |
| Punducherry | | | NA |
| Punjab | | | |
| Rajasthan | | | |
| Sikkim | 2.24 | NA | 0.00 |
| Tamil Nadu | 68.84 | 0.00 | 0.00 |
| Telagana | 51.80 | 13.71 | 9.03 |
| Tripura | | | |
| Uttar Pradesh | | | |
| Uttarakhand | 0.00 | 0.00 | 19.04 |
| West Bengal | 8.79 | 0.00 | 0.00 |

*Source*: Devolution Report 2015-16, Ministry of Panchayati Raj, Government of India

Table 6 presents the availability of functionaries at different levels. At the GP level, it may be seen from Table that Andhra Pradesh, Chattisgarh, Himachal Pradesh, Lakshadweep, Madhya Pradesh and Tamil Nadu have cent percent availability of functionaries followed by Sikkim with 99 per cent, Karnataka, Haryana and Chhattisgarh with 98% availability. Maharashtra has reported 97 per cent and Kerala has reported figures of 94 per cent. Uttar Pradesh is having the lowest (37%) in all the States. The average national availability at this level is 81 per cent .At intermediate level the figures of availability in Andhra Pradesh, Chandigarh, Chhattisgarh, Madhya Pradesh, Tamil Nadu and Uttar Pradesh are 100 per cent while that of Kerala and Himachal Pradesh is 99 per cent. Rajasthan is having the lowest (43%) in all the States. The average national availability at this level is 83 per cent. At district level, Andhra Pradesh, Chhattisgarh, Kerala, Manipur, Sikkim, Tamil Nadu and Uttar Pradesh have reported 100 per cent availability where as Karnataka and West Bengal have reported availability of 97 per cent. Jharkhand is having the lowest (25%) in all the States. The average national availability at this level is 84 per cent.

The issue of personnel could only be addressed properly if functional domain of the Panchayats is delineated properly. Further, the issue of availability of personnel could be considered seriously by the State Governments if there is pressure from the villagers for the delivery of various services at local levels. However, problem is serious in the sense that at the average manpower at the GP level in States like Uttar Pradesh and Bihar are one- sixth of the national average and need to be addressed immediately to enable the Panchayat Raj Institutions to have their legitimate share in local governance, planning and development (Planning Commission, 2001).

## CONCLUSIONS

To conclude, two Hindi saying aptly describe the present status of the PRIs in the country. One, 'P*anchon kee baat seer matha patnala yahin girega* '(We appreciate your point of view, but the status

**Table 6:** Proportion of availability of functionaries by state across tier of Panchayat 2015

| *Name of State/UT* | *Gram Panchayat* | *Block Panchayat* | *District Panchayat* |
|---|---|---|---|
| Andaman and Nicobar Islands | 0.94 | 0.94 | 0.98 |
| Andhra Pradesh | 1.00 | 1.00 | 1.00 |
| Arunachal Pradesh | 0.48 | 0.97 | 0.93 |
| Assam | 0.49 | 0.63 | 0.67 |
| Bihar | 0.78 | 0.59 | 0.90 |
| Chandigarh | 0.98 | 1.00 | 1.00 |
| Chhatisgarh | 1.00 | 1.00 | 0.92 |
| Dadra and Nagar Haveli | | | |
| Daman and Diu | 0.93 | | 0.98 |
| Goa | 0.58 | | 1.00 |
| Gujarat | 0.92 | 0.70 | 0.41 |
| Haryana | 0.98 | | 0.29 |
| Himachal Pradesh | 1.00 | 0.99 | 1.00 |
| Jammu and Kashmir | 0.43 | | |
| Jharkhand | 0.74 | 0.52 | 0.25 |
| Karnataka | 0.98 | 0.88 | 0.97 |
| Kerala | 0.94 | 0.99 | 1.00 |
| Lakshadweep | 1.00 | | 1.00 |
| Madhya Pradesh | 1.00 | 1.00 | 1.00 |
| Maharashtra | 0.97 | 0.94 | 0.86 |
| Manipur | 0.53 | | 1.00 |
| Odisha | 0.97 | 0.72 | 0.84 |
| Punducherry | | | |
| Punjab | 0.63 | 0.56 | 0.71 |
| Rajasthan | 0.50 | 0.43 | 0.64 |
| Sikkim | 0.99 | | 1.00 |
| Tamil Nadu | 1.00 | 1.00 | 1.00 |
| Telangana | 0.85 | 0.82 | 0.92 |
| Tripura | 0.69 | 0.64 | 0.39 |
| Uttar Pradesh | 0.37 | 1.00 | 1.00 |
| Uttarakhand | 0.83 | 0.76 | 0.62 |
| West Bengal | 0.77 | 0.96 | 0.97 |

*Source*: Devolution Report 2015-16, Ministry of Panchayati Raj, Government of India

quo will remain). Two:' *Ghar- bar sab tumhara, kothi kuthala ke hath maat lagana* (Everything of the house belongs to you, but do not touch the money and other precious things). There have been a number of meetings and conferences between central and the

State Governments. All- India Panchayat Adhyakshas Sammelans were also held in the past. The result has been as expected. The Central and the State Governments, instead of initiating such policies which could strengthen the PRIs, have used these institutions as conduits for distributing funds to the target groups (Mahipal, 2004). The Schemes such as the MP Local Areas Development Scheme and strengthening the District Rural Development Agency have been initiated which are in essence and in practice, anathema to the motto of decentralisation through the PRIs. It was also expected that the constitution of the PRIs would create a new leadership at local levels which would not only abjure obscurantism and backward- looking attitude but also would be instrumental in changing the anti-development outlook of the traditional caste leaders in the villages so that the people could achieve their collective aspiration of developing themselves holistically. But the hopes have been belied because there is no urge for decentralisation at the grassroots. Remedy of the malady lies in creating effective demand on the part of the people at the grassroots in terms of asking more powers from the Governments. For this, it is necessary for Panchayats leaders to get organized and to form their associations at the local, district, state and national levels in order to enhance Panchayats' bargaining powers and enable themselves by learning from each other and by extensively deliberating matters of common interest.

## REFERENCES

Govt. of India. (1992). The Constitution (Seventy Third) Amendment Act 1992 retrieved from https://mhrd.gov.in/sites/upload_files/mhrd/files/upload_document/73amend.pdf on 20.04.2019.

Govt. of India. (1996). The Provisions for Panchayats (Extension to Scheduled Areas) Act 1996. Retrieved from https://tribal.nic.in/actRules/PESA.pdf on 20.04.2019.

Mahipal. (2000). Panchayats in the Fifth Scheduled Areas. Economic and Political Weekly. Vol. 35, Issue No. 19. May 6.

Mahipal. (2004). 'Panchayati Raj and Rural Governance: Experience of a Decade', Economic and Political Weekly. Vol. 39, Issue No. 02, 10th Jan.

Ministry of Rural Development. (2001). Report of the Task Force on Devolution of Powers and Functions Upon Panchayati Raj Institutions. August.

Planning Commission. (2000). Mid-Term Appraisal of the Ninth Five- Year Plan (1997-2002). October.

Planning Commission. (2001). Report of the Task Force on Panchayati Raj Institutions(PRls). December.

Planning Commission. (2001). The Report of the Working Group on Decentralised Planning and Panchayati Raj Institutions for the Tenth Five Year Plan (2002-07). November.

TISS and MoPR. (2016). Devolution Report 2015-16, Ministry of Panchayati Raj, Government of India.
Retrieved from https://www.panchayat.gov.in/documents/20126/0/devolution2015-16.pdf/d5e26984-5783-3a14-e7f7-6113a6cfa7c4?t=1554884884392 on 22.04.2019.

---

***Dr. Mahipal*** is Indian Economic Services (Retd.) Officer. Presently, Visiting faculty, School of Planning and Architecture, New Delhi and Adjunct Professor in the Institute of Business Management, Mangalayatan University, Aligarh. Earlier he has served Ministry of Rural Development Government of India and Haryana Institute of Rural Development. He has authored several books and papers on Panchayati Raj and Rural Development.

4

# Rural Development and Democratic Decentralization in India: Analyzing the Role of PRIs

PRADIP PARIDA[5]

## INTRODUCTION

A cursory look into the rural development programmes since Independence will give us a rough picture regarding issues, problems, strategies, programmes and policies implemented to address various dimension in the rural development sectors of contemporary India. Though the post liberalization period has taken a dramatic change in many ways, still then the primary focus to address poverty and related issues of rural development has not changed from the centre stage of this sector. As there was a watershed development at macro level in terms of policy input, in terms of role of market *versus* the role of state in many sphere, more particularly economic sphere. As matter of fact discourse on development always focuses on 'rural development' as the focal point, whatever may be the issue, notion and parameters of development (Singh, 1999). The Human Development Indicators (HDI), Gender Development Indicators (GDI), basic amenities to civic life, *i.e.* basic amount of food, cloth, shelter- housing, primary education, primary health care facilities, transportation and

[5] Rajiv Gandhi Institute of Petroleum Technology, Amethi U.P.
**Corresponding author*: E-mail: paridapradip1@gmail.com

communication and so also entitlement to freedom- rights of an individual in given state structure- his legal entitlement.

## PROGRAMMES IN INDIA TO ADDRESS RURAL DEVELOPMENT

Since independence with the beginning of First Five year plan till the recent one, always there are efforts and targeted intervention to address various issues on 'rural development'. Though the approaches were different on many occasion, depending upon the political regime and issues they are highlighting, *i.e.* 'Garibi Hatao' during Ms. Indira Gandhi's time, none the less providing the basic amenities of civic life and a decent life in terms of income, access to food, cloth, shelter- housing and other necessary facilities have always been the prime concern for the successive central and state governments across the board (Dandekar and Rath, 1971). The constitution of India solemnly declares India to adopt 'socialistic pattern of society'. In other words the state will come forward to create a society in India at least, where the basic amenities of civic life will be available to all.

The central sponsored programme implemented by Panchayat but sponsored by the government of India, since independence till date are as follows:

- MNERGA – Mahatma Gandhi National Rural Employment Guarantee Programme, to cater to the needs of the population in rural areas, where they can get 100 man days job per family and create assets. It will stop migration to cities for job purpose and can give employment opportunity at local level.
- NRHM – National Rural Health Mission caters to need of the issue related to health sector, primarily to address IMR, MMR, Malaria, diarrhea, polio and common diseases at local level by providing doctors, nurses, paramedics, medicine, ambulances etc.
- NRLM – National Rural Livelihood Mission aims at providing livelihood options at local by opening up various avenues, starting from agriculture, horticulture, cottage industry, non-

agriculture based activities, primarily to address the creation of livelihood opportunities.

- SSA – Srava Siksha Abhiyan cater to the need of making right to education as a fundamental right by creation of new school, community based teaching, teacher from the local community, availability of school in neighborhood or village level, para teacher, reading materials etc.
- Mid Day Meal Schemes in Schools in recent time has added value to it. In one way it gives minimum nutritious food to poor children and in other it is aloes increasing the attendance of students in schools.
- IAY – Indira Awas Yojana cater to the need of housing for the house less persons and below poverty line people (BPL) at rural areas, so that at least they have one room house to live in. Modified version is Prdhan Mantri Awas Yojana.
- ICDS – Integrated Child Development Scheme is meant to provide nutritious food and medicine to pregnant mother and child in rural areas and can take care of their food and health till certain level. The AnganWadi workers appointed under the schemes are expected to provide all these support to these groups of targeted beneficiaries.
- National Watershed Mission – It caters to the need of arid and semi-arid region to create water resources for consumption of human being, other animals, restoration of ecology, stopping soil erosion, and can be utilized for agriculture and related livelihood activities.
- National Horticulture Mission – It cater to the need of creation of a buffer stock of fruits and vegetables, starting from seasonal to annual and throughout the year, so that people at least can avail vegetables in all parts of the country.
- White Revolution: Operation Flood was meant to create surplus milk production for the country, so that people can utilize raw milk, milk products and the excess can be exported to other parts of the country or the world.
- Blue Revolution – It was implemented to make India sufficient in terms of fish production, so that we won't be importing fish from outside, rather with technological input we can produce from inland and from ocean, to cater to the

need of our own consumption, rest we can preserve can send to open market, even if abroad.

- IRDP – Integrated Rural Development Programme aimed at providing a holistic approach to rural development by composing number of issues, primarily to address rural poverty.
- FFW – Food for Work programme aimed at providing food or ration to needy poor people, while they work, apart from providing monetary benefit to them. This was an innovative programme to address the food scarcity in the rural areas. In recent time the flag ship programmes like MUDRA, Swachha Bahrat Abhyan, Jan Dhan Yojana, Deen Dayal Antoday Yojana, Rashtriya Madhyamik Sahayak Yojana (RSMY) and many more implemented in Rural India through the help of PRIs. A microscopic analysis of various central sponsored programmes by the successive governments will give us a picture, where the followings are observed/ reflected from the flagship programmes:
- Poor have a strong desire to come out of poverty, and, have innate capabilities
- Social mobilization and building strong institutions of the poor is critical for unleashing their capabilities
- An external dedicated and sensitive support structure is required to induce social mobilization
- Providing employment opportunities to people
- To create livelihood opportunities through Self Help Groups
- To give opportunities to marginalized sections to have some avenues to lead life with dignity.

## PANCHAYAT AS AN INSTITUTION OF GOVERNANCE

The 73$^{rd}$ amendment by the Parliament of India and subsequent legislation by various states and amendments by parliament of India has brought a sea change in the context of grass roots democracy in India. However, there was somewhat slow progress in terms of implementation of various provisions. None the less all most all the states followed the 73$^{rd}$ amendment in later rather than spirit. Hence there is some inherent contradiction within the administrative system itself while implementing various provisions of 73rd amendment in the context of grassroots democracy. Among all the states, Kerela came out with a 'peoples plan' through active participation of people at all the three tiers of Panchayats (Maheswari, 1987). The state devolved funds, functions, functionaries and prepared a campaign, which is unparalleled in the country in terms of its scale and scope. The Ministry of Panchayati Raj document also mentioned that the statutes enacted by the States in conformity with the 73rd Constitutional Amendment Act had merely incorporated the 29 subjects of 11th Schedule without significantly altering the functional domain of the Panchayats. There was also vagueness in the listing of responsibilities or duties of Panchayats. It has also mentioned that most of the states after devolving several responsibilities upon the PRIs have not transferred the requisite staffs needed by the Panchayats to carry out the responsibilities entrusted to them. Hence it seems as is half hearted attempt. Similarly the first round table conference of Ministers of Panchayati Raj which was held in Kolkata in July 2004, categorically mentioned about devolution in three dimensions- 'functions', 'functionaries', 'funds'. As a matter of fact most states have devolved the funds and functions but not the functionaries. This is commonly visible across the board with a few exceptions (GoI, 2006; 2008).

## ROLE OF PANCHAYATS IN RURAL DEVELOPMENT PROGRAMMES

The issue of forging links between CSSs and PRIs has been seen as a possible solution both to help the CSSs to shed their top-down character, and enable PRIs to emerge as institutions of self government. All the programmes in their guidelines/frameworks are making fairly elaborate provisions to involve PRIs at various levels. But what is found from the field that the actual linkage is being approached more in an instrumental rather in an integrated way. This could be discerned both with regard to the purpose as well as the method adopted for such a linkage. In the context of involvement of PRIs and the role they are able to play; wide variations could be seen across schemes. Even within a scheme there were variations across states and across three layers of PRIs (GoI, 2008). The variations could be attributed to factors like difference in the degree of devolution achieved by the states, the nature of the programme, and the guideline provisions for involving the PRIs. The bureaucracy and parallel agencies continue to dominate over PRIs. At the district level across schemes and sates, the district collector or magistrate remains a key person for governing and administering the CSSs. Hence it is found that the involvement of PRIs is being attempted merely out of the compulsion of following the programme guidelines. Given a choice, many states may prefer an arrangement which is convenient to them. Moreover, there has been resistance across many states from the bureaucracy for transferring functionaries to PRIs. The states have shown reluctance for any large scale transfers of regular functionaries. In some of the cases states have even reversed such transfers (Garg, 2006).

When a CSS gets recast and comes up with a newer mandate for decentralization like SSA and NRHM, there is inadequate response to shed powers in the well entrenched bureaucracy. This is also one of the reasons as to why the committees of these CSSs get constituted mostly as parallel bodies to PRIs. Many of the programme guidelines insist that such committees be constituted as sub-committees of PRIs. However, not in many schemes / states such integrated committees could be seen. The officials are found not even fully sharing the information about these schemes with the PRIs. The women PRIs leaders especially from weaker sections are found facing even greater hurdles in dealing with the officials. Given the nature of CSSs in recent times, the PRIs are found involved largely in the some aspects of implementation of these programmes. Monitoring is another role taken up to a certain extent.

## LOCAL GOVERNANCE AND DECENTRALIZATION PROCESS IN CONTEMPORARY INDIA

The 73rd amendment by the Parliament of India and the subsequent legislation by various states and amendments by parliament of

India has brought a sea change in the context of grass roots democracy in India. However, there was somewhat slow progress in terms of implementation of various provisions. None the less, all most all the states followed the 73rd amendment in letter than spirit. Hence there is some inherent contradiction within the administrative system itself while implementing various provisions of 73rd amendment in the context of grassroots democracy. Among all the states, Kerala came out with a 'peoples plan' through active participation of people at all the three tiers of Panchayats. The state has devolved funds, functions, functionaries and prepared a campaign, which is unparalleled in the country in terms of its scale and scope. Similarly Madhya Pradesh has done considerable amount of progress in this field during this period. Devolution in the context of the Panchayats, means that when the authority in respect of a specific activity is to be transferred from the state to the local government, the later should have the prerogative of taking decisions in respect of planning and implementation of such activity. For effective implementation of their decisions, the panchayats need staff support and resources along with transfer of functions. In fact '*functions, funds* and *functionaries*' are complementary to one another in the process of devolution of responsibilities and powers upon the Panchayats. There are 29 'subjects' listed in the Eleventh Schedule, which could be devolved upon the Panchayats.

The Ministry of Panchayati Raj document also mentioned that the statutes enacted by the States in conformity with the 73rd Constitutional Amendment Act had merely incorporated the 29 subjects of 11th Schedule without significantly altering the functional domain of the Panchayats. There was also vagueness in the listing of responsibilities or duties of Panchayats. It has also mentioned that most of the states after devolving several responsibilities upon the PRIs have not transferred the requisite staffs needed by the Panchayats to carry out the responsibilities entrusted to them. Hence it seems as if half hearted attempt. Similarly the first round table conference of Ministers of Panchayati Raj which was held in Kolkata in July 2004, categorically mentioned about devolution in three dimensions-

'functions', 'functionaries', 'funds'. *As a matter of fact most states have devolved the 'funds' and 'functions' but not the 'functionaries'.* This is commonly visible across the board with a few exceptions (GoI, 2006).

However, devolution must come through the process of evolution. It should not be bureaucratic driven. If Panchayat members are not aware about their role, power, duties and responsibilities, then it cannot be implemented properly. For that purpose, the capacity building process of Panchayats must be strengthened. It has to be in a missionary zeal. It must be voluntary, genuine devolution and participation of all the stake holders. Unless all the elected representatives including people, imbibe and develop the qualities necessary to run Panchayats, the inclusive governance with genuine participation may not be possible. Only then the democratic process can be strengthened. Hence there is urgent need of exploring the ways a Gram Sabha functions in Panchayat set up as well as suggesting some remedial measures for its improvement. As tribal areas of our country are undergoing a metamorphic change in terms of its economic and political structure, it is natural that the epi-center of governance system, that is a village, how does decisions are being taken care of. If we try to understand this, the role of Gram Sabha becomes the focal point. Despite having constitutional backing, Gram Sabhas across the States have been deliberately degraded to act as 'beneficiary Sabhas' or 'register Sabhas' or 'activity Sabhas'.

## MAJOR PROBLEMS IN STRENGTHENING GRASS ROOTS DEMOCRACY

Manifestation of poor service delivery (adversely affecting achievement of MDGs); economic, social and political exclusion (despite reservations for women and other marginalised groups) and weak accountability (at all levels: downward vertical, upward vertical and horizontal). Slow progress during first decade in terms of transfer of funds not matched by concomitant transfer of funds and functionaries. Similarly Central ministries dealing with panchayat-mandated subjects are spending substantial funds at local level bypassing panchayats, relying on parallel structures, leaving little incentive for states to devolve powers to panchayats (Choudhry, 2007). Conflicting signals – our policies are centralizing and we are still proliferating central schemes, but expect states to devolve and PRIs to implement. Strengthening of Gram Sabha, social audit, right to information (linked to programmes). PRIs still functioning as implementing arms of line departments and not institutions of self-government. If it has to function as 'government', it should be empowered to legislate on its matters (there is no panchayat list along with union, state and concurrent lists), collect revenue and regulate. As government, it should 'provide' and not necessarily 'produce' basic services. The difference between providing education and building schools must be clear.

With some exceptions, DRDAs have not yet been merged with district panchayats. In some states, DRDAs are chaired by ZP chairperson and in some others by district collector. A number of jurisprudential issues remain unresolved (harmonization of subject laws with panchayati raj acts). Availability of funds at panchayat level is inadequate, unpredictable and adhoc. PRIs are highly dependent on transferred funds which are tied. Devolution is not linked to activity mapping or functional domain.Administrative devolution not attended to, personnel still report to line departments, little control of elected authority over personnel, PRIs' administrative structure needs re-engineering, jobs re-profiled, DRDAs still strong, activity mapping again is a pre-requisite. PESA implementation is tardy, conflicts with subject laws, no harmonization achieved, strong resistance by subject departments - critically important for economic, social and political inclusion of scheduled tribes. There are institutional and substantive weaknesses in decentralized planning. These include lack of capacity, technical knowledge and authority and lack of focus on women, dalits and social issues in the plans and corresponding budget.

## PROBLEMS OF DECENTRALIZED DEMOCRACY

As a matter of fact let us admit that Gram Panchayat is the custodian of grassroots governance. There are number of suggestions on how to strengthen Gram Panchayat. These suggestions are already available in public domain as well as in government files. Let us not keep experimenting with local self governance. We should first work towards making local governments relevant to people. And this could be possible only when every citizen in his/her Panchayat is obliged to remain connected with his/her Gram Sabha or Gram Panchayat. This will ensure a sense of ownership, participation and pride as the self decision maker. The village can function as a unit of republic at a micro-level. As planning in our country is bureaucratic driven and directed from the centre, there is lack of peoples participation. Hence lack of proper involvement of Panchayats. Panchayats are becoming simply implementing agents of various developmental activities, which can be carried out by line departments. In that case, the panchayats do not have any control over local bureaucracy.

The PRIs have also faced several limitations or constraints for effective programme implementation. Lack of technical expertise and capacity was found to be a major problem faced by PRIs for execution. Lack adequate information on schemes was another major constraint faced by PRIs leaders coming in the way of their participation. The standing committees of PRIs at all three levels were found to be inactive or dormant leading to ineffective role in monitoring. A common feature reported across different states was equal sharing of funds by the PRI leaders under several schemes. The funds in such cases were being found utilized more as per individual preferences than based on the real need in the community. Many PRI leaders demand that they should be provided with adequate remuneration or honorarium so that they are able to fully participate in the local governance. It is also found that the PRI representatives from poorer communities were found constrained from playing their role as elected leaders due to the compulsion of meeting their own livelihood needs.

The role of PRIs in planning is highly insignificant. Even in schemes like SSA and NRHM which visualize decentralized district and local plans, line agencies carry out planning with only a perfunctory involvement of PRIs. In NREGS, the PRIs are able to participate in the planning process to an extent. However the planning by PRIs is confined merely to identification shelf of projects. A major fall out of such a planning process is the absence or lack of local ownership for these interventions among PRIs. The PRIs, as such are found not identifying themselves fully with these schemes. At the same time, the PRIs have been constrained to come up with their own initiative for local development. Invariably, much of their time and effort is focused on implementation only.

## CONCLUSIONS

Though in theoretical sense PRIs are ought to play great role in ameliorating the poverty condition in rural areas and play a role of catalyst in addressing the critical mass in all the rural development programmes, the findings from the field is not much encouraging. The attempt to bring PRIs and CSSs together has not produced any dramatic change. Neither the purpose of improving the programme delivery nor the objective of empowering the PRIs has been realized significantly because of the linkage that exists presently. There are both systemic and programmatic hurdles coming in the way of forging an effective linkage between the two. Systemically, the inadequate and slow progress towards devolution by the states is the major constraint for the PRIs to make a significant contribution. The continued top-down nature of the CSSs is the programmatic constraint which nullifies the potential role of PRIs for bottom up planning and development. Hence strengthening the provisions in the programme guidelines to include PRIs alone becomes perfunctory which can produce only limited outcomes for decentralization. The way forward for a meaningful linkage lies not only in restructuring the CSSs to shed their top-down character but also in simultaneously enabling states to appreciate and deepen the decentralization process further as envisaged under the constitution.

## REFERENCES

Choudhry K. (*Ed*). (2007). Globalization, Governance Reforms and Development in India. Sage. New Delhi.

Dandekar, V.M. and Rath N. (1971). Poverty in India. Indian School of Political Economy. Pune.

Garg S.C. (2006). 'Transformation of Central Grants to States: Growing Conditionality and Bypassing State Budgets'. Economic and Political Weekly. 41 (48).

Garg, S.C. (2006). 'Transformation of Central Grants to States: Growing Conditionality and Bypassing State Budgets'. Economic and Political Weekly. 41 (48).

GoI. (2006). Planning at the Grassroots Level: An Action Programme for the Eleventh Five Year Plan, Report of the Expert Group. New Delhi.

GoI. (2006). The State of the Panchayats: A Mid-term Review and Appraisal. New Delhi.

GoI. (2008). 'Centrally Sponsored Schemes: Identifying a Domain for the Panchayati Raj Institutions'. In The State of Panchayats: 2007-08, Vol. 3: Supplementary. New Delhi.

GoI. (2008). Report of the Empowered Sub-Committee of the National Development Council on Financial and Administrative Empowerment of the Panchayati Raj Institutions. New Delhi.

GoI. (2008). The State of Panchayats: 2007-08. Vol. 1. New Delhi.

Maheswari S. (1987). 'Voluntary Action in Rural Development in India'. Indian Journal of Public Administration. Jul-September.

---

***Dr. Pradip Kumar Parida*** is working as Associate Professor in Rajiv Gandhi Institute of Petroleum Technology, Amethi. Before he served as Assistant Professor in Indian Institute of Public Administration (IIPA) New Delhi. His areas of interest and specialization include rural development and Panchayati Raj Institutions; community based disaster management (CBDM); human rights and policing; people's participation in development process; globalization, Governance and Welfare; micro-models of development in developing countries. He has contributed chapters in several edited books and research papers to journals.

# 5

# Working of Panchayati Raj Institutions in Odisha: An Overview

ATANU MOHAPATRA[6] AND RAMAKRUSHNA PRADHAN

## INTRODUCTION

Panchayats have been the backbone of Indian villages since the beginning of recorded history. The institution of Panchayati Raj happens to be as old as Indian civilization itself. It was in existence since ancient periods, having an effective control over civil and judicial matters in the village community. Vivid impression and account of Panchayat system in the form of local administration can be found in the *Rigveda, Manusamhita, Dharmashastras, Upanishads, Jatakas* and others (Ghosh and Pramanik, 1999).

The word Panchayat is derived from the word *pancha panchasvanusthitah,* referring to the existence of Grama Sanghas or rural communities. Panchayati Raj Institutions, as the grass root units of local self government have been considered as instruments of socio economic transformation in rural India with involvement of people at the grass root level for bringing about socio-economic development. PRI has been identified as institutional expression of democratic decentralization in India. Decentralization of power to the Panchayats is seen as a means of

[6] Central University Gujarat; Fakir Mohan University, Balasore.
**Corresponding author*: E-mail: atanu.mohapatra@gmail.com

empowering people and involving them in decision making process. Local governments being closer to the people can be more responsive to local needs and can make better use of resources. The democratic system in a country can be ensured only if there is mass participation in the governance. Therefore, the system of democratic decentralization popularly known as Panchayati Raj is considered as an instrument to ensure democracy and socio-economic transformation.

However, its operations were not sanctioned by any legal or juridical body, therefore had inherent weaknesses in its operation. It is only after Mohandas Karmachand Gandhi, the father of the nations, had aptly remarked in 1946 that, "the Indian Independence must begin at the bottom and every village ought to be a Republic or Panchayat having powers", the institution of Panchayati Raj got wider publication and acceptance (Singh, 1996). The dream of having self government at local level has been translated into reality with the introduction of Panchayati Raj system in Indian Constitution under Article 40 of Part IV called Directive Principles of State Policy (Basu, 2012). Nevertheless, the local self government was introduced not before than 1992 under 73rd Amendment Act as three-tier Panchayati Raj system to ensure people's participation in village levels (Bakshi, 2012). Although, the institutions of Panchayati Raj came into operation in Indian villages under the umbrella protection of Indian Constitution, the very idea and ideals for which it was so talked about is quite often missing from the agenda of PRI. The chapter is a modest attempt and endeavor to look into the ideas of Panchayati Raj, such as: Decentralization, expanding democratic space, participatory governance, issue of historicity and inclusive politics. An effort in this chapter has been made to examine whether the above mentioned ideas are found in the operation of Panchayati Raj Institutions in India and especially in Odisha. The chapter tries to give space to the contemporary debate on the apolitical nature of PRI and goes on to suggest certain recommendation to maintain its apolitical sanctity and yet functioning as an effective body of rural reconstruction.

## PANCHAYATI RAJ INSTITUTIONS: IN RETROSPECT

India has a long tradition of local governments, going back to more than 4000 years (Ghosh and Pramanik, 1999). This institution has survived numerous political changes and upheavals in the ancient and medieval periods till the advent of the British Raj. With the coming of the colonial administration, the patterns of the working of the local bodies also underwent marked changes.

Historically speaking, the earliest reference to Panchayat is derived from the word ***Pancha***, refering to an institution of the five (pancha panchasvanusthitah) is found in the Shanti-Parva of Mahabaratha, pancha and panchavanustitah are semantically close to Panchayat (Singh, 1996). A description of these village councils are also found in ***Arthashastra*** of Kautilya who lived in 400 B.C. ***Arthashstra*** gives a comprehensive account of the system of village administration prevailing in its time. During this period, the village administration was carried under the supervision and control of *Adyaksha* or headman. There were other officials such as *Samkhyaka* [accountant], Anikitsaka [veterinary doctor], Jamgh karmika [village couriers], Chikitsaka [physician]. The village headman was responsible for ensuring the collection of state dues and controlling the activities of the offenders. In Ramayana of Valmiki, there are references to the *Ganapada* (village federation) which was perhaps a kind of federation of village republics (Ghosh and Pramanik, 1999).

It is well mentioned in *Rigveda* about the Self-governing village community that dates from approximately 200 B.C. (Mathew, 2000). The village was the basic unit of administration in the Vedic period. The institution of popular assembliesof '***Sabha***', and the '***Samiti***' traced their origin to this period (Ibid). The office of the village head man (***Gramani***) indicates the emergence of the village as a unit of administration. In the later Vedic period, the Samiti disappeared as a popular assembly while the Sabha sank into anarrow body corresponding to the kings Privy Council.

In the *Mouryan* period, the village was the basic unit of administration. Villagers used to organize works of public utility and recreation, settle disputes, and act as trustees for the property of minors. But, they had not yet evolved regular councils. The village council appeared to have evolved into regular bodies in the *Gupta* period as well. They were known as ***Panchamandalas*** in central India and ***Gramajanapadas*** in Bihar (Altekar, 1997). During the *medieval and Mughal* periods, village bodies were the pivot of administration. In the *Mughal* period, particularly in the regime of Sher Shah, the villages were governed by their own panchyats. Each panchayat comprised of village elders wholooked after the interest of the people and administered justice and imposed punishment ondefaulters. The head man of the village, a semi government official, acted as a coordinator between the village Panchayat and the higher administrative hierarchy. *Akbar* accepted this system and made it an indispensable part of civil administration. In this period, each village had its own Panchayat of elders. It was autonomous in its own sphere and exercised powersof local taxation, administrative control, justice and punishment (Ghosh and Pramanik, 1999).

The *Mughals* introduced elaborate administrative machinery with a hierarchy of officials, particularly in the field of revenue. The Mughal local administrative system lasted over centuries. It was with the collapse of the Mughal strong hold, the British established their hegemony in India. Local self government as a representative institution was the creation of the British. It was Lord Mayo, the then viceroy of India (1869 to 1872), who felt the need to decentralize powers in order to bring about administrative efficiency and introduced the concept of elected representatives in the urban municipalities in 1870 although with some fiscal connotations. The imperial financial strains resulted due to 1857 revolt compelled to finance local services out of local taxation. Therefore it was out of fiscal compulsion that Lord Mayo's resolution on decentralization came to be adopted (Mathew, 2000).

The beginning of the revival of the traditional village Panchayati system for first time started in Bengal with the Bengal Chowkidar Act of 1870 (Ibid). The Chowkidar Act empowered district magistrates to set up Panchayats of nominated members in the villages to collect taxes to pay the chowkidars or watchmen engaged by them.

Lord Ripon widely regarded as the pioneer of local self governance in India has made remarkable contribution towards its developments. In 1882, through government resolution of 18th May, landmark structural evolutions were made to local governments. It provided for local boards consisting of a large majority of elected non-official members and presided over by a non-official chairperson. This is considered to be the Magna Carta of local democracy in India. This resolution proposed the establishment of rural local boards where 2/3rd of whose membership was composed of elected representatives. He brought in the concept of self-government in urban municipalities. Ripon's resolutions followed a series of Committees, Commissions and Acts in this line. The Royal Commission on Decentralization in 1909 elaborated further the principles of Ripon Resolution. But this remained merely on paper. Ripon's scheme did not make much progress in the development of local self government institutions.

The Montagu Chelmsford reforms passed in the year 1919 was enabled the transfer of the subject of local government to the domain of provinces (Stephen, 2001). It also recommended that as far as possible there should be a complete popular control in localbodies and the largest possible independence for them, of outside control. However, due to certain organizational and fiscal constraints this reform could not get much result as far as democratization of Panchayats was concerned.

Government of India Act, 1935 is proved to be another important stage in the evolution of Panchayats in British India. With popularly elected government in the provinces, almost all provincial administrations felt duty bound to enact legislations for further democratization of local self government institutions, including village Panchayats. Although the popular government in the provinces governed by the Congress vacated office following the declaration of Second World War in 1939, the position as regards local government institutions remained unchanged till August 1947, when the country attained independence (Ibid).

Even though the British government did not have interest in the village autonomy, they were forced to do so, in order to continue their rule in India and moreover to meet financial necessities. The Indian rural republic had flourished till the advent of British. It received a set back during the British rule. Self contained village communities and their Panchayats ceased to get substance. They were replaced by formally constituted institutions of village administration. In the highly centralized system of British rule, village autonomy seems to have lost.

After independence from British raj, India constituted its own constitution for self rule. Although, it was widely believed that in India – the republic of villages and where Gandhji was the beacon light having unbound faith in *Gram Swaraj*, Panchayat System ironically find no place in the draft constitution prepared in 1948. It was only after Gandhi took it seriously and fought for it, Panchayat could find a place in the constitution only under Directive Principle of State Policy. Article 40 of the constitution as it prescribe for Village Panchayat reads as, 'the states shall take steps to organize village Panchayats and endow them with such powers and authority as may be necessary to enable them function as units of self governments' (MoLaJ, 2008). Since Directive Principles are not legally binding on the government, the strengthening of grass root democracy was grossly neglected over the years.

The first organized effort has been taken in the form of Community Development Programme in 1952 to deal with rural problems in India. For this purpose National Extension Services was launched in 1953 with the objectives to promote self help and self reliance among the rural people, to generate a process of integrated social, economic and cultural change with the aim of transforming social and political life of the villagers. This programme though intended to bring socio-economic development in rural India failed to materialize the objectives due to lack of people participation in grass root level.

## BALWANTRAI MEHTA COMMITTEE

Balwantrai Mehta Committee was the first Committee set up in 1957 to look into the problems of democratic decentralization in independent India has made far reaching recommendations in the direction of democratic decentralization and rural reconstruction. It pointed out that the community development programme was not successful because it failed to evoke local initiative and that in the absence of local initiative and local interest, development would not be possible. The committee laid down five fundamental principles.

1. There should be three-tier structures of local self government bodies from village to the district level and these bodies should be linked together.
2. There should be genuine transfer of power and responsibility to these bodies to enable them to discharge their responsibility.
3. Adequate resources should be transferred to these bodies to enable them to discharge their responsibilities.
4. All welfare and developmental schemes and programmes at all three levels should be channeled through these bodies, and
5. The three tier system should facilitate further devolution and disposal of power and responsibility in future. The committee envisaged three tire systems of Panchayats known as Zilla Parishad, Panchayat Samiti and Gram Panchayat and recommended encouragement of peoples' participation in community work, promotion of agriculture and animal husbandry, promoting the welfare of the weaker sections and women through the Panchayats (Mishra, 1998).

For the first, time the Committee made recommendations for co-opting of two women who are interested to work for women and children. However, like the rest of the male members, women were not to be elected but were to be co-opted.

The recommendations of the Balwantrai Mehta Committee came into effect on 1$^{st}$April 1958. Rajasthan was the first state to implement it on 2nd October 1959 (Mathew, 2000). By mid 1960s, Panchayat had reached all parts of the country. There was enthusiasm in rural India and people felt that they had a say in the affairs affecting their daily life. These were considered as the promising days of Panchayati Raj Institutions in India. The report of the Ministry of Community Development had stated in 1964-65 that younger and better leadership was emerging through Panchayati Raj Institutions and there was a fairly high degree of satisfaction among the people with the working of the Panchayats (Ibid).

The recommendations of Balwantrai Mehta Committee were implemented by many states in the country. Till the mid sixties, Panchayati Raj system flourished in India. But there was decline in Panchayati Raj Institutions after the mid sixties mainly because of centralized tendencies of functioning all over the country (Singh, 2002). The elections were not held regularly and the participation of people weakened in these bodies. Inefficiency, corruption, favoritism, uncertainty and irregularity led to their decline. Most of the development programmes were kept out of their preview. Centrally sponsored schemes were initiated; parallel administrative bodies were created and government reduced funds considerably. During the period of national emergency, bureaucracy got the upper hand and these institutions lost their significance. The village panchayats were made subordinate units of government to implement its programmes.

## ASHOK MEHTA COMMITTEE (1977)

The Janata government in 1977 appointed a Committee with Ashok Mehta as chairman and was entrusted the task of enquiring into the causes responsible for the poor performance of Panchayati Raj Institutions. It was also asked to suggest measures to strengthen Panchayati Raj Institutions. The committee suggested two tire system of Panchayati Raj consisting of Zilla Parishads at the district level and Mandal Panchayats at the grass root level as against three tier system suggested by the Balwantrai Mehta

Committee. The committee recommended constitutional protection to the Panchayati Raj Institutions and further decentralization of power at all levels. A noteworthy feature of the report is that it recommended regular elections to these bodies and open participation of political parties (Ghosh, 1999).

## THE ASHOK MEHTA COMMITTEE SUGGESTED

- Reservation of seats for the weaker sections
- Two seats for women
- Adequate financial resources for the Panchayats
- Requirement of Constitutional sanctions
- To extend people's participation in developmental activities (Ibid).

Due to the fall of the Janata government, the Ashok Mehta Committee recommendations were not implemented. Few states have formulated new legislation on the basis of the recommendations of this Committee. Both the Committees overlooked the importance of Panchayats as units of self government.

During 1980's, two important Committees were appointed to look into local governments: GVK Rao Committee in 1985 and Dr. L.M. Singhvi Committee in 1986. The GVK Rao committee recommended the revival of Panchayati Raj Institutions such that greater responsibility of planning, implementation, and monitoring of rural development programmes could be assigned to them (GoI, 1986). L.M. Singhvi Committee recommended that the Panchayati Raj Institutions should be constitutionally recognized and protected. New chapter in the constitution should be provided to define their powers and functions and free and fair election to be conducted through the election commission. Committee recommended for the appointment of finance commission and all the rural development programmes are entrusted to the Panchayati Raj Institutions by amending schedule VII of the constitution (Ibid).

## $73^{RD}$ AMENDMENT ACT, 1992

Following these circumstances, Rajiv Gandhi the then Prime Minister of India introduced the $64^{th}$ Amendment bill on local government on the $15^{th}$ May, 1989 in the Parliament, but it failed to get the required support. A second attempt was made in September 1990 to pass the bill in the Parliament. The bill however was not even taken up for consideration. In September 1991, a fresh bill on Panchayati Raj was introduced by the Congress government under P.V. Narasimha Rao, the then Prime Minister. It was passed in 1992 as the $73^{rd}$ Amendment Act 1992 with minor modifications and came into force on $24^{th}$ April 1993.

## SALIENT IDEAS FOR PRI UNDER THE ACT

The Act provided for the establishment of Grama Sabha in each village comprising of all the adult members registered as voters in the Panchayat area. Three shall be a three-tier system of Panchayat at village, intermediate and district levels. Smaller states with population below 20 Lakhs will have option not to have intermediate level Panchayat. Seats in Panchayats at all three level shall be filled by direct election. In addition, the chairperson of the village Panchayat can be made member of the Panchayat at the intermediate level. MP, MLA, MLC, could also be member of Panchayat at the intermediate and the district level. In all the Panchayats, seats should be reserved for SCs and STs in proportion to their population and 1/3 of the total number of seats will be reserved for women. Offices of the chairperson of the Panchayat at all levels shall be reserved in favour of SCs and STs in proportion in the state. One-third of the offices of chairperson of Panchayats at all levels shall also be reserved for women.

Legislature of the state shall be at liberty to provide reservation of seats and office of chairperson in Panchayat in favour of backward class citizens. Panchayats shall have a uniform five year term and elections to constitute new bodies shall be completed before the expiry of term.

In the event of dissolution, election will be compulsorily held within six months. There constituted Panchayat will serve for remaining period of five year term. It will not be possible to dissolve the existing Panchayats by amendment of any Act before the expiry of its duration.

A person who is disqualified under any law, election to the legislature of the state or under any of the state will not be entitled to become a member of a Panchayat. Independent election commission will be established in the state to superintendence, direction, and control of the electoral process and preparation of electoral rolls. Specific responsibilities will be entrusted to the Panchayats to prepare plans for economic development and social justice in respect of matters listed in XI Schedule. For the implementation of development schemes, main responsibility will be entrusted to the Panchayats. The Panchayats will receive adequate funds for carrying out their plans. Grants from state government will constitute an important source of funding but state government is also expected to assign the revenue of certain taxes to the Panchayats. In some cases, Panchayat will also be permitted to collect and retain revenue it raises. In each state, finance commission will be established within one year and after every five years to determine principles on the basis of which adequate financial resource would been trusted for Panchayats. Panchayats existing on the 24th April 1993 will be allowed to complete their full term except when they are dissolved by the house by resolution (GoI, 1992).

## ARTICLE 243 G OF THE XI SCHEDULE INCLUDES THE FOLLOWING ACTIVITIES

Agriculture, including agricultural extension; Land improvement, implementation of land reforms, land consolidation and soil conservation; Minor irrigation, water management and watershed development; Animal husbandry and poultry; Fisheries; Social forestry and form forestry; Small- scale industries, including food processing industries; Khadi, village and cottage industries; Rural housing; Drinking water; Fuel and fodder; Roads, culverts, bridges, waterways and other means of communication; Rural electrification including distribution of electricity; Non conventional energy sources; Poverty elevation programme; Education, including primary and secondary schools; Technical training and vocational education; Adult and non-formal education; Libraries; Cultural activities; Market and fairs; Health and family sanitation including hospital, primary health centers anddispensaries; Family welfare; Women and child development; Social welfare, including welfare of the handicapped and mentally retarded, Welfare of the weaker sections and particular of the scheduled cast and scheduled tribes and Public distribution system (Ibid).

The 73$^{rd}$ Amendment Act is an attempt to restructure the Panchayati Raj to reach the grass root level. The bill for the first time gave constitutional status to Panchayati Raj institutions and it became mandatory on all state governments to implement it. This Amendment brought about uniformity in structure, composition, powers and functions of Panchayats. It gave impetus to Panchayati Raj to promote social and economic development and improvement in living condition of rural India.

## SOME REFLECTIONS ON PANCHAYATI RAJ IN ODISHA

Panchayat system was in existence inthe rural Odisha since time immemorial although in different names and varied types. During colonial period it was under state of dormant. After independence Odisha for the first time tried to empower its Gram Panchayats and later followed the guidelines of the union government, consequent upon the adoption of Balwantrai Mehta Committee report, adopted three tier of Panchayati Raj system in the state. To make it participatory grass root democracy Panchayati raj was reconstructed in 1992 through the 73$^{rd}$ constitutional amendment. Odisha was the first state in the country to make provisions in favour of weaker sections, even before the enforcement of the 73$^{rd}$ Amendment (Pradhan, 2011).

## PANCHAYATS IN PRE-INDEPENDENCE PERIOD

Like other states, Odisha has a long tradition of Panchayat system. Generally, day-to-day problems and small disputes were solved through the village Panchayat system. Except for major crimes like murder etc. they take the help of police but other small crimes were solved through the village Panchayat. First land settlement in Odisha was taken place during the last decade of $12^{th}$ century. And the second settlement was introduced by Emperor Akbar. Under Maratha rule multiple tax system was introduced in 1751. The State came under British rule in 1803. During the Colonial period Britishers tried to initiate some formal type of division to have control over the local administration for their own benefit but there was no local administration in the rural areas. In order to control and collect revenues from rural areas they appointed some local Zamidars or local elites as agents. Zamindari was put to auction for collecting revenues effectively. This created Land Boards in the State. So their main objective was not to give power to the people and also for no self-government. But, their main aim was the protection of imperial interests and hence paid more attention to urban administration rather than rural (Joshi and Narwani, 2002). Thus they concentrated mainly around the trading centers; their interest in the beginning was limited to the creation of local bodies of nominated members in the major cities and towns.

But the Great Famine of 1866 was a severe blow to the continuing village administration. Colonial administration set up a Commission in 1880 to investigate famine in India which understood the importance of rural local self-governance. This helped introduction of local self government (Mishra, 2010). The Royal Commission (1907) laid emphasis on the establishment of Gram Panchayat. It recommended that the members of the village Panchayat should be elected by the villagers and village head be made Chairman of the Panchayat (The Royal Commission, 1907). The Reform Act (1919) provided that the provinces would legislate on Panchayats (Mitra, 1919). Thus, among others the Bihar Local Self Government Act was enacted in 1920. Odisha was covered under this Act (Bihar and Odisha Legislative Department, 1921).

## PANCHAYATS IN POST-INDEPENDENCE PERIOD

Odisha became separate state in 1936. During that period there was realization to empower the grassroots people. After independence realizing the rural governance at the village level, Orissa Panchayat Act, 1948 was enacted. During the Chief Ministership of Sri Naba Krushna Choudhury a new innovative attempt was made through the Constitution of Anchal Sasan and Creation of Anchal Fund under the Odisha Estates Abolition Act of 1951. The Anchal Sasan Act (1955) intended to accord full powers to Anchal, a local authority which was at a higher level than the Gram Panchayat so that representatives of the villagers could have played visible role in the working of the system related to Public Health, Education, Agriculture, Cottage Industries etc. Thus, Odisha had already tried to empower its Panchayats even before the formal Panchayati Raj system came into existence.

The Anchal Sasan was a body with corporate capacities enabling fund raising out of land revenue, fees, tolls, cesses and taxes. Out of this fund provision were made to meet the expenditures on educational programmes of the Sasan. The institutions of Anchal Sabha and Anchal Adhikari were made to be paid out of Anchal Fund. However, the Act remained only in files and official records and was never implemented to proper practice (Dhal, 1992).

In the meantime, the Central Government had initiated some programmes to empower the rural people like Community Development Programme (GOI, 1973), National Extension Service (MoRD, 1953). However these programmes were also grossly failed to yield any result in the direction of Community Development. In 1956, Balwantrai Mehta Committee was appointed by the centre to review these programmes. This resulted in the creation of a three-tier system of Panchayati Raj Institutions to organize and manage the rural development activities. The fate of Gram Panchayat in Odisha during 1950s and early 1960s was under the mercy of several departments. Till 1956 it was under the Board of Revenue and the Revenue Department. The Panchayats came under the Department of Agriculture and Community

Development in 1956 and then moved to the Political and Services Department which was under the Chief Minister. In December, 1959 it was placed under the Department of Planning and Coordination with a Secretary to head the Department. With the B.R. Mehta recommendations were given effect, the Odisha Anchal Sasan Act, 1954 was repealed and the three-tier Panchayati Raj system was introduced onthe lines of Balwantrai Mehta Committee Report in 1959 (GoO, 1954).

Since the gram panchayat had already been constituted at the village level in 1948, Odisha Panchayat Samiti and the Zilla Parishad Act, 1959 was passed. The framework of the new institutional arrangement comprised Village Panchayats at the village level, Panchayat Samiti at the middle and Zilla Parishad at the apex level. After this Odisha accepted three tiers Panchayati Raj system in 1960-61. In July 1962 under the new, young and dynamic Chief Minister Sri Bijayananda Patnaik a new Department of Community Development and Panchayati Raj was created. The Panchayats, Samitis, Parishads and former District Boards came under its purview. The Panchayat wing was separated and it waskept under Commissioner, Panchayati Raj who also looked into functioning of the Community Development. Two posts of Directors from IAS cadre were also created. Afterwards the Commissioner post was abolished and the Departments were kept under one Secretary (Mishra, 2010).

A new act called the Odisha Gram Panchayat act, 1964 was passed in 1965 relating to the gram panchayats in the state and empowered the state government to establish and constitute the grama, the grama sasan. Though many rural development programmes such as IRDP, NREP, and DPADP were introduced by the central and state governments during this period but they were not under these three tiers Panchayati Raj system. Instead, under a separate society (DRDA) all the programmes have been implemented (Mohanty, 2003). So power was vested among the higher authorities or the agencies which are not related with PRIs. There was no attempt made by the government to reform the Panchayati Raj system in Orissa after 1966. During that period even the Panchayats in general were neglected. Other states at least tried to make some efforts to reform their Panchayat system, there was no such interest shown by Odisha government. Many committees were appointed by different states to review the failure and give suitable suggestion on Panchayati Raj system. But states like Odisha were not having separate committee because the politicians did not take interest to revise their Panchayat system.

Though many committees were formed during this period to give a suitable form to Panchayati Raj system no one could succeed. Over all these committees reported that all the development programmes are politicized and failed to achieve the goal of the rural people. There was realization that without the participation or involvement of the grass roots people it is not possible to fulfill the target. So there was a link of the developmental programmes with the Panchayati Raj system.

From the recommendations of various committees the Central Government decided to give a constitutional status to the PRIs and passed the 73$^{rd}$ Constitutional Amendment Act, 1993 to provide uniformity to the Panchayati Raj system throughout India (Basu, 2012).

## POST 73$^{RD}$ AMENDMENT AND PANCHAYATS IN ODISHA

Until 1990 there was no attempt were made by the government for devolution of power to people. Only in 1992, an attempt was made by the Biju Patnaik led Janata Government to ensure rural populations effective participation in their self governance. One-third reservation for women in all the tiers of PR bodies was introduced. It made provisions for reservation of SC and ST members' according to their population and reservation of one third seats, including office bearers for women. He also pressed for transfer of eight important departments like small scale industries, food processing, rural housing, poverty alleviation programme, women and child welfare, social welfare and public distribution system. Thus, the devolution of powers envisaged in the 73$^{rd}$Amendment Act and the women empowerment scheme were effectively incorporated by visionary Biju Patnaik (Mishra, 2010).

Odisha became the first state in the country to make provisions for the reservation of seats for elective functionaries in the local institutions at the village level in favour of weaker sections, even before the enforcement of the 73rd Amendment (Mohanty, 2009). Nevertheless, 73rd Amendment was implemented in Odisha through confirmatory legislation by J.B. Patnaik – the new Chief Minister of Odisha elected in fresh election conducted in 1997 (Mishra, 2010). This new Act enabled in ushering in socio-economic inclusiveness among the village people and empowered them to rule over themselves.

## EVALUATION OF PRI AND ITS FUNCTIONING IN ODISHA

Under the State laws, wide powers of suspension and dismissal have been vested in the State bureaucracy and places Panchayati Raj Institutions in a position of disadvantage. It also takes away the essential characteristic of PRIs as elected representative bodies and reduces it to a position of subordination *vis-a-vis* Intermediate Panchayats and so on.

A scrutiny of State laws reveals that the State Government has kept enough powers with it to deal with PRIs as far as ensuring checks and balances is concerned. These provisions had existed even before the introduction of 73rd Constitution Amendment Act and had been in use widely.

Another important aspect of the administrative restructuring process is the merger of District Rural Development Agencies (DRDAs) with Zilla Parishads. In the light of the 73rd Constitution Amendment Act, DRDAs need to be restructured to suit the changed scenario. They should work under the overall control and supervision of the Zilla Parishads. In case of Orissa, the Chairman of Zilla Parishad is also the Chairman of the DRDAs (Ibid).

It is widely in practice in Odisha as noticed from first hand information that the Gram Panchayat Sarapanches have to spend a good lot of time visiting Block Offices/Block Chairman's Chamber and of harassment by block level officials. Systems which require Gram Panchayat Sarpanch to approach Block office for funds and/ or technical approval need drastic change. Village bodies should be able to spend funds on their own without having to take technical approval from government officials. These interactions with Block staff distort the role of Sarapanch as elected representatives of the Gram Sabha and induct them into bad old ways of official dom and also encourage corruption.

The Constitution Amendment Act itself has certain provisions, which adversely affect the sustainability of these institutions. For instance, while there are reservations for women and scheduled castes/scheduled tribes, these seats are to be allotted by rotation to different constituencies. In practice, this implies that a woman or a scheduled caste/tribal elected to a Panchayat will normally have a term of five years, with no prospect of re-election. This goes against the spirit of democracy as people work hard for their constituencies in the expectation that they would be returned to power in the next elections. The existing provisions provide no incentive for the elected persons to deliver on their promises; on the contrary, self-interest would dominate, with little concern for the community at large.

The three tiers also compete for funds and powers. The lower tiers are normally the losers in this process. This would make decentralized development, within adistrict plan, infructuous and non-sustainable. It is imperative in the given framework that the state legislatures clearly delineate the work to be done by each of the three tiers in each of the sectors which fall within the purview of Panchayats, in order to ensure that the Panchayats at the village level can be effective institutions for local governance.

Empowerment of Gram Sabhas would require efforts at mobilization of the village community for mass participation in meetings of the Gram Sabha. Further, a massive awareness generation programme needs to be taken up to inform Gram Sabhas about their rights in planning, implementation and audit of development programmes and in control over natural resources, land records and conflict resolution. Ironically, the Block Chairman enjoys the power due to his/her political advantage over the Sarapanch in the administration and control of development programmes under Panchayat jurisdiction. The high handedness of the Block Chairman in Grama Panchayat affairs although is unwarranted and uncalled for, is a reality practiced in present political situation in Odisha. Thus it gives way for ambiguity in the functioning of the Sarapanch and the Panchayat at large and probably emerges as the greatest stumbling block in the process of realizing the Gandhian ideals as prescribed under Indian constitution.

In the prevailing situation in Odisha, the Panchayat must follow the following norms very carefully for ensuring transparency and accountability of the institution. These are: first, the Panchayati Raj Institutions, especially Gram Panchayats, should display all vital information about development projects (especially receipt of fundsand how they are being spent) in the Panchayat Offices or on a prominent board outside the village school for the information of the public. Second, all relevant records should be open to inspection.Third, members of public should also be able to obtain photocopies of documents related to development projects as also matters of general public interest by paying anominal charge. Such documents would extend in particularly to all bills, muster rolls, vouchers, estimates and measurement books as well as information about the criterion and procedure for selection of beneficiaries. A list of beneficiaries should not only be available for inspection, but photocopies of it should be given on demand from a convenient place such as Block or Tehsil Office.

In the opinion of the villagers, devolution as implemented may not have brought about development, but it has on the other hand reinforced the unequal access to power. References to the works are often accompanied by sneering remarks about the money which has gone down the drain, or has disappeared into the pocket of the party in power, Sarapanch, the block chairman and the block officials. Much of what comes from the government, they feel, is snatched away by the important people.

However, this rather negative assessment of omissions and commissions should not lead us to the conclusion that Panchayats and local level planning have lost their attractiveness for the villagers. It is a general perception that the responsibility of village level development should be reposed with Panchayats and the Block Chairman or official shouldn't force their views over the Panchayat. In the prevailing system of party penetration into the PRI and very recent carder based politics on the rise, important party functionaries and Block Chairman without any contention believes himself to be the boss of all the Panchayats falling under his block/constituency. To get rid of this corrupt and unhealthy practice, the Panchayats need to be much stronger but with more accountable Sarapanches. The Block chairman/Development Officers whosoever it may be should act only as an important tier of PRI not as a superior agent or ultimate authority over the village Panchayat.

From the outset it appears that the Panchayat is stronger and has the potential to bring in the fruits of development to the people at grassroots level. It is indeed true, if not hindered by Block Chairman/Official/Party influential. Corruption is though singled out as the most important cause for the ineffective functioning of these institutions, multiple control mechanisms exercised by the Block Chairman/officials/party in power over Village Panchayats and Gram Sabhas has not only buttressed corruption, but it has also led to pessimism that villagers on their own and at their level cannot change or improve things because of heavy dependence on elected functionaries and Block officials. The present system is, therefore, seen to have actually reinforced dominance and unequal access to power, besides rendering the villagers helpless and alienated.

## CONCLUSIONS

The prime objectives of the three-tier Panchayati Raj System are to ensure popular participation at rural level, decentralization of power and authority for ensuring transparency and effectiveness in administration, village autonomy, for bringing in democratic decentralization at the grass root units of local self government, empowering people and involving them in the decision making process, for bringing about socio-economic transformation in rural areas, development to eradicate poverty, uplift standard of living of people in the rural areas, and bring about a healthy society by creating awareness for hygiene, sanitation and eradication of illiteracy. The state has established a State Election Commissioner to conduct the election of PRIs. The 73rd amendment of the Constitution mandates Government to endow the Panchayati Raj Institutions with such powers and authority as may be necessary to enable them to function as institutions of self-Government. It also provides that powers and responsibility shall be devolved upon PRIs subject to such conditions as may be specified therein, with respect to the preparation of plans for economic development and social justice and implementation of schemes for economic development and social justice as may be entrusted to them including those listed in the 11th Schedule. However, ironically, at political side democratic decentralization couldn't properly taken place as the Sarapanch remains a mere rubber stamp due to existence of multiple power centers at Block Chairman/Official level. At economic self sufficiency front, progress on fiscal and functional decentralization has taken back seat due to operational problems at fund devolvement, function and functionaries to the PRIs. Although, the State Finance Commissions have submitted their recommendations, very few steps have taken so far to ensure fiscal viability of the PRIs. Above all what seems important in the ill functioning of the Panchayats is the meddling of the intermediary rung in the affairs of the village unit and forcing its decision of the Panchayat and the Sarapanch. Therefore, to ensure effectiveness and transparency at grass root unit of local self governance, autonomy of the Panchayat is very essential while clearly demarcating the powers and functions of the Panchayat and Panchayat Samiti needs to be specified. The Panchayat should be placed under the control and guidance of the District Collector in order to free it from unwarranted Block level monopoly, financial discrimination and political subjugation. Probably, the Panchayat will get its due as mandated by the Constitution of India under

73rd Amendment Act, 1992, if the Panchayat Samiti's control over the Panchayats either be unchained or inspected by District level non-political authority.

## REFERENCES


Altekar A.S. (1997). State and Government in Ancient India. Motilal Banarasi Das Publications. New Delhi.

Bakshi, P.M. (1996). Indian Constitution, 3rd Edition, Universal Law Publishing Company.

Basu, D.D. (2012). Introduction to the Constitution of India. 20th Edition. Lexisnexis.

Bihar and Odisha (India), Legislative Department (1921), The Bihar and Odisha Local Self-government (amendment) Act, 1920, Bihar and Odisha Act V of 1920, Printed at the Bihar and Odisha Government Press.

Dhal, S. (1992). 'Rural Development and Panchayati Raj: A study of Odisha (1952-1989)'. Ph.D Thesis (unpublished) submitted to the University of Delhi.

George M. (2000). Panchayati Raj in India, An Overview. Status of Panchayati Raj in India, Concept Publishing Company, New Delhi.

Ghosh R. (1999). 'Panchayati System in India: Historical and Constitutional Perspective'. In Ghosh R. (*ed*), Panchayati System in India: Historical, Constitutional and Financial Analysis. Kanishka Publishers, New Delhi.

Ghosh R. and Pramanik A.K. (1999). Panchayat System in India. Historical, Constitutional and Financial Analysis. Kanishka Publication. New Delhi.

GOI. (1973). Department of Community and Development, Community Development Programme in India - 1952-72. Govt. of India Press.

GOI. (1986). Report of the Committee on Revitalization of Panchayati Raj Institutions, L.M. Sanghvi, Chairman. Delhi.

GoO. (1954). Law Department, Acts, Ordinances and Regulations, Odisha Anchal Sasan Act, 1954, Government of Orissa. Retrieved from http://www.orissa.gov.in/law/acts/default.html on 15.04.2019.

Joshi, R.P. & Narwani, G.S. (2002). Panchayati Raj in India: Emerging Trends across the States. New Delhi. Rawat Publications.

Malik S.S. (2002). The New Panchayati Raj, Rural Traformation in the State of Haryana, Aalekh Publication. Jaipur.

Mishra S. (1998). Women and the 73rd Constitution Amendment Act, A Critical Appraisal. In Sabstin R. and Mathias E. (*eds*). People's Power and Panchayati Raj: Theory and Practice, Indian Social Institute, New Delhi.

Mishra S.N. (2010). Panchayati Raj in Orissa: Some Reflections, Odisha Review, February-March.

Mitra H.N. (1919). The Reform Act (1919), Montague-Chelmsford Reform Act 1919, N N. Mitter, Annual Register Office, Calcutta.

Mohanty B.B. (2003). 'Panchayati Raj in Maharastra and Orissa: An Overview'. Indian Association of Social Science (IASSI), Vol. 21, No. 3&4.

Mohanty B.B. (2009). 'Power to the Excluded Groups and Panchayati raj in Coastal Orissa'. In Baviskar B.S. & Mathew G. (*eds.*) *Inclusion and Exclusion in Local Governance,* Sage Publications India.

MoLaJ. (2008). Ministry of Law and Justice, Constitution of India, Government of India, July.

MORD. (1953). National Extension Services.

Pradhan B. (2011). Panchayati Raj and Tribal Development in Orissa: An Overview, International Journal of Current Research, Vol. 3, Issue. 11, November.

Singh R. (1996). Panchayat Raj Manual: A Socio-Historical Cum Legal Perspective. Anmol Publications. New Delhi.

Stephen F. and Rajasekaran. (2001). An Empirical Study of Women in Local Self Governance in Karnataka, Search publications, Bangalore.

---

***Dr. Atanu Mohapatra*** is Associate Professor in Central University Gujarat. He holds Ph.D. in International Relations from JNU, New Delhi. ***Dr. Ramakrushna Pradhan*** is Assistant Professor in Political Science, Department of Social Science, Fakir Mohan University, Balasore. A Ph.D from Centre for Russian and Central Asian Studies, School of International Studies, Jawaharlal Nehru University.

6

# State of Panchayati Raj System in India: Inferences from Selected Border Villages

SATYAKI DATTA[7] AND RASANAND PANDA

## INTRODUCTION

Mahatma Gandhi, the father of the nation believed in the power of the people, he believed that the love and not authority to the common person, could earn the power to rule. He actually was a solicitor for the local self-government, through the three tier Panchayat System, for rural India. It was in the year 1992 that by the 73rd amendment of the Indian Constitution finally the current shape of the three tiers system came into existence. The year 2017 marks the silver jubilee of that occasion. Though the Panchayat system has shown considerable benefits for many parts of the rural region of the country, yet, there are several interior pockets, where the benefits are still difficult to find. The paper strives to find the cases of few of the interior most rural regions of the country, analyze the standard of living with respect to three parameters of education, employment and health care, and thereby evaluate the works of the Panchayati system in India.

India is a vast country. The figures of 2011, conveys there are 2,40,355 village panchayats and 5407 rural local bodies, 6,317 block

[7] MICA, Ahmedabad.
**Corresponding author*: E-mail: rasananda.panda@micamail.in

samitis and 40 equivalent local bodies and 585 district councils in India (Ministry of Panchayati Raj, 2012-2013). Here, one thing is to be included is that, it does feature the self-proclaimed "*khaap*" Panchayats found in few places of North India.

The Balwant Rai Mehta Committee was appointed by the Government of India in January 1957 to examine the work of the Community Development Programme (1952) and the National Extension Service (1953) and to suggest measures for improving their work. The recommendation of the committee in January 1958 set the stage for the launching of Panchayati Raj Institutions throughout the country. The committee recommended the establishment of the scheme of 'democratic decentralization', which finally came to be known as Panchayati Raj. This led to the establishment of a three-tier Panchayati Raj system: Gram Panchayat at the village level, Panchayat Samiti at the block level, and Zila Parishad at the district level. While the grass root level consists of five elected members with one leader or the Sarpanch, the next level is the block or tehsil, which consists of members of each of the village that makes up the block and finally the highest hierarchy in the pyramid, is the representatives from each of the blocks that constitute a district.

The Panchayat Raj system was first adopted by the state of Rajasthan in Nagaur district on 2$^{nd}$ of Oct 1959. State governments during the 1950s and 60s adopted this system. It also founded backing in the Indian Constitution, with the 73$^{rd}$ amendment in 1992 to accommodate the idea. The Amendment Act of 1992 contains provision for devolution of powers and responsibilities to the panchayats, both for the preparation of economic development plans and social justice, as well as for implementation in relation to 29 subjects listed in the eleventh schedule of the constitution, and the ability to levy in addition, collect appropriate taxes, duties, tolls and fees.

## CHALLENGES AND ISSUES

Though the present form of the three tier Panchayati Raj came into existence with the 73$^{rd}$ amendment of the Indian constitution, things were nothing to be overwhelmed so much, as there were cases of problems of intervention from political parties, stake groups and bureaucrats. The common basis for this discord is redistribution of power.

The constitution of India through its list of duties scheduled under national, state and concurrent list has endowed the Panchayats with several duties and has empowered them with funds and facilities either from the central government or from state government. Education, employment and health care are three very important services featuring on these lists and are therefore considered as the parameters in this paper, wherein, we try to find the status quo of these few regions of the vast nation, with respect to the said parameters. The reason for considering these extreme and interior regions is that of their proximity to the neighbors than to the mainland India. Most of these regions are at a continuous threat both culturally and economically from the neighboring countries and hence requires better look out from the Indian Union in order to safeguard the sovereignty.

Education, employment, health care are all in the vicious circle with no starting or end points, but, the rationale behind choosing these three basic amenities are because every household requires some kind of financial earnings to sustain the family. Money is the sole medium of exchange for availing any goods and services, in any section of the society, and therefore, employment status is very important for any society. Education falls into an important factor. Every generation might not fall in the shoes of their ancestors' livelihood, but aspire higher and even if they continue the tradition, education will help in the betterment of the same old trade. Education also helps the mass understand the treatment meant to them from the administration. Health care is of utmost important. India still faces crisis of high maternal and child mortality rate. Coupled with these are the problems of high disease burden and high cost of medical treatment, which often impoverishes a large section of the population.

## TOPOGRAPHY

The blocks and villages to be studied spreads across the length and breadth of the country. The Pamban block in Tamil Nadu, is a part of the Ramanathapuram district and consists of the infamous Dhanuskhodi village, once a vibrant suburb that was transformed to a desolate barren land after the super cyclone of 1964. Hasnabad block is a part of Basirhat sub division of the North Twenty Four Parganas district in West Bengal. Tawang is on the far eastern part of India, in the state of Arunachal Pradesh and is at close proximity with the line of actual control of McMahon Line. Longewala in the district of Jaisalmer of Rajasthan lies in the Thar Desert of western India and is only few kilometres from Pakistan. Minicoy is the lowermost troll of the archipelago of Lakshadweep, about 400 kms from Trivandrum and very close to the island neighbor Maldives.

## PAMBAN VILLAGE

Pamban village off the coast of Dhanuskhodi lies in the Rameswaram tehsil and Ramanathapuram district of Tamil Nadu. Bordered on both sides are the Park Strait and Gulf of Mannar. It has the highest population in the district (Directorate of Census Operations, 2011) and is the lonely inhabited village in the taluk. The village of Pamban has a total area of 3599 hectares with a total population of 37819 at a healthy gender ratio of 0.973, further it is the home for 503 scheduled castes and four scheduled tribe people. (Directorate of Census Operations, 2011). About 13000 are employed in either agriculture, household industry or any marginal works but an alarming 24,703 are non-workers (Directorate of Census Operations, 2011). For a village of size about 36 square kilometres, it is poor in health care facilities. The following Table-1 would make it clear, that the Panchayat system has severely failed in the health care sector, which is an important duty of the Panchayat and is an important requirement for an island village, separated from the mainland by two large water bodies. The census and other reports on the districts and blocks of Tamil Nadu, speaks clearly of the inabilities of the Panchayat.

**Table 1:** Health Care Facilities in Pamban

| *Item* | *Units* | *Nearest Unit* |
|---|---|---|
| Community Health Center | NIL | at least 10 kms away |
| Primary Health Center | 2 | |
| Primary Health Sub Center | 5 | |
| Maternity and Child Welfare | 2 | |
| Hospital - Alopatheic | NIL | at least 10 kms away |
| Hospital - Alternative Medicine | NIL | at least 10 kms away |
| Family Welfare Center | 2 | |

*Source*: District Census Handbook 2011, T.N.

## TAWANG

The serine location in the eastern most state of India, Arunachal Pradesh. However it is equally claimed by People's Republic of China and Republic of China (Taiwan). Area wise the district is quite big about 2085 square kilometres. The literacy is 52% for a total population of 49,977 (Census 2011, 2015). Of these total population of the district, some 28,561 are engaged in some kinds of work, either agriculture, cultivation, husbandary, other house hold industries. The entire district has 8 pre primary, 19 primary, 13 middle and only one secondary school only (District Census Handbook, Arunachal Pradesh, 2011). Further, the general health care sector are as shown in the Table-2 below.

The district council, should be more empowered in the fields of health care specially. It has to be kept in mind that the foreign neighbors are always a threat to the sovereignity of this region.

**Table 2:** Health Care facilities in Tawang

| *Item* | *Units* | *Nearest Unit* |
|---|---|---|
| Community Health Center | NIL | at least 10 kms away |
| Primary Health Center | 2 | |
| Primary Health Sub Center | 3 | |
| Maternity and Child Welfare | 3 | in the vicinity of 5-10 km |
| Hospital - Alopatheic | NIL | at least 10 kms away |
| Hospital - Alternative Medicine | NIL | at least 10 kms away |
| Family Welfare Center | 1 | |

*Source*: District Census Handbook 2011, Arunachal Pradesh

The only way to apease the population and make them pro India, is by providing the basic facilities of living and therefore, three tier Panchayat system of these district has to be more active and look for their sustainable and continuous supply of these amenities.

## HASNABAD

Hasnabad block is bounded by the river Ichamati on the East, which separates it from Bangladesh. Quite close to the metropolitan Kolkata, yet an interior borderland block. It comes into limelight, only once a year and that too in the regional media for the cross country immersion of goddess *Durga*, during Dussehra. Of the total 155.4 square kilomtres, only 2 square kilometres are of urban and the rest are rural county. About 1,97,014 people resides in this block only 33,400 people are barely literate here. Some 77,619 (District Census Book, West Bengal, 2011) are employed in some kind of work like agriculture or small scale industry, but the rest are unemloyed. This is very alarming, considering its proximity from Kolkata. The block has not done great in health care sector too, as shown in the Table-3 below.

**Table 3:** Health Care facilities in Hasnabad

| *Item* | *Units* | *Nearest Unit* |
|---|---|---|
| Community Health Center | NIL | at least 10 kms away |
| Primary Health Center | NIL | Less than 5 km away |
| Primary Health Sub Center | NIL | at least 10 kms away |
| Maternity and Child Welfare | NIL | at least 10 kms away |
| Hospital - Alopatheic | NIL | at least 10 kms away |
| Hospital - Alternative Medicine | NIL | at least 10 kms away |
| Family Welfare Center | NIL | at least 10 kms away |

*Source*: District Census Handbook 2011, West Bengal

## LONGEWALA (JAISALMER)

The block is situated in the westermost part of the Indian Union. The region is of immense strategic importance to the defense of the country, as it is vulnerable to the attacks from Pakistan. There has been possible intrusion from the Pakistani army through

Longewala in 1971 and its twin village of Saddewala in 1965. Infact, if any enemy attacks and wins it, they can straightaway run up to Jaisalmer through Ramgarh. Longewala is one of thoses scarcest populated villages of India, with a combined population of just 188 people of which just 20 people can read and write. 97 people are reported to have some livelihood and 91 people do not have any (District Census Handbook, Rajasthan, 2011). Naturally there have been no report of individual educational institutes in these block, however the entire Jaisalmer block which has 226 villages alongside Longewala (Jaisalmer.rajasthan.gov.in, 2017), has 55 pre-primary, 111 primary, 59 middle, 36 secondary and 9 senior secondary schools (District Census Handbook, Rajasthan, 2011). The medical care facilities are as per Table-4 below.

**Table 4:** Health Care Facilities in Longewala

| *Item* | *Number of Villages* |
|---|---|
| Community Health Center | 3 |
| Primary Health Center | 9 |
| Primary Health Sub Center | 94 |
| Maternity and Child Welfare | 11 |
| Hospital - Alopa theic | 0 |
| Hospital - Alternative Medicine | 5 |
| Family Welfare Center | 4 |
| Medicine Shops | 19 |
| No Medical Facilities | 131 |

*Source*: District Census Handbook 2011, Rajasthan

It is quite clear from the data in the table and the statistics provided, that the facilities are quite inadequate considering the entire Jaisalmer block which has an area of about 11,411 square kilometres, a total house hold of about 29,300 and a population of about 1,67,700 (District Census Handbook, Rajasthan, 2011). As mentioned earlier, that this region is strategically important from the defense point of view, therefore, better standard of living is expected by the residents of this land, who can fall easy victim from the cross border intrusion both physically and psychologically and will in turn be detrimental to the internal peace and security of the country.

## MINICOY

One of the islands of the Lakshadweep archipelago, about 400 kilometres West of Trivandrum, lies the island of Minicoy, in the Arabian Sea. Like, all other places discussed in this paper, this tiny island is of utmost importance to the sea routes to India and for the diplomatic relation with SAARC neighbors Maldives. The island almost completely has urban inhabitation but still is under the jurisdiction of the Panchayat system. Its area is of about 4.8 square kilometres and inhabited by about 10,447 people. Out of these total population an estimated 8768 people are literate, keeping par with the historically high rate of literacy percentage of Lakshadweep, but out of these only 3,138 people are having livelihood, which is a matter of concern (District Census Handbook, Lakshadweep, 2011).

Minicoy has 11 primary level schools, 3 middle level schools and 2 schools each for matriculation and senior secondary level, per 10000 people (District Census Handbook, Lakshadweep, 2011). The health care facilities of this island is as per shown in the Table-5 below.

**Table 5:** Health Care facilities in Minicoy

| *Item* | *Units* | *Nearest Unit* |
|---|---|---|
| Health Center | 3 with no beds | |
| Maternity and Child Welfare | 3 | 398 KMS AWAY |
| Hospital – Allopathic | 1 with 20 beds | |
| Medicine Shop | NIL | |
| Family Welfare Center | NIL | 398 KMS AWAY |

*Source*: District Census Handbook 2011, Lakshadweep

The table number 6, that follows provides a vivid picture for the overall scenario, both at the respective state level and also, with respect to the all India level. The comparisons have been made on some detailed paramters in line with the main criteria of employment, education and health care. The selected papramters, gives a strong sign of what actually is happening in these villages.

**Table 6:** Overall scenario w.r.t. state level as well as All India level.

| | *I* | | *II* | | *III* | | *IV* | | *V* | | |
|---|---|---|---|---|---|---|---|---|---|---|---|
| | ***Pamban (Block)*** | ***Tamil Nadu*** | ***Tawang (District)*** | ***Arunachal Pradesh*** | ***Hasnabad (Block)*** | ***West Bengal*** | ***Longewala (Village)*** | ***Rajasthan*** | ***Minicoy*** | ***Lakshadweep*** | ***India*** |
| Total Area (Sq. Km) | 35.99 | 130060 | 2085 | 83743 | 155.4 | 88752 | 296 | 342239 | 4.8 | 32 | 3287000 |
| Percentage of state's area | 0.028 | – | 2.49 | – | 0.175 | – | 0.086 | – | 15 | | |
| Total Population | 37819 | 72100000 | 49977 | 1383727 | 197014 | 91276115 | 188 | 68548437 | 10447 | 64473 | 1310000000 |
| Percentage of state's population | 0.052 | – | 3.612 | – | 0.216 | – | 0.00027 | – | 16.20 | | |
| Total Workers | 13116 | 32884681 | 28561 | 587657 | 77619 | 34756355 | 97 | 29886255 | 3138 | 18753 | 481743311 |
| Percentage of Population working | 3.46 | 45.61 | 57.14 | 42.47 | 39.4 | 38.1 | 51.5 | 43.6 | 30.04 | 29.09 | 36.7 |
| Number of Literates | 28304 | 51837507 | 26073 | 766005 | 33400 | 61538281 | 20 | 38275282 | 2914 | 59219 | 969924000 |
| Gender wise Literacy ratio | 0.92 | 0.84 | 0.47 | 0.74 | 0.77 | 0.82 | 0.05 | 0.62 | 0.95 | 0.96 | 0.797 |
| Absolute Literacy ratio | 74.84 | 71.90 | 52.17 | 55.36 | 16.95 | 67.42 | 10.64 | 55.84 | 27.89 | 91.85 | 74.04 |

(*Source*: Indiastat.com, 2017)

## ANALYSIS AND INFERENCE

The conjecture of all the table, gives a vivid picture of the conditions of the sites considered in this paper the performance of the sites based on the two of the selected parameters, employment and literacy (or education), and as compared to their respective state averages and national averages. When it comes to working population (as a measure of employment), it reflects that except Pamban, all the other selected regions fare better than their respective state average. Pamban alongside Minicoy have poorer averages than the national average. The reason for poor performance by Pamban might be due to the lack of attention from the authorities post the super cyclone of 1964, the aftermath of which led to the administration to complete abandon Dhanuskhodi, a prominent locality within Pamban. While the marginally lower performance of Minicoy with that of the national standard is due to the heavy dependence on tourism industry for livelihood. It is to be noted that Minicoy have fared better than the average of its domicile state Lakshadweep. The superior performance of Tawang and Hasnabad cannot be directed as the good result of the Panchayati Raj solely, as Tawang has good income resource from tourism and trading with neighbors Bhutan and Tibet. Hasnabad has good amount of population often migrating to or travelling daily to the city of Kolkata for livelihood. Interesting is to see the good performance of Longewala in matter of livelihood, which is attributed to the herding of camels and petty jobs to the nearest town of Jaisalmer.

The gender average of most regions are equal to their respective state averages, except Tawang and Longewala. The results clearly show that Arunachal Pradesh and Rajasthan have yet not been able to implement the National Literacy Mission for all, properly. Again, the overall literacy rates are mostly at par for each of these sites, which signify the appreciable performance of the respective Panchayats, when it comes to the basic education.

The earlier part of the paper have shown glimpse of the condition of the health care sector, for each of these location. In most cases, the village or the block does not have the basic medical units and have to rely on facilities, situated 5 to 10 kms away.

## CONCLUSIONS

Separate ministries of the Government of India administer the Panchayat system and defense in India. However, it is an opinion that for the administration of such borderline villages, the ministry of defense should also be involved, especially as these villages, blocks or districts have heavy deployment and strategic involvement of the armed forces or the coast guards for the safeguard of the peace and order of the mainland.

In many cases, it is seen that for the greater cause of the security of the country the armed forces has to intervene in the activities of these localities and again in many cases it is found, that the existing protocols cause harassment to the natives and hamper their lifestyle.

Again, on the contrary, since most South Asian people resemble each other, it becomes quite difficult for the armed forces guarding the international land and water bodies, to differentiate in between an Indian citizen or a foreigner.

The problem becomes intense, in case of some occasions or turmoil. For example, *Durga Puja* is an important festival amongst Hindus and is immensely popular in the Eastern Indian state of West Bengal and its international counterpart Bangladesh. The five days annual ceremony ends with much pomp and joy, with finally immersing the idols of Goddess *Durga*, in the water bodies. Hasnabad in West Bengal and Khulna and Satkhira divisions of Bangladesh, meet each other on the common river boundary of Ichamati during this and often after the program, the local civic bodies accuse the armed forces of strictness and hampering the local customs. However, the localities often do not understand that a good amount of infiltration and trafficking happens during this time (Times, 2014). Again a lot of illegeal asylum have been sought by the Sri Lankan Tamils from Jafna and Thalaimmar during the LTTE[8] civil war in the island country (India Today, 2016) through Pamban in Tamil Nau. The close proximity of the people of these region makes it difficult for the armed forces to control the huge number of illegal infiltration.

Again, Arunachal Pradesh has been long been claimed by China as their integral part and had in the recent past intruded inside Indian territory on number of ocassions (India Today, 2016). The proximity of the clan of the people of this region with the Chinese and also with their language, makes it difficult for the Indian army to keep track of disguised trafficking through the long unfenced border.

Things are almost equal in Longewala. Spying and smuggling by Pakistan, through the Thar by camels can be easy mode. Again this camels can be owned by the localites and can be easily hired out for easy money, in case of lack of livelihood opportunities by local authorities from the Indian side.

Finally, Minicoy, though far from the madding crowd, is not far from Maldives. Maldives till date has been pro India, but, one can never rule out the use of these two places by any third country for infiltration and intrusion to the Indian mainland.

The Panchayati system has done commendable efforts through out the country and their efforts in the discussed regions are not too bad. However, considering their location and their importance to the defense of the country, a better and special attention should be given to these places. A separate ministry might actually be a spoil sport, so should be avoided, but some better strategic decisions along side the consultation of the ministry of defense for the better empowerment and upliftment of these regions should happen on priority basis.

[8] LTTE – Liberation Tigers Tamil Eelam, a radical Tamil separatist group once active in North Sri Lanka

## REFERENCES

AllIndiaFacts.Com. (2017). Hospitals in Hasnabad. Retrieved from AllIndiafacts.com: http://allindiafacts.com/school/west-bengal/north-twenty-four-pargana/hasnabad.html on 24.04.2019.

GoI. (2011). *District Census Handbook - Ramanathapuram, Series 34, Part 12A.* Directorate of Census Operations, T. N. New Delhi.

GoI. (2011). District Census Handbook, Ramanathapuram. Directorate of Census Operations, T. N. New Delhi.

GoI. (2015). Tawang District: Centsus 2011-2019 Data. Retrieved from Census 2011: http://www.census2011.co.in/census/district/465-tawang.html on 24.04.2019.

GoR.(2017). Retrieved from Jaisalmer.rajasthan.gov.in: http://jaisalmer. rajasthan.gov.in/content/raj/jaisalmer/en/about-jaisalmer/blocks-tehsils-panchayats.html on 24.04.2019.

India Today. (2016, June). Retrieved from http://indiatoday.intoday.in/story/ sri-lankan-refugees-tamil-nadu-plight-camps-war/1/687724.html 25.04.2019

India, G.O. (2011). District Census Book, West Bengal, Series 20, Part 12B. Kolkata: Directorate of Census Operations, West Bengal.

India, G.O. (2011). District Census Handbook, Lakshadweep, Series 32, Part 12 A. New Delhi: Directorate of Census Operations, Lakshadweep.

India, G.O. (2011). District Census Handbook, Lakshadweep, Series 32, Part 12 B. new Delhi: Directorate of Census Operations, Lakshadweep.

India, G.O. (2011). District Census Handbook, Rajasthan, Series 9, Part 12A. New Delhi: Directorate of Census Operations.

India, G.O. (2011). District Census Handbook, Rajasthan, Series 9, Part 12A. New Delhi: Directorate of Census Operations, Rajasthan.

India, G.O. (2011). *District Census Handbook, Tawang, Arunachal Pradesh, Series 13, Part 12A.* New Delhi: Directorate of Census Operations, Arunachal Pradesh.

India, G.O. (2017, June 7). *Data Net India Pvt Ltd.* Retrieved from Indiastat. com: https://www.indiastat.com/default.aspx on 25.04.2019

India, G.O.(n.d.). Retrieved from Wkipedia: https://en.wikipedia.org/wiki/ Balwant_Rai_Mehta_Committee 24.04.2019.

Indiastat.com. (2006.). Retrieved from Indiastat.com: https://www. indiastat. com/table/administrativeunits/1/panchayats/200/410708/data.aspx on 25.04.2019.

Indiatoday. (2016). Retrieved from http://www.news18.com/news/india/ chinese-army-intrudes-inside-arunachal-pradesh-1296041.html on 24.04.2019

Indiatoday.in. (2016). Retrieved http://indiatoday.intoday.in/story/sri-lankan-refugees-tamil-nadu-plight-camps-war/1/687724.html on 25.04.2019

MoPR. (2013). Annual Report 2012-13. New Delhi.

OneFiveNine.Com (2017). Retrieved from http://www.onefivenine.com/india/Listing/Town/hospitals/24-Paraganas-North/Hasnabad

ToI. (2014). Retrieved http://timesofindia.indiatimes.com/india/India-Bangla-joint-Durga-idol-immersion-cancelled/articleshow/44306018.cms 25.04.2019

---

***Mr. Satyaki Datta*** is currently a Research Associate at MICA, Ahmedabad. Started career as a graduate engineer and holds a postgraduate degree in Marketing from KIIT University. ***Dr. Rasananda Panda*** is working as a Professor of Economics at MICA, Ahmedabad. A person from Odisha, he has 24 years of experience in academics.

# 7

# Participation in Development: Decentralized Governance and Development in Andhra Pradesh and Madhya Pradesh

RADHIKA KUMAR[9]

## INTRODUCTION

The Panchayati Raj Institutions (PRIs) in the State of Andhra Pradesh (united Andhra Pradesh) and Madhya Pradesh were pivotal to the welfarist/populist program pursued by the government in power. In both states, wide scale institutional changes were effected for purposes of promoting participatory local government. However the method of doing so varied in both. Madhya Pradesh effected decentralisation through the panchayats themselves while in Andhra Pradesh, parallel institutions of decentralisation were established in the form of stake-holder associations for purposes of promoting participation. Given the different institutional paths of decentralisation, the comparison is made meaningful. This is because it will provide the context of distinguishing between the development trajectories of the two states with regard to their efficacy in promoting participation and development. In doing so one will also briefly look at legal, financial and administrative viability of panchayats given that all these

[9] Motilal Nehru College, Delhi University.
*Corresponding author*: E-mail: radhikaku@gmail.com

factors are crucial in determining the functioning of local level institutions. This paper concludes that the process of institutional decentralisation in both the states has been an evolving process. It identifies two types of shortcomings: first, the legislations for decentralisation are not in place or where legislation has been enacted, in practice funds, functions and functionaries have not been devolved and second, the government has fortified itself with so many caveats in the laws relating to decentralisation that the panchayati raj institutions have no maneuverability to perform their assigned role.

## DECENTRALISED INSTITUTIONS IN THE STATE OF MADHYA PRADESH

Madhya Pradesh was amongst the first states to adopt the provisions of the 73$^{rd}$ amendment act and set up the three tiered panchayati raj system. Besides adopting panchayati raj, the government also made a series of amendments to the act to deal with various limitations that were noticed during its implementation. To promote women's participation which continued to be low despite reservation for women in panchayati raj institutions, the government made it compulsory for the quorum to include one third women members. Also members of parliament or the legislative assembly who were elected from urban constituencies were denied membership to district or block level panchayat. This too was effectuated by amending the state panchayati raj act. This was to ensure that the rural areas would not be short-changed for the urban. Further it was decided that a meeting of the gram sabha should be held at least once in three months (Samarthan, 2001). Another empowering provision was the right to recall. This allows the gram sabha (> 2/3) to pass a motion to recall the elected representatives, sarpanch / panch after a period of two and a half years (PRIA, 1999).

Apart from these representational changes in the panchayati raj institutions the government also aimed to clearly define and also expand administrative capability and financial viability of these institutions Therefore as has been argued, the purpose of the amendments has been to operatinalize the panchayats consistent with the ideology of 'power to the people' and democratic decentralization (Behar and Kumar, 2002).

However it is argued that in practice however, the administration has been reluctant to decentralize power, authority and finances. Functions performed by panchayats are mostly subsidiary in nature involving drawing up of beneficiary lists, overseeing development works or dispensing routine administrative formalities. Panchayats do not have final decision making powers and departments continue to exercise overriding authority (Behar and Kumar, 2002). Other problem areas include no clear demarcation of the roles of the bureaucracy and the zila panchayat particularly since the merger of the two. Panchayat functionaries remain unaware of government rules and procedures and therefore are unable to act effectively or deal with the government system.

The Madhya Pradesh government made a number of efforts to strengthen the financial position of panchayats. Some of the important measures are:

Following recommendations of the State Finance Commission (SFC) put forth in 1997, 2.91% of state income was devolved to the panchayati raj institutions. Also in a bid to synchronise administrative and political functions and functionaries; the Block Development Office (BDO) was merged with the janpad panchayat.The janpad panchayat now came to be headed by a chief executive officer.

Gram panchayats could now give permission for extracting minor minerals. By transferring this power another revenue source was made available to them.

The government also transferred functions relating to 22 departments to the panchayats. These included education, women and child development and rural industries amongst others.

Following the Tenth Finance Commission's recommendations the government transferred funds to all the three tiers of local governance. In terms of ratio of funds, the zilla panchayat received 3.45%, the janpad panchayat got 8.04% while the bulk of funds *i.e.* 88.52% were devolved to the gram panchayat (Behar and Kumar, 2002).

It is the central and the state governments which make finances available to the zilla panchayat. These grants from the state government contributed 96.38% of the total income till 1996-97. Once the DRDA was merged with the zila panchayat in 1997-98 the quotient of central government contribution went up. However grants received by zilla panchayats are essentially tied grants. Questions of fiscal autonomy and discipline become difficult to deal with under such a system where grants are the main source of funding (Behar and Kumar, 2002). The higher tiers like zilla panchayat receive funds for various schemes and disburse it to lower levels with little input on any aspect of the same. They are said to function as a 'post-office' *i.e.* an administrative conduit. On the other hand it has been noted that "utilization ratio for the social sector schemes are very high. The selection of beneficiaries is much more effective" (PRIA, 1999).

## EMPOWERING THE INSTITUTION OF THE GRAM SABHA IN TRIBAL AREAS

Carrying the democratic experiment a step further the Madhya Pradesh government enacted the Panchayati Raj Dwitiya (Sansodhan) Adhiniyam 1997 (hereinafter amendment Act 43 of 1997) to conform to the central legislation of Panchayat Extension to Scheduled Areas Act or PESA (ELDF, 2011).The state which has a tribal population of 12.23 million constitutes 20.27% of the total population of the state. The PESA is seen as path breaking in many respects as it attempts to change the terms of engagement between the village community and panchayat by strengthening the institution of the gram sabha. Also a deliberate attempt has been made under the act not to disturb prevalent customs, traditions and practices of the tribal groups and communities.

Under the act, gram sabhas in the tribal areas have the following functions *i.e.* (i) "approve the plan, programmes and projects for social and economic development before the plans, programmes and projects are taken up for implementation by the panchayat at the village level; (ii) be responsible for the identification or selection of persons as beneficiaries under the poverty alleviation and other programmes" (ELDF, 2004). Another important provision is that the panchayat must obtain a 'certificate of utilization of funds'from the gram sabha. Planning and management of major water bodies in the scheduled areas as also in case of grant of prospective license or mining lease for minor minerals the approval of the gram sabha or panchayats has been made mandatory. Besides the above, the panchayat and gram sabhas are also endowed with the ownership of minor forest produce and have, "the power to prevent alienation of land in the scheduled areas and to take appropriate action to restore any unlawful alienated land of a scheduled tribe" (ELDF, 2004).

Further the state legislature is expected to ensure that panchayats are able to act as autonomous entities embodying the spirit of 'self-government' without the higher tiers of governance usurping any of their powers. However, in practice it has been observed that the gram sabhas were largely ignorant regarding their legal jurisdiction over village forests. Land ownership in tribal communities which is essentially customary has as yet not been given any legal recognition.

## ELECTIONS AND PANCHAYATI RAJ INSTITUTIONS

Given these institutional constraints and achievements, it is imperative to also undertake an electoral analysis of panchayati raj institutions, as lack of mobilization of civil society has been one of the main impediments to successful democratic decentralization and governance. As already stated Madhya Pradesh was the first state in the country to hold elections after the 73rd amendment to the Constitution was adopted. Elections to 45 zilla panchayats, 459 janpad panchayats and 30922 gram panchayats were held in 1994 and then again in 2000. This definitely reflected a strong political commitment to decentralize power to the people.

The experience of the campaign reflected that the gram sabha was not in favour of electing again the candidates who had not performed satisfactorily during the tenure. There was lack of knowledge about the provisions of the elections as many women did not contest on the general seats as they perceived such seats to be reserved for men. However, as compared to the first round of elections, enthusiasm and awareness amongst the voters was much more in the second round. Further, while political parties did not overtly participate in the elections, covert party affiliation of the candidates was seen (Bandhu, 2000).

## INAUGURATING 'GRAM SWARAJ'

On 21st January, 2001, the Madhya Pradesh government amended the 'Madhya Pradesh Panchayati Raj Adhiniyam' (Act), 1993. This act now came to be known as the Madhya Pradesh Panchayati Raj (Sanshodhan) Adhiniyam, 2001. With this amendment the words 'Panchayati Raj' was substituted by words 'Panchayati Raj Avam Gram Swaraj' in the act. The purpose of the amendment was to establish gram swaraj. Gram swaraj by involving all adult members of the village community in deliberation and decision making regarding local issues was meant to realise the concept of 'direct democracy'. In practice this has meant strengthening the gram sabha. Changes envisaged are many. At present the gram panchayat exercises limited but significant powers over many but not all government developmental projects. These include selection of beneficiaries for many programmes and taking decisions regarding the location of projects funded under earmarked schemes devised at higher levels. All of these powers would now be vest in the gram sabha and the eight permanent committees that it is expected to elect (Behar and Kumar, 2002).

Institutionally one of the main shortcomings of the panchayati raj system which had emerged during the first phase of its implementation was excessive centralization of power in the sarpanch and hence the reference 'sarpanch raj'. Another issue was that while the village to which the sarpanch belonged would monopolise all development related work and funds, other constitutive villages do not get their due share of attention. Also as there would only be one gram sabha for a group of villages included within gram panchayat, participation from these 'dependent villages' would be limited. It is argued that the chief minister initiated these changes upon receiving particular feedback from the various development projects. The general perception was that elected 'user committees' for various projects were more successful than when members to these committees were appointed officially (Behar and Kumar, 2002).

The government intended to achieve twin goals by these changes. They were expected to be popular and to demonstrate that a government led by the Congress party is more innovative and geared towards fulfilling the needs of the people when compared to other political parties. Another reason for their popularity was that these changes were also expected to reduce corruption. Officials argue that corruption among sarpanches and their associates often occurs because those people are not beneficiaries of the programmes from which funds are diverted. By requiring the new 'user committees' to consist mainly or entirely of beneficiaries of the projects that they oversee, the incentives for corruption are expected to decline. The new system is also intended crucially to please the ruling party's state legislators. The latter were often at loggerheads with the village sarpanches within their constituencies (Manor, 2001).

The sarpanch lobby definitely felt threatened by the implementation of the system fearing that their powers would be diluted and their political importance reduced within the context of the local community. A sarpanch mobilization took place against the introduction of the gram swaraj act leading to filing of a case questioning the constitutional validity of the new system in the Jabalpur High Court. The government buckling under pressure exerted by the sarpanch lobby back tracked and inducted them into the gram swaraj system by making them co-signatories for operating the gram swaraj account. The gram swaraj system was expected to have a separate finance committee with a separate treasurer working according to the instructions of the gram sabha.

However, the step to make the sarpanch, co-signatory to the gram swaraj account, led to dilution of financial autonomy of the gram sabha. The lack of financial devolution by the state government also remains a major bottleneck (Behar, 2003).

Operationalising the system has led to identification of many problems. Committee members are usually nominated and not elected and even when elected, are unaware of their powers and functions. Often there is overlapping of roles between committees and there is lack of a clear cut dispute resolution system. 'Sarpanch Raj' continues as the sarpanch still chairs the meetings of the gram sabha.

Further the gram sabha has not been entrusted with governance functions like justice or security. The Gram Nyaylaya Adhiniyam (Village Court Act) and Gram Suraksha Adhiniyam (Village Protection Act) adopted on 26$^{th}$ January 2001 with the gram swaraj act, negate the task of self-governance assigned to the gram sabha (Behar and Kumar, 2002).

The panchayati raj system envisaged under the 73$^{rd}$ amendment act was based on a set of laws, rules and expected to function within a specific framework. However ground reality has been very different. Persistence of traditional mechanism's and hierarchies as also informal interactions at the level of the village reflect the existence of a different operating system. Hence it is argued that the panchayat system imposes a rational construct on the village culture of interpersonal relationships which affects the functioning of panchayats (Samarthan, 2001).

Madhya Pradesh's performance with regard to panchayati raj is usually lauded. One of the reasons cited for the same is that the top level political leadership is strongly committed to the institution of panchayats as an integral part of the governance system. Various legislations and policies taken with regard to devolution of powers and functions to panchayats reflect the same. However gaps between policy and practice as also resistance to change have diluted the extent of change that these laws were expected to bring about. On the basis of the Devolution Index (D.I.) which ranked states on the basis of framework, functions, finances, functionaries, capacity building and accountability, Madhya Pradesh was ranked sixth out of 24 states and 4 union territories. It scored 47.26 while the national average score on overall devolution was 38.52 (Alok, 2013).

## DECENTRALISED INSTITUTIONS IN ANDHRA PRADESH

Development relating to panchayati raj in Andhra Pradesh from the Balwant Rai Mehta Committee report of 1957 to the coming into force of the 73$^{rd}$ constitutional amendment in 1994 can be divided into 5 phases. While each phase added new dimensions to the system, institutionally and functionally, the phase beginning in 1986-1994 is interesting in terms of the political dynamics and various functional changes involved in the same. The Telugu Desam government which came to power in 1983 had promised in its elections manifesto that it would work for revitalization of panchayati raj institutions. The proclaimed purpose of the reform was to decentralize planning and administration, with a view to taking administration closer to the people. The idea was to retain the old zilla parishads and establish mandal panchayats by abolishing the panchayat samities and gram panchayats. As this proposal did not find favour, it was decided to introduce a four tier system. It abolished 330 panchayat samities and created 1,104 Mandal Praja Parishad (MPPs) in their place. As already stated, the objective behind the creation of the mandals had been to take administration to the door-step of the common man. However, doubts were expressed regarding realization of this objective especially after the defeat of the Telugu Desam party and the return of the Congress to power in 1989. Scarce resources and inadequate staff at the disposal of the mandals had certainly been impediments to the realization to this objective, but the mandals undoubtedly proved more accessible to the people than the earlier panchayat samities.

## ELECTIONS AND PANCHAYATI RAJ INSTITUTIONS

For eleven years since the inception of panchayati raj in 1959 till 1970, elections had been conducted in the state only thrice in 1959, 1964 and 1970. The next elections to Panchayati Raj bodies in the state had been scheduled for 1979 but were deferred owing to a writ petition, filed in the high court challenging certain statutory provisions pertaining to the reservation of elected offices for scheduled castes. After the disposal of the writ petition, elections were slated for 1980, but were again postponed in view of the impending reorganization of the Taluks to make them co-terminus with blocks. This apart, the approaching decennial census (1981) and another writ petition in the high court led to the elections being deferred once again. They were finally held in December 1981.

Elections were again held after the coming into effect of the 1986 act. Elections were held in March 1987 to panchayati raj bodies at all levels except the gram panchayat since these had already been held in March 1986, and as stipulated were not conducted on party lines. At the Mandal and Zilla Praja Parishad levels the elections had been party based with a ban imposed on defections. With the introduction of direct elections for the post of chairperson (ZPP) and President (MPP) and with the provision of ex-officio membership to these bodies, an internal conflict was built into the organization. There were cases where a majority of the members of ZPP belonged to one party, for example the Telugu Desam party while the chairperson belonged to the opposition party (in this instance the Congress party). There were also instances where a majority of the members of the MPP belonged to the Congress party and the Bhartiya Janata party (BJP) but the president belonged to the Telugu Desam party.

## THE 1994 ACT AND FEATURES OF THE PANCHAYATI RAJ INSTITUTIONS

The state government amended the existing laws governing the panchayati raj institutions in the light of the 73$^{rd}$ amendment.

Accordingly, the 'Andhra Pradesh Panchayati Raj' bill was passed by the state legislative assembly on March 3rd, 1994. Henceforth a three tiered structure consisting of Zilla Parishad (ZP) at the district level, Mandal Praja Parishad (MPP) at the intermediate level and gram panchayat at the village level were constituted in the state.

The Act provides for direct election of members to the panchayati raj institutions at all the three levels on the basis of wards for the gram panchayat and territorial constituencies in the case of mandal parishad and zilla parishad, with reservations for the scheduled castes, scheduled tribes, backward classes and women. It provides for the participation of political parties in the elections for the intermediate and district tier bodies. Also all three tiers have been 'organically' linked such that elected heads at the lower level are permanent invitees to meetings held at the next higher level body (Rajiv Gandhi Foundation, 1999).

The role of the gram sabha is largely consultative. The gram panchayat is expected to consider the gram sabha's suggestions with regard to various development programmes.However as provided for under the act, the gram panchayat is not bound to implement the suggestions of the gram sabha. Therefore if the decisions of the gram sabha are not suitable to the panchayat the latter may just ignore the same and chart its own course in various matters.

Further it is argued that in most of the cases gram sabha meetings are not convened regularly. Also often local level politics tend to dominate such meetings. As no specific quorum is mandated for such meetings manipulating the same has become even easier. Often fictitious meetings are recorded. The resolutions of these meetings are authenticated by collecting signatures from individuals sympathetic to the panchayat sarpanch (Rajiv Gandhi Foundation, 1999).

Elections to mandals and zilla parishads were held in 2 phases on 6th and 10th March 1995. About 70% of the voters exercised their franchise. Out of the total 1,093 zilla parishad territorial constituencies, the Telugu Desam won 695 (64%) and the Congress won about 25%. In the elections of the mandal parishad territorial constituencies the Telugu Desam party won 52% and the Congress won 34% of the total seats. Apart from local level political and party affiliations that may impede functioning of the panchayats the state government too continues to exert its influence over panchayati raj institutions. Under the 1994 act the government can cancel or suspend any resolution of the gram panchayat or mandal or zilla parishad if in its opinion any such resolution abuses the provisions of any act. The government also has the powers to dismiss panchayati raj institution heads at all the three levels, and has stipulated that such persons cannot seek re-election for two years from the date of their removal. It can dissolve the zilla parishad/ mandal parishad/ gram panchayat and any of its standing committees (Rajiv Gandhi Foundation, 1999).

In 1999 the state government did transfer 13 out of the 29 subjects to panchayati raj institutions. Identification of beneficiaries for various employment oriented schemes like Jawahar Rozgar Yojana (JRY), Employment Assurance Scheme (EAS) and the recently introduced 'Adarna' scheme (for distribution of tools to poor village artisans) and other departmental schemes should be done through the gram panchayat and approved by the same. However except for JRY which is given directly by the central government to the gram panchayats for implementation, the sarpanches allege that they are not involved in identifying local beneficiaries for other schemes being implemented directly by the concerned state government departments. This criticism has been made particularly with regard to the Janambhoomi programme initiated by the state government in 1997. It has been alleged that the latter is essentially a government programme with local bureaucracy playing a pivotal role. There is only 'guided involvement' of the gram sabhas and sarpanches. In fact it has been argued that there are two gram sabhas operating at the local level. One is the gram sabha organised for Janambhoomi which has high participation of villagers as all the line departments of the state government are involved (PRIA, 2001). On the other hand is the gram sabha held by the gram panchayat which has poor attendance. Secondly, inspite of specific guidelines of the government, mandal and district level leadership is not deeply involved. Also while the sarpanch and the ward member of the concerned habitation are members of the programme, their participation is muted. The programme agenda and its enactment are mainly decided by officials and political leaders (PRIA, 2001).

While the Janambhoomi programme was launched for the purpose of promoting people's participation it has actually led to panchayats becoming weaker. It is argued that,"....although the programme is people oriented, the involvement of panchayats is superficial and at times, counter-productive is terms of political factionalism and group rivalry. Thus the' programme poses a serious challenge to the system of panchayats" (PRIA, 2001). In fact in May 2004, The Andhra Pradesh Sarpanches' Association demanded that the state government withdraw the Janambhoomi programme as it had led to dilution of powers of the panchayats (Institute of Social Sciences, 2004).

In the subsequent elections held for the zilla parishads and mandal parishads in 2001, the TDP won only 10 zilla parishads as opposed to all the 22 zilla parishads that it had won in the March 1995 elections. The Congress got a majority in four zilla parishads on its own and in three zilla parishads with the support of the Communist party. The Telangana Rashtra Samiti (TRS) which made its debut in the panchayat elections won 84 seats as also the chairmanship of Nizamabad zilla parishad. Party wise tally was as follows *i.e.* TDP 512 seats, Congress 44, Left parties 24, BJP 13 and TRS 84 (Institute of Social Sciences, 2001).

Looking at the financial aspect, the powers of taxation are exclusively given to the lower rung of panchayati raj system *i.e.* gram panchayat (Vittal, 1999). The gram panchayat has both compulsory and discretionary taxation powers. The mandal and zilla parishad's own resources account for only 5% of the total income. The remaining 95% income is received as assigned revenues and grants. Thus panchayati raj institutions in general have not been able to mobilize their own resources.

The state of Andhra Pradesh essentially represents a case wherein the panchayati raj bodies, after having an initial successful beginning could hardly regain the status they had enjoyed. Though there seems to be total conformity with the 73rd constitution amendment at least in legal terms, the situation in the field does not conform to the governments' commitment to the process of decentralization.

## COMPARING PANCHAYAT RAJ INSTITUTIONS IN MADHYA PRADESH AND ANDHRA PRADESH

While panchayati raj institutions in both Andhra Pradesh and Madhya Pradesh have been plagued by various shortcomings, for a comparative understanding some parameters may prove useful. The status of panchayati raj institutions can be reviewed in terms of the following:

Conduct of panchayat elections

Devolution of financial powers

Devolution of functions and functionaries

Constitution of district planning committees (DPCs)

Status of gram sabha

Act 40 of 1996

Checks and balances of panchayati raj institutions and accountability.

While two rounds of elections to panchayat were conducted in both Madhya Pradesh and Andhra Pradesh they were however, delayed in both cases. Madhya Pradesh recently held elections to panchayat institutions, marking completion of the third round of elections.

Both the states constituted State Finance Commissions (SFCs). Of the 84 financial and non-functional recommendations made by Andhra Pradesh State Finance Commission in 1997, the government accepted 55. Out of the Rs 979.16 crores recommended by the state finance commission for purposes of devolution to various panchayati raj institutions, government accepted devolutions to an extent of Rs. 434.42 crores. These mainly related to doubling the per capita grants, increase of pension grants for various other basic services such as sanitation, drinking water etc.

Amongst the non-financial recommendations made by the commission and accepted by the government has been release of grants based on a backwardness index used to classify various gram panchayats. This is note worthy as it includes assigning weightage to ordinary, backward and tribal gram panchayats for purposes of giving grants. The weightage would be based on the pace of development as measured by the state planning department.

With regard to devolution of functions and functionaries, 29 subjects have been identified in the eleventh schedule, which need to be devolved by the various State governments. In the case of Madhya Pradesh 18 departments, have been handed over to the panchayati raj institutions with administrative control over class III and class IV employees deputed to the panchayats. In the case of Andhra Pradesh given the parallel running programme of 'Janambhoomi', protests were launched by the sarpanches which led to 13 subjects being transferred to the panchayati raj institutions by the state government. Madhya Pradesh has then given certain additional functions to the panchayats in particular with regard to developmental tasks. The powers related to education, social forestry, agriculture, maintenance and repair of roads, street lighting etc. As per the Ministry of Rural development, Government of India's report the position regarding transfer of funds, functions and functionaries as in July 2001 was found as given in Table 1 below (Govt. of India, 2001).

**Table 1:** Transfer of Power to Panchayats

| ***State*** | ***Funds*** | ***Functions*** | ***Functionaries*** |
|---|---|---|---|
| Andhra Pradesh | 5 | 13 | 2 |
| Madhya Pradesh | 10 | 23 | 9 |

It has been argued that it is essentially in the case of funds that Madhya Pradesh scores over Andhra Pradesh. In the case of Andhra Pradesh, out of the three tiers of panchayats, panchayats at the district level are strong while the other two at the block and village levels are treated as subordinate to the district panchayats and thus they are not independent.

However, one caveat in the case of Madhya Pradesh is that though the functions of 23 departments have been transferred, staff and budget continue to be with line departments. Further, the state government has retained the powers not only to add to the functions but also withdraw the entrusted functions and duties when it decides. Thus, not only are functions and duties subject to executive discretion, but they are relevant only so far as funds allow.

While contracting out of works is not allowed in the case of Andhra Pradesh as also most other states, under the Janambhoomi programme it has been seen that not only were work contracts handed over to private contractors but also that the state government awarded contracts without the consent of the gram panchayats.

The Andhra Pradesh government has started curbing the panchayat powers since 1999. It not only took away the power of panchayats to draw cheques, but also vested the district collectors and other officials with most other executive powers, bypassing elected representatives of the panchayati raj institutions.

It is with regard to the gram sabha, that Madhya Pradesh has greatly advanced the process of decentralization. By granting legal status to the gram sabha, the government has made the advice of the gram sabha binding on the gram panchayat. The state laws with regard to gram sabha in all other cases including Andhra Pradesh set out highly ritualistic functions for the same.

The provisions of the Panchayats (extension to scheduled areas) Act 1996 (PESA) came into force in December 1996. Both the Andhra Pradesh and Madhya Pradesh governments adopted the acts with some modifications. In Andhra Pradesh, the gram sabhas in scheduled areas have no role to play with regard to grant of prospecting license or mining lease for minor minerals. Also in the case of Andhra Pradesh it is the gram panchayat which oversees matters of land acquisition and resettling persons displaced on account of such acquisition. On the other hand, Madhya Pradesh has given primacy to the gram sabha with regard to all the above subjects. Additionally the 'power to prevent and to restore tribal alienated land, to exercise control over institutions and functionaries in all social sectors as also control over local plans and resources including tribal sub-plans' have been assigned to the gram sabhas (Planning Commission, 2002).

On the question of accountability, if one were to assess the relationship between the bureaucracy and the panchayati raj institutions, it becomes evident that most of the state governments including those of Andhra Pradesh and Madhya Pradesh have not devolved all powers to panchayats. However, with regard to administrative restructuring, one positive development in Madhya Pradesh has been the merging of the DRDA with the zilla parishad. With the passage of the 73$^{rd}$ constitutional amendment act DRDA's were expected to function under the zilla parishads. In Andhra Pradesh the DRDA is headed by the district collector, whereas chairperson of district panchayat is its vice president (Planning Commission, 2002).

With regard to transparency, in Madhya Pradesh and Andhra Pradesh, development works of panchayati raj institutions are subject to social audit.

## CONCLUSIONS

Some general observations that can be made are that, the process of institutional decentralisation in both the states has been an evolving process. The shortcomings have essentially been of two types. Firstly the legislations for decentralisation are not in place or where legislation has been enacted, in practice funds, functions and functionaries have not been devolved. Secondly the government has fortified itself with so many caveats in the laws relating to decentralisation that the panchayati raj institutions have no manoeuvrability to perform their assigned role. Apart from this general experience that is shared by both Andhra Pradesh and Madhya Pradesh regarding panchayati raj institutions, the difference lies in the extent to which the two governments have pushed for the establishment of local governance bodies. As already stated, in the case of Madhya Pradesh, the government has repeatedly attempted to strengthen panchayats and an effective feedback mechanism has ensured that decentralization could be taken to the level of the Gram Sabha.

In the case of Andhra Pradesh the initial impetus to strengthen panchayats came from thepeople and not from the government. While this may point towards greater level of awareness and political activism in the rural areas, in practice the degree of decentralisation has largely depended on the commitment of state governments. This is because there is no direct devolution of powers and functions from the central government to the panchayati raj institutions. Further the development strategy adopted by the Andhra Pradesh government has led to its preferring parallel organizations to deliver development rather than allowing for development goals to be defined and implemented by the panchayati raj institutions.

Thus while in practice, the performance of panchayats in both Andhra Pradesh and Madhya Pradesh may show mixed results, in the case of the former the possibility for improvement is negligible as the panchayati raj institutions have been bypassed. In a sense the Andhra Pradesh model provides for administrative decentralisation without any political decentralization (Mooij, 2003).

## REFERENCES

Alok, V.N. (2013). Strengthening of Panchayats in India: Comparing Devolution across States; Empirical Assessment- 2012-13, April, New Delhi: Ministry of Panchayati Raj, Government of India and Indian

Institute of Public Administration (IIPA). Retrieved from *www.iipa.org.in* / upload/Panchayat_devolution_Index_Report_ *2012-1...* · PDF file on 28.04.2019.

Bandhu R. (2000). Jansatta. 20 January.

Behar A. (2003). 'Experiment with Direct Democracy-Time for Reappraisal'. Economic and Political Weekly. Vol.38, No.20, 23 May.

Behar A. and Kumar Y. (2002). Decentralisation in Madhya Pradesh, India: from Panchayati Raj to Gram Swaraj (1995 to 2001), Overseas Development Institute. Working Paper 170.

ELDF (2004). Hamara Gaon, Hamara Raj: A Booklet on Tribal Self-Rule Law in Madhya Pradesh. Retrieved from http://www.pria.org/publication/Hamara%20Gaon%20Hamara%20Raj%20%20%20A%20Guid%20Book%20on%20Tribal%20Self%20-Rule%20in%20Madhya%20Pradesh.pdf on 26.04.2019.

GoI. (2001). Report of the Task Force on Devolution of Powers and Functions upon PRIs., New Delhi: Ministry of Rural Development in Bandhyopadhyay *et al.* (2002). 'Convergence of Programmes by Empowering SHGs and PRIs'. Economic and Political Weekly. Vol. 37, No. 26, 29 June, pp. 2556-2561

Institute of Social Sciences. (2001). Andhra Pradesh. Panchayati Raj Update. New Delhi.

Institute of Social Sciences. (2004). Panchayati Raj Update 2004, *Andhra Pradesh*, New Delhi, pp.04

Manor J. (2001). 'Madhya Pradesh Experiments with Direct Democracy'. Economic and Political Weekly, Vol. 36, No. 9, 03-09 March.

Mooij J. (2003). Smart governance? Politics in the Policy Process in Andhra Pradesh'. Working Paper 228. Overseas Development Institute, London. Retrieved from http://www.odi.org.uk/sites/odi.org.uk/files/odi-assets/publications-opinion-files/2464.pdf on 26.04.2019.

Planning Commission. (2002). 'Decentralisation and Panchayati Raj Institutions (PRIs)'. In Mid-Term Appraisal of the Ninth five year plan(1997-2002). Retrieved from http://planningcommission.nic.in/plans/mta/mta-9702/mta-ch10.pdf

PRIA. (1999). Finances of Panchayats in Madhya Pradesh. New delhi.

PRIA. (2001). Parallel Bodies and Panchayati Raj Institutions (Experiences from the States). National Resource Centre. New Delhi.

Rajiv Gandhi Foundation. (1999). Task Force on Panchayati Raj 1999, Panchayati Raj in India Status Report. New Delhi.

Samarthan. (2001). Status Report on Panchayati Raj Institutions in Madhya Pradesh (1995-2000). Bhopal.

Vittal, C.P. (1999), 'Aspects of Panchayati Raj Finances in Andhra Pradesh: An Overview' in *Panchayat System in India: Historical, Constitutional and Financial Analysis, eds.* Ratna Ghosh and Alok Kumar Pramanik, Kanishka Publishers, New Delhi.

---

***Dr. Radhika Kumar*** is Assistant Professor in the Department of Political Science in Motilal Nehru College, Delhi University. A Ph.D. degree holder from JNU New Delhi she has contributed several research papers.

# 8

# Challenges of Panchayati Raj in Jammu Region: An Observation

ARCHANA KUMARI[10]

## INTRODUCTION

The evolution and history of Panchayati Raj system in Jammu & Kashmir is as unique as the history of the state itself. The Jammu & Kashmir Panchayati Raj Act, 1989 was introduced in the J&K assembly in April 1988 and passed in March 1989. This paper examins the provisions of Jammu & Kashmir Panchayati Raj Act and its implementation challenges in Jammu region. On the basis of empirical study of three Gram Panchayats Satriyan (R S Pura), Panjar Kalsote (Udhampur) and Bainglar (Samba) it has been observed that the government interventions are hampering the participatory character of local self governance leading to politicisation and controlling of these institutions. Panchayats are not perceived as fair, active and effective institutions. A lot of control is still with government, so the participatory and self governance nature of panchayats is being compromised. The villagers are unaware of many policies related to panchayats like reservation policies, administrative policies and financial policies, due to which they have to remain dependent on local government officers. In spite of so many acts and amendments, the Panchayati

[10] Central University, Jammu.
*Corresponding author*: E-mail: archanaiimc@gmail.com

Raj System in Jammu region is still facing these challenges, and suggests that an honest effort is required for implementation of local self governance in this region.

## PANCHAYATI RAJ IN INDIA: A GLANCE

Panchayati Raj or decentralised governance system is not a new concept rather it has been practiced since long in India; however constitutional status was given to this system in the year 1992 by 73rd amendment in the constitution (www.panchayat.gov.in). Though, the spirit of panchayati raj system had always been the integral part of the village system of India, it was Mahatma Gandhi who first foresaw and highlighted its importance for the growth and prosperity of Indian villages. He wrote,

> It (the Indian village) is a complete republic, independent of its neighbours for its vital wants, and yet inter-dependent for many other wants in which dependence is a necessity. Thus every village's first concern will be to grow its own crops and cotton for its cloth............As far as possible, every activity will be conducted on a cooperative basis. (Jain, 2013)

It was from this visualisation that formalisation of Panchayati Raj was thought off and Article 40 related to village panchayats was incorporated under the Directive Principles of Constitution. These principles are only guiding principles, neither mandatory nor legal; so Panchatyati Raj was also not legal till 73rd amendment in constitution was introduced which approved and made the participatory governance mandatory at all levels and established the provision of Gram Sabha in villages.

According to Article 243(B) of 73rd amendment (www.panchayat.gov.in):

> "Gram Sabha" means a body consisting of persons registered in the electoral roles relating to a village comprised within the area of panchayat at the village level. A Gram Sabha may exercise such powers and perform such functions at the village level as the legislature of a state may, by law, provide.

Thus Gram Sabha is a statutory body which acts as a watchdog of Gram Panchayats. However in current scenario; it has been sidelined at many places. (Jain, 2013)

Panchayati Raj in India has a four tier structure, in which Gram Sabha is at the lowest level and after it there are Gram Panchayat, Panchayat Samiti and Zila Parishad. In order to evaluate the prospects and challenges of Panchayati Raj, first the functions of each of these four bodies must be discussed. The functions of Gram Sabha as per constitution are:

> The main functions of Gram Sabha are to review the annual accounts of Panchayat, discuss audit, administrative reports of its Panchayat and schemes for Panchayat works. Also discuss the tax proposals and accept community service and voluntary labour. The members of Gram Sabha also elect the members of Gram Panchayat. In one year at least two meetings of the Gram Sabha are held.

Gram Sabha and Gram Panchayat both ensure the participation of the rural people in all types of social welfare, financial growth and smooth administration of village related work. Only difference is that, when the former is a guiding and regulating body, latter is an executive body and thus it has to remain very active. The functions of Panchayat are:

i. Municipal work broadly related to public health, social education, public safety and public construction.

ii. Physical planning of the village

iii. Social welfare

iv. Representational

v. Civil defence to maintain the public safety

vi. Conciliative in order to resolve the disputes

vii. Agency functions such as small savings, insurance and revenue collection.

(ibid)

However though the expectations are high from the Gram Panchayats as apparent from the above list of functions; it is a matter of study how much of these functions are actually undertaken by the panchayats in India. There is a link structure between Gram Panchayat and district administration; called Panchayat Samiti. It has following functions:

i. To implement and co-ordinate the policy directives of the State Governments related to development and extension programmes
ii. Implementation of production and social welfare programmes
iii. Supervise the work of Gram Panchayats.

(ibid)

At the apex of the Panchayati Raj system, there is Zila Parishad. Since its functions vary from state-to-state, it cannot be generalised.

The Panchayati Raj Institutions (PRIs) have not evolved nor functioning in uniform manner in all the states of India. Its functioning, impact, practices varies from place-to-place depending upon their political, economical and social conditions. In general there is a strong opinion that PRIs are mere constitutional body and not effective considerably. On the basis of studies conducted on decentralisation, reports submitted, conferences conducted on the same theme, following problems and challenges of Panchayati Raj System across India, have been inferred:

i. Excess government control and lack of will to decentralise the powers. Practically neither centre nor state governments are interested in decentralisation of powers. The control over PRIs is maintained through financial and administrative measures. The developmental fund becomes one of the sources to control over the PRIs. These funds are allocated through the MPs and MLAs to panchayats keeping in mind their political interests.
ii. The party politics has entered to the grassroots through PRIs and involvement of MLAs and MPs has led to different set of problems. The rural population has also been divided on not

only political lines but also on the narrow lines of caste, community, religion etc. The villages have been converted into the grounds of all kinds of political activities.

iii. The deep rooted feelings of caste system have divided the village population into many groups, sub-groups and factions. Instead of efficiency of the candidate, people vote them on the basis of his caste and sub-caste which has resulted in division and rivalries among the rural people and dilution of the purpose of PRIs.

iv. Even though there is 33% reservation for women in Panchayat elections as per 73$^{rd}$ and 74$^{th}$ amendment, the functioning of PRIs is dominated by males. In the Indian patriarchal society, politics is considered to be male domain and even if women are elected as pradhans the male family members or male representatives take decisions on her behalf. Report of conference of Elected Women Representatives (March, 2009) also reveals the fact that women are less politically socialised.

v. Shortage of funds is also one of the major problems for local bodies. They highly depend upon the State government for grants and due to inadequate grant they fail to implement the development programmes.

vi. Elections are not held regularly for local bodies which hampers the regular functioning of these bodies.

vii. Apart from all above mentioned specific problems the Panchayats are also struggling with the general issues of corruption, illiteracy, urbanisation, migration etc. The educated people of village tend to migrate to urban areas leaving behind only uneducated people to run the local bodies.

(Sharda, 2010; Jain, 2013; Ram, 2013)

## EVOLUTION AND GROWTH OF PANCHAYATI RAJ SYSTEM IN JAMMU & KASHMIR

The evolution and history of Panchayati Raj system in Jammu & Kashmir is as unique as the history of the state itself. The state of Jammu & Kashmir owes the initiation of grassroot governance to the popular mass movement in 1931 as a result of which Maharaja of J & K promulgated the J & K Village Panchayat Act No. 1, 1935 (Kumar, 2014). After independence, the National Conference came to power in March 1948. At that point of time, the development scenario of the State was characterised by economic stagnation and educational backwardness. The Zamindars had accumulated large chunks of land through manipulation. The majority of the people were impoverished. In view of this situation, abolition of landlordism became the top priority of the Government. It resulted in the introduction of Big Landed Estates Abolition Act, 1950. This was a landmark in the history of J & K as it was the first experiment of its kind in land reforms in the sub-continent. The introduction of this Act brought about appreciable changes in the socio-economic scenario of the state. (Panchayati Raj in Jammu & Kashmir, n.d., para 10)

All these measures created a conducive environment for reactivation of the Panchayati Raj system in reshaping the rural economy in the state (Aslam, 1977). Realizing this, the government replaced the Panchayat Act of 1935 (as amended in, 1941) with Act-V of Samvat 2008 in 1951. This Act provided for the establishment of panchayat of villages. However local self-governance entered a long period of dormancy before it could be revived in the year 1958 (Kumar, 2014). Though it went into the state of dormancy for a long period; it awoke and became active much before the whole nation awoke towards the panchayati raj system. No policy was working and still cannot work without people's active participation and their involvement at each and every level. Perhaps this is why, the study team on Community Development and National Extension Services headed by Balwant Rai Mehta (1957) expressed concern about the lack of people's participation and made a strong plea for devolution of power to lower levels through panchayats. Before the Panchayati Raj system could be introduced in the whole country, the Jammu & Kashmir State took a lead by passing the Jammu & KashmirVillage Panchayat Act of 1958 and repealing the earlier Acts. (Panchayati Raj in Jammu & Kashmir, n.d., para 18). However, even after passing the Panchayat Act of 1958, the panchayats at village level could not fulfil their purpose of local self governance due to not so active people's participation and lack of linkages with developmental institutions. For almost two decades the village level panchayats remained dysfunctional until the state government realised the importance of people's participation in development programmes. Then the State Government took a bold step by introducing an innovative concept of 'Single Line Administration', to secure the participation of the people through their representatives in the developmental process. "The twin objectives of the Single Line Administration was to secure a mechanism for developing the planning process at the district level to take full account of the resource endowments the potentialities and needs structure and also to initiate a process of equitable development of various areas within the district" (Choudhary, 1990).

Inspite of the introduction of this innovative developmental strategy in the mid-1970s, the Panchayati Raj system in the state of J & K could not be reinvigorated. However, the implementation of this innovative model led to the realization that "human potential which is available at the grassroots level should be mainstreamed into the movement of development to purvey a sound and strong basis to the democratic structure. It was in this context that the desire to have a sound institutional framework to give a definite and positive role to the community in the matter of self-governance has provided a sense of urgency for restructuring the institutional framework of Panchayati Raj" (ibid). This realization led to the introduction of Jammu & Kashmir Panchayati Raj Act, 1989.

## THE JAMMU & KASHMIR PANCHAYATI RAJ ACT, 1989

This Act was introduced in the J&K assembly in April 1988 and passed in March 1989. For the first time an Act was named a "Panchayati Raj Act" rather than a "Village Panchayat Regulation Act". This is certainly a very positive initiative as 'Panchayati Raj Act' gives an impression of interlinking the local self governance at all (village, block and district) levels and not only confined to the village level.

The preamble of the 1989 Act (http://drdk.nic.in) states: "Whereas it is expedient to promote and develop Panchayati Raj in the State as an instrument of vigorous local self government to secure effective participation of the people in the decision making process and for over-seeing implementation of development programmes". The salient features of the Act are:

a) Reduction of voting age from 21 to 18 years;
b) Holding of elections within six months of super session of a panchayat;
c) Direct election of the Sarpanch (Chairperson);
d) Constitution of Panchayati Adalat (Panchayat Courts) comprising five members who shall be nominated by the prescribed authority out of the panel prepared and recommended by the halqa panchayat;
e) Empowering panchayats to prepare plans and implement schemes for poverty alleviation and employment generation, agriculture and allied activities, rural industrialization, health, universalisation of elementary education, etc.;
f) No bar on holding elections on party lines.

The Act provides for a three-tier system consisting of Halqa Panchayat, Block Development Council and District Planning and Development Board. In addition, the Act provides for a Panchayati Adalat for every Halqa.

***Halqa Panchayat*:** The Act provides for a halqa panchayat for every halqa. Halqa means the area comprising a village or such contiguous number of villages as may be determined by the government from time to time. The important powers and functions allocated to Halqa Panchayats as enshrined in the Act are:

- To prepare and implement the plans for the development of the Halqa ;
- Preparation and implementation of special developmental plans for alleviating poverty and employment generation;
- The Halqa Panchayat shall be involved in the implementation of scheme of universalisation of elementary education and other educational programmes;

- The Halqa Panchayat shall also perform such other functions and duties as may be assigned or entrusted to it by the Government, the District Planning and Development Board and the Block Development Council within the area of which Halqa Panchayat is located.

(ibid)

***Block Development Council*:** The Act provides for the constitution of a Block Development Council. The main functions of the Block Development Council are:

- Construction, maintenance and supervision of inter-Halqa Panchayat communication system;
- Administrative and technical guidance to Halqa Panchayats and review of their work;
- To supervise plans relating to agriculture, rural development, animal husbandry/sheep husbandry, social forestry, education and public health;
- To supervise and monitor the implementation of poverty alleviation programmes;
- To carry out such other functions as may be entrusted to it by the Government or by the District Planning and Development Board.

(ibid)

***District Planning and Development Board*:** Further, the Act provides for the constitution of a District Planning and Development Board. The main functions of the DPDB are:

- To consider and guide the formulation of development programmes for the district and indicate priorities for various schemes and consider issues relating to the speedy development and economic upliftment of the district;
- To review periodically progress and achievements of development plans and schemes and make recommendations as it considers appropriate;
- To function as a working group for formulation of periodic and annual plans for the district;

- To formulate and finalise the plan and non-plan budget for the district;
- To lay down the policy guidelines for the Block Development Councils and Halqa Panchayats;
- To approve the budget of the Block Development Council and supervise and coordinate their work;
- To undertake special measures for alleviating poverty and employment generation and extending assistance to Halqa Panchayats in this behalf;
- To promote and assist cooperative institutions;
- To perform such other functions and duties as may be assigned or entrusted to it by the government from time to time.

(ibid)

***Panchayati Adalat*:** Panchayati Adalat is another important feature of Jammu & Kashmir Panchayati Raj Act. Apart from the Indian Penal Code, there is equivalent The Ranbir Penal Code applicable only to J&K State. The constitution of Panchayati Adalat at halqa level is therefore a very welcome step as it would provide great respite to the rural people from the complicated legal system and running from pillar to post in hostile townships (Kumar, 2014).

In spite of all these endeavours and provisions, the Jammu & Kashmir Panchayati Raj Act of 1989 cannot in any way claim to decentralise power or create a democratic environment at the grassroots level. On the basis of studies conducted on Panchayati Raj Act of Jammu & Kashmir, reports and conferences conducted on the same theme, following problems and challenges of Panchayati Raj System of J&K, have been inferred:

i. Just like the flaw of Panchayati Raj system across India, the most serious flaws in the Jammu & Kashmir Panchayati Raj Act, 1989 is related to government intervention in the composition of panchayats. Unlike the 73$^{rd}$ Amendment to the Constitution that provides that all the seats in the panchayats shall be filled by persons chosen by direct election from territorial constituencies in the panchayats, this Act provides for nominations at every level – the Halqa

Panchayat, the Block Development Council and the District Planning and Development Board thus enabling the government and political parties to not only take control of it but also serve their own interest. The principle of direct election of panchayats is applied only at the village level.

ii. Another critical flaw of the Act is its inability to provide for reservation of seats for women, scheduled castes and the scheduled tribes (SCs/STs). Unlike the 73rd Amendment of the Constitution which provides for reservation of 33 per cent seats for women through direct election, the State Act empowers the government to nominate women to the panchayats if it feels that their representation is needed (Kumar, 2014).

In order to overcome the problems and challenges of 1989 Act, the State Government had adopted many positive features of 73rd Amendment Act over the years. The various important changes made in the original Panchayati Raj Act of 1989 are:

*i.* ***Halqa majlis*:** Theprovision of Halqa Majlis equivalent of Gram Sabha in Jammu and Kashmir was made by the Jammu and Kashmir Panchayati Raj Rules, 1996.

*ii.* ***Provision for Reservation:*** The J&K Panchayati Raj (Second Amendment) Act, 2003 was solely passed with the objective to strengthen the representative character of the Halqa Panchayats, and also to ensure effective participation of women and scheduled castes/scheduled tribes (SCs/STs) in the functioning of grassroot level democratic institutions. State government agreed to adopt this important provision of 73rd Amendment although partially as only panch seats are reserved- because representation of women in panchayats that set up after 2001 elections was very less (ibid).

*iii.* ***State election commission:*** The J&K government amended the Act in 2011 and made a provision for State Election Commission.

*iv.* ***State finance commission:*** It is already mentioned above that financial autonomy is one of the challenges with Panchayati Raj system across India. In order to overcome this challenge, the Jammu and Kashmir State Finance Commission for Panchayats and Municipalities Act, 2011 was passed.

## RECENT OBSERVATION

In the backdrop of above mentioned scenario, the researcher visited some of the panchayats and observed the current situation and prevailing practices in the panchayat there. Some of the points tried to be minutely observed and questioned were – functioning of the Gram Sabha, people's participation in Gram Sabha, meetings of Gram Panchayat, planning and estimation of annual budget, implementation of various schemes (*e g.* SBM, MGNREGA etc).

Three panchayats were visited and their functioning was observed. These three panchayats were – Satriyan (R S Pura), Panjar Kalsote (Udhampur) and Bainglar (Samba).

***Satriyan Gram Sabha (R S Pura):*** This is situated only 3-4 kms away from the Indo-Pak border in R S Pura. It seems to be very sensitive Gram Sabha considering its geographical location. The participation of people in Gram Sabha is also very less. It depends upon the people whether they want to attend it or not and mostly only those attend it whose issues have to be discussed or any other matter concerning them is to be discussed there. The meetings of Gram Sabha happen only when there is any kind of problem not on regular intervals. Also there is no concept of annual budget so it seems to be an arbitrary and informal arrangement instead of an organised and formal one. The implementation of schemes and the benefits of schemes are being enjoyed only by the close ones of panchayat members with whom they have good relations and these schemes are kept beyond the knowledge and reach of the other villagers.

***Panjar Kalsote (Udhampur):*** This panchayat is situated in the Udhampur district, which is third largest city of Jammu region and considered to be a connecting line between Jammu region and Kashmir region. Here in Udhampur, particularly in this panchayat, people's participation in Gram Sabha is very less as they think that it has no power to make things better. The meetings also do not take place regularly and there is no specific time frame for the meetings. Usually meetings take place once or twice in a month. Since most of the things are decided by the Block

Development Officers, people do not give much importance to the Gram Sabha. Even panchayat and Gram Sabha approve the annual budget under the guidance of Block Development Officer. Also people say there is huge problem in implementing some centre sponsored schemes like SBM, MGNREGA etc. as it is concentrated in the hands of few powerful people. In MGNREGA, the identification of work is done by few people who facilitate their known ones, payments are not given on time, women and poor cannot raise their voice, no payment of medical charges are being paid in case of any accident during work. There is no unemployment allowance given to the people. In the whole district, there is no panchayat ghar at few panchayats and Panjar is one of them.

***Bainglar (Samba)*:** This Bainglar panchayat falls in Samba district of the state of Jammu & Kashmir. Comparatively this panchayat is doing well for its people. People elect few panchs and a sarpanch and they constitute the panchayat. Sarpanch can be a woman or a man and the developmental issues of the village are discussed and sometimes the family issues or property issues are also discussed and solved in the panchayat. The condition of roads, transport and certain other issues related to the progress of the village are also discussed and resolved. People actively participate in panchayat, attend the meetings and share their problems. Meetings generally take place every month or once in six months and in those meetings various issues are discussed. They prepare their budget regularly and work according to it. There is an important role of the Gram Sevak; who implies the rules and regulations and plans for the village. He directly describes and explains the problems of the village to the MLA and gets the work done. Gram Sevak passes the bills of the contractors who have done some work in the village. BDO works hand-in-hand with the village panchayat. Schemes like MGNREGA, SBM have been effectively implemented in the villages. People get employment under the scheme and get their wages in their bank accounts which have been opened under Jan Dhan Yojana. These schemes are implemented in some villages but not all the people of all the villages are aware of these schemes.

## CONCLUSIONS

It is also proved from these recent observations that the government interventions are hampering the participatory character of local self governance leading to politicisation and controlling of these institutions. Out of three panchayats visited, two are facing such problem suggesting that there could be many similar cases. However, from the example of the third panchayat, it seems to be imperative to have local level dedicated leaders who are always ready to serve their community and locality. Perhaps the reason of the success of Bainglar panchayat of Samba district is the dedicated person known as Gram Sevak in the village. In spite of few such sparkling experiences, the larger picture of panchayati raj system in Jammu region is gloomy. The main challenges emerged are: -

- Panchayats are not perceived as fair, active and effective institutions.
- A lot of control is still with government, so the participatory and self governance nature of panchayats is being compromised.
- The villagers are unaware of many policies related to panchayats like reservation policies, administrative policies and financial policies, due to which they have to remain dependent on local government officers.

In spite of so many acts and amendments, the Panchayati Raj System in Jammu region is still facing these challenges, which gives a clear message that an honest effort is required for implementation of local self governance in this region.

## REFERENCES

Aslam M. (1977). Land Reform in J&K. Social Scientists. Volume 6. No. 4, November edition, 45-48.

Choudhary S. (1990). Does the Bill give power to people? In Panchayati Raj in J&K. George M. (*Ed.*). Concept Publishing House. New Delhi.

Jain, T. (2013). Panchayati Raj Administration and Rural Development. Book Leaf Publishers. New Delhi.

Kumar A. (2014). Panchayati Raj Institutions in Jammu and Kashmir: A Critical Analysis. Journal of Rural Development, Vol. 33, No. 1, pp. 73-82. NIRD, Hyderabad.

Panchayati Raj – A Retrospect. (*n.d.*). Retrieved from http://documents.gov.in/JK/8939.pdf on 25.04.2019.

Panchayati Raj Act – 1989 & Panchayai Raj Rules – 1996. (n.d.). Agriculture & Rural Development Department, J&K Govt. Retrieved from http://drdk.nic.in/J&K%20Panchayati%20Raj%20Act%201989%20and%20Rules%201996.pdf on 25.04.2019.

Panchayati Raj in Jammu & Kashmir. (n.d.) Retrieved from http://shodhganga.inflibnet.ac.in/bitstream/10603/51984/10/10_chapter%203.pdf on 25.04.2019.

Sharda, M. (2010). Evolution of Panchayati Raj in India. Kanishka Publishers, New Delhi.

Sultan M. (1995). Jammu & Kashmir. In Status of Panchayati Raj in the States of India-1994. Concept Publishing House. New Delhi.

***Dr. Archana Kumari***, is an alumni of Indian Institute of Mass Communication and is working as Assistant Professor in the Department of Mass Communication and New Media at Central University of Jammu. She has been the faculty of IIMC, Central University of Kashmir and Central University of Bihar in her academic experience of last 10 years. Her area of expertise is Media Economics, Development Communication, Media Research and Print Media.

# 9

# Panchayats in Fifth Schedule Areas: A Review of Implementation of PESA Act

RAJESH KUMAR SINHA[11]

## INTRODUCTION

In order to protect the interests of Scheduled Tribes with regard to land and other social issues, various provisions have been enshrined in Fifth Schedule and Sixth Schedule of the Constitution. The Fifth Schedule under Article 244(1) of the Constitution defines "Scheduled Areas" as areas, as the President may by order declare to be Scheduled Areas after consultation with the Governor of that State. The criteria for declaring any area as a "Scheduled Area" under the Fifth Schedule are: preponderance of tribal population, compactness and reasonable size of the area, a viable administrative entity such as a district, block or taluk, and economic backwardness of the area as compared to the neighbouring areas. The specification of "Scheduled Areas" in relation to a State is by a notified order of the President, after consultation with the State Government concerned. The same applies in the case of any alteration, increase, decrease, incorporation of new areas, or rescinding any orders relating to "Scheduled Areas".

[11] National Institute of Rural Development and Panchayati Raj, Hyderabad.
*Corresponding author*: E-mail: rajeshksinha@gmail.com

The Fifth Schedule Areas notified in 10 States, are characterized by poverty, illiteracy, weak infrastructure and deprivation in general. These areas are found in districts/blocks/clusters which are having predominant tribal population. Some of these are also facing left wing extremism. The Provisions of the Panchayats (Extension to Scheduled Areas) Act, (PESA) was enacted in 1996 to empower the Schedule Tribes with special powers of self governance through Gram Sabhas. It is strongly felt that effective implementation of PESA will not only bring development and deepen democracy in these areas, but will also help contain left wing extremism. PESA brings the community in the form of Gram Sabha at the centre of governance at the village level. Gram Sabha comprises of the people themselves, whereas all other institutions are representative bodies. However, Gram Sabha in these areas are not functioning as envisaged under the Act due to, inter-alia, lack of awareness of provisions of PESA, specially for empowering Gram Sabhas, low participation of people in meetings of Gram Sabhas, lack of administrative support and non-implementation of Gram Sabha resolutions. Generating awareness in the villages, orienting the Gram Sabhas in carrying out their statutory role and increasing levels of participation and ownership of members of Gram Sabha are critical inputs required for effectiveness of the Gram Sabhas.

## EVOLUTION OF PESA ACT

Article 243M (1) of the Constitution exempts Scheduled Areas and tribal areas referred to in Clause (1) and (2) of article 244 from application of the provisions of Part IX of the Constitution. However, article 243M (4) (b) empowers the Parliament to legislate and extend the provisions of Part IX to Scheduled Areas and tribal areas referred to in clause (1), subject to such exceptions and modifications as may be specified in such law and no such law shall be deemed to be an amendment of the Constitution for the purpose of article 368. "The Provisions of the Panchayat (Extension to the Scheduled Areas) Act, 1996" (PESA), extends Part IX of the Constitution with certain modifications and exceptions, to the

Fifth Schedule Areas notified under Article 244(1) of the Constitution. At present, Fifth Schedule Areas exist in 10 States *viz.* Andhra Pradesh, Chhattisgarh, Gujarat, Himachal Pradesh, Jharkhand, Madhya Pradesh, Maharashtra, Odisha, Rajasthan and Telangana.

Government constituted a Committee under the chairmanship of Shri Dilip Singh Bhuria in 1994, popularly called "Bhuria Committee" to examine various dimensions of self-rule for tribals, the constitutional requirements and to make recommendations for extending the provisions of Part IX of the Constitution to the Scheduled Areas. On the basis of report of Bhuria Committee submitted in 1995, the Parliament enacted PESA Act, 1996 for its applicability to Fifth Schedule Areas and tribal areas as per article 243M of the Constitution (Bijoy, 2006).

## KEY PROVISIONS OF PESA ACT

Following are key provisions of the PESA Act:

- Every village shall have its own Gram Sabha. A village may consist of one or more habitations or hamlets comprising a community and managing its affairs in accordance with traditions and customs.
- Every village shall have its own Gram Sabha. A village may consist of one or more habitations or hamlets comprising a community and managing its affairs in accordance with traditions and customs.
- Gram Sabha is "competent" to safeguard and preserve the traditions and customs of the people, and their cultural identity, community resources, and customary mode of dispute resolution; Gram Sabha has mandatory executive functions to (i) approve plans, programmes and projects for social and economic development; identify persons as beneficiaries under the poverty alleviation and other programmes; issue a certificate of utilisation of funds by the Panchayat for the plans, programmes and projects referred to in clause.

- Powers exclusive to Gram Sabha/Panchayat at appropriate level including right to mandatory consultation in land acquisition, resettlement and rehabilitation of displaced persons; Panchayat at an appropriate level is entrusted with planning and management of minor water bodies; mandatory recommendations by Gram Sabha or Panchayat at appropriate level for prospective licenses/lease, concessions for mines and minerals.
- Powers endowed to Gram Sabha and Panchayat at appropriate level to regulate sale/consumption of intoxicants; ownership of minor forest produce; prevent land alienation and restore alienated land; manage village markets; control over money lending to STs; control over institutions and functionaries in social sector, local plans including Tribal sub plans and resources (MoPR, 2015).

## IMPORTANCE OF PROVISIONS OF PESA ACT FOR THE FIFTH SCHEDULE AREAS

Effective implementation of PESA Act will institutionalize self-governance and people's participation in decision making. By notifying Gram Sabha at village *(hamlets or group of hamlets / habitation or group of habitations)* level, people will feel more comfortable in taking part in the governance of the village. It will reduce alienation in tribal areas as they will have control over the utilization of public resources in the village through Gram Sabha. Reduction of alienation and resentment among tribal population will have a positive impact in reducing left wing extremism in the districts affected by it. Effective implementation of PESA Act is also likely to reduce poverty and out-migration among tribal population as they will have control over natural resources such as minor water bodies, minor forest produce, minor minerals, etc. Control over and management of these resources will improve their livelihoods and incomes. Another positive impact could be on reduction of exploitation of tribal population as they will be able to control and manage money lending, consumption and sale of liquor and also village markets. PESA has the potential to check illegal land alienation and also restore unlawfully alienated tribal land. This will not only reduce conflict but will also improve socio-economic status of tribal population if these areas through better implementation of developmental schemes and programmes due to enhanced people's participation in planning and identification of beneficiaries. Local administration is likely to be more accountable and responsive due to control over functionaries of social sector and also power to issue utilisation certificates. Last but not the least, effective implementation of PESA will also promote cultural heritage through preservation of traditions, customs and cultural identity of tribal population (Bijoy and Kamodang, 2014).

## INITIATIVES TAKEN BY GOVERNMENT OF INDIA

For implementation of PESA, Ministry of Panchayati Raj (MoPR) is the responsible Ministry. Government of India has taken a number of initiatives in the past in this direction. Such initiatives can be categorised into constitution of committees to assess implementation of PESA, commissioning of research studies, organising review workshops, issuing guidelines and advisories, providing capacity building and administrative support etc.

Various Committees to assess different aspects of PESA implementation have been constituted in the past. The Ministry of Panchayati Raj constituted three sub-committees, one chaired by Shri B.D.Sharma on *'Model Guidelines to vest Gram Sabhas with Powers as envisaged in PESA'*; another chaired by Shri Raghav Chandra on *'Land Alienation, Displacement, Rehabilitation and Resettlement'* and a third chaired by Shri A. K. Sharma *on Minor Forest Produce.* A Committee under the chairmanship of Dr. T Haque was constituted by MoPR on August 23, 2010 to suggest appropriate measures on *Ownership, Price Fixation, Value Addition and Marketing of Minor Forest Produce (MFP).* The Committee submitted its report in May 2011. The Government launched a Centrally Sponsored Scheme of "Mechanism for Marketing of Minor Forest Produce (MFP) through Minimum Support Price and Development of Value Chain for MFP". This

Scheme has not been expanded to entire country. Based on the recommendations of the Second Administrative Reforms Commission in its Seventh Report 'Capacity Building for Conflict Resolution–Friction to Fusion', a Committee on Harmonization of Central Laws with the Provisions of the Panchayats (Extension to the Scheduled Areas) Act (PESA), 1996 was set up on December 14, 2011 under the chairmanship of the Union Law Secretary.

The Ministry of Panchayati Raj has also commissioned some Studies related to PESA Act. In the year 2008, the MoPR commissioned a study by the Indian Law Institute on three Central laws viz. The Mines and Minerals (Development and Regulation) Act, 1957, the Indian Forest Act (IFA), 1927 and the Forest (Conservation) Act, 1980 to suggest amendments to make them compliant with PESA. The study report was sent to the Central Ministries concerned during 2009 for necessary action. The Ministry of Environment, Forest & Climate Change (MoEFCC) has agreed for amendments to the Indian Forests Act, 1927, particularly, amendment to section 68 of the Act for recording the views of the Gram Sabha concerned while compounding offences under the Act. MoPR has also shared its suggestions on certain provisions of the Wild Life (Protection) Act, 1972 to the MoEFCC to make the Act PESA compliant. MoPR commissioned an action research study for preparation of training modules on PESA by the National Institute of Rural Development. The training module prepared by NIRD was forwarded to all the PESA States in May 2009 and were advised to prepare training modules to train District and Block level officers and elected representatives of PRIs. MoPR commissioned a study by Enviro-Legal Defence Firm (ELDF) during January, 2011 on the compliance of State Panchayati Raj laws and other subject laws with the provisions of PESA. The State-wise reports also suggest changes/amendments to be made in each of the State laws to bring them in consonance with PESA. The ELDF reports have been sent to the States with the request to make necessary amendments, frame rules, etc. All the States having Fifth Schedule Areas have examined the reports and have initiated action to amend their laws/rules, accordingly (ELDF, 2011).

In addition to constitution of committees and commissioning studies, MoPR has taken several other initiatives to facilitate implementation of PESA. In view of prevailing incidences of extremism in many Fifth Schedule Areas and their vicinity, consolidated guidelines on implementation of PESA were issued on 21.5.2010 to all the States having Fifth Schedule Areas. States have also been advised that full videography of all Gram Sabha meetings be done. It will help in improving the transparency and accountability in the Panchayati Raj system at grassroots level. Further, in July, 2013 these States were requested to take appropriate steps to ensure participation of SC/ST members in Gram Sabha meetings. Constant reviews of the implementation of the PESA Act in the States having Schedule Areas, through visits to States, correspondence and meetings in the Ministry have been undertaken. During 2014-15, State level workshops were held in eight States for improving awareness and coordination between various line departments, district officials and other stakeholders on implementing the Act in each State. A National Workshop was organized at New Delhi on February 4-5, 2016 to review the progress of implementation of PESA in States, issues and challenges being faced and the way forward. The workshop was attended by Union and State Ministers of Panchayati Raj, State Secretaries, officials of Union Ministries and other stakeholders. Under RGSA, the Fifth Schedule Areas are being assisted financially by making provision for one Gram Sabha Mobiliser in each Gram Panchayat to help in ensuring maximum participation of members of Gram Sabha and its decision-making process; one PESA Coordinator in each Block, one PESA Coordinator in each district. A Handbook on "Community Mobilisation in Fifth Schedule Areas" containing basic information about the provisions of PESA, methods of community mobilization and role of Gram Sabha/community mobilisers and PESA coordinators has been prepared and disseminated widely. The States have been requested in July, 2015 to frame strategy to ensure inclusion of implementation status of PESA provisions in the Governor's Annual Report; fill up vacancies, create Panchayat cadres and give hardship allowance to Panchayat functionaries so that they come forward to work in these areas; create information-cum-grievance redressal mechanisms. All the States having Fifth Schedule Areas have been asked to place PESA Coordinator at the State level in the State Panchayat Resource Centres (SPRCs) established/to be established under RGPSA to strengthen the training component related to PESA and also support the Department of Panchayati Raj on policy matters which also calls for coordination with various line departments. Financial assistance under theFourteenth Finance Commission (FFC) award is also available to the Fifth Schedule Areas for supporting and strengthening the delivery of basic services – water supply, sanitation including septage management, sewerage, storm water drainage and solid waste management, street lighting, local body roads and footpaths, parks, playgrounds, burial and cremation grounds. It is expected that the enhancement of direct and untied funding to the local bodies in LWE areas will improve systems of administration as basic services to the people will be attended to, instilling faith in government institutions. On the initiation of the MoPR, all the States have issued detailed guidelines for preparation of Gram Panchayat Development Plans (GPDP) including those in most affected LWE GPs to improve utilisation of resources which are available with them. These are participatory plans, which are prepared by involving people in planning for resources available with the Panchayats. This planning process will be supported by the State under RGPSA and will make the Gram Sabhas involved in the planning process, transparent and accountable. The PESA Act does not provide for rule making powers. The MoPR is moving a Draft Cabinet Note for approval of the Government for introducing PESA Amendment Bill, 2016 (MoPR, 2016).

## IMPLEMENTATION STATUS OF PESA IN THE STATES

All the ten States having Fifth Schedule Areas are required to make their State Panchayati Raj Acts and concerned subject laws compliant with the provisions of PESA Act, 1996. All the States have taken action and made the Panchayati Raj Acts and some of their subject laws PESA compliant. As reported by the States, the status of compliance of Panchayati Raj Acts and Subject Laws with PESA as on February 06, 2016 is given in the Table 1 and Table 2 below:

**Table 1:** Compliance of State Panchayati Raj Acts with Section 4 of PESA Act

| ***States*** | ***Provisions under clauses of Section 4 of PESA*** | | | | | | | | ***Sub-clauses of Section-4(m)*** | | | | | |
|---|---|---|---|---|---|---|---|---|---|---|---|---|---|---|
| | ***D**** | ***E**** | ***F**** | ***H**** | ***I**** | ***J**** | ***K**** | ***L**** | ***(i)*** | ***(ii)*** | ***(iii)*** | ***(iv)*** | ***(v)*** | ***(vi)*** |
| Andhra Pradesh | Y | Y | Y | Y | Y | Y | Y | Y | Y | Y | Y | Y | Y | Y |
| Chhattisgarh | Y | Y | Y | Y | Y | Y | Y | Y | Y | N | Y | Y | N | Y |
| Gujarat | Y | Y | Y | Y | Y | Y | Y | Y | N | Y | Y | Y | Y | Y |
| Himachal Pradesh | Y | Y | Y | Y | Y | Y | Y | Y | Y | Y | Y | Y | Y | Y |
| Jharkhand | Y | Y | Y | Y | N | N | N | N | N | N | N | Y | N | Y |
| Odisha | Y | Y | Y | Y | Y | Y | Y | Y | Y | Y | Y | Y | Y | Y |
| Maharashtra | Y | Y | Y | N | Y | Y | Y | Y | Y | Y | Y | N | Y | Y |
| MP | Y | Y | Y | Y | Y | Y | Y | Y | N | N | N | Y | N | Y |
| Rajasthan | Y | Y | Y | Y | Y | Y | Y | Y | Y | Y | Y | Y | Y | Y |
| Telangana | Y | Y | Y | Y | Y | Y | Y | Y | Y | Y | Y | Y | Y | Y |

'Y' denotes the provision has been made PESA compliant. 'N' denotes action is yet to be completed. *Source*: Ministry of Panchayati Raj, 2017.

D* (Customary mode of conflict resolution by the (Gram Sabha)

E* (Selection of programme beneficiaries by Gram Sabha)

F* (GP to obtain UC from Gram sabha)

H* (Nomination by State Government of persons of ST not represented in intermediate & district PRIs)

I* (Consultation with Gram Sabha or PRI before land acquisition and resettlement & rehabilitation)

J* (Planning & management of water bodies by Gram Sabha or PRI)

K* (Recommendation by Gram Sabha or PRI before grant of prospecting license or mining lease)

L* (Recommendation by Gram Sabha or PRI before exploitation of minor minerals)

(i) (Restrict sale of intoxicant)

(ii) (Own MFP)

(iii) (Prevent land alienation)

(iv) (Manage village markets)

(v) (Control money lending)

(vi) (Control social sector institutions & functionaries)

**Table 2:** Compliance of important Subject Laws with PESA

| ***States*** | ***Land acquisition*** | ***Excise*** | ***Forest produce*** | ***Mines and minerals*** | ***Agri produce market*** | ***Money lending*** |
|---|---|---|---|---|---|---|
| Andhra Pradesh (Includes Telangana) | N | N* | N | N* | N* | N |
| Chhattisgarh | Y | Y | N | Y | Y | Y |
| Gujarat | N | Y | N | Y | Y | Y |
| Himachal Pradesh | Y | Y | Y | Y | N | N |
| Jharkhand | N | N | Y** | N | N | N |
| Odisha | N | Y | Y | Y | N | Y |
| Maharashtra | N | N | Y | N | N | N |
| Madhya Pradesh | Y | Y | N | Y | Y | N |
| Rajasthan | N | N | N | Y | N | Y |

*Govt. of AP has informed that the amendment in subject laws is under consideration. **Jharkhand Govt. has adopted a resolution on 8.2.2007 conferring ownership right over MFP to GP. *Source*: Ministry of Panchayati Raj, 2017.

## RECENT INITIATIVES IN SELECTED STATES

In Maharashtra, aspecial section has been introduced in the Maharashtra Village Panchayat Act to define village and in other sections. Thereafter changes have been brought about in Maharashtra Money lending Regulation Act, Maharashtra Prohibition Act, Maharashtra Livestock Improvement Act, Maharashtra Agriculture Pests and Diseases Act. The thrust is to ensure that the village/ Gram Panchayat is involved in decision making process. The State has brought changes in legislation through Hon'ble Governor's notification. The State has gone far ahead to bring about the change in the Indian Forest Act in which Minor Forest Produce has been defined especially with regard to Bamboo and Tendu leaves. Maharashtra has also empowered Gram Panchayats in Fifth Schedule Areas for issues related to issuing of transit passes and taking other decisions. Maharashtra land revenue code has also been changed to ensure that no auction of minor minerals takes place without the approval of Gram Panchayat. Maharashtra has made changes in Markets and Fairs Act, Water and Pollution Act and brought changes to ensure that that five percent of the TSP funds should be earmarked as untied funds to Gram Sabhas in Fifth Schedule Areas. The definition of Village as mentioned in the PESA has been introduced in all hamlets and settlements in Fifth Schedule Areas. The State therefore has statutory Gram Sabhas. PESA rules have been notified and as a result the following achievements have been made: (i) fishery rights have been handed over; (ii) a separate Gram Kosh has been established in each hamlet; (iii) Rules for Natural Resources; (iv) Rules for prevention of illegal land alienation and (v) PESA rules includes rules for restoration of land alienated, consultation before land acquisition, planning and management of water resources, powers of Gram Sabha, markets and fairs, regulation of intoxicants. He shared the fact that as a result of legislation change regarding Bamboo, 25 Gram Panchayats are selling their own bamboos. In future more than 200 Gram Panchayats would be doing so and as a result their income has increase many fold from nothing to crores of rupees. Five percent of the TSP funds (Rs.258.5 crore) is given directly to tribal communities for informed decision making on local issues (Infrastructure, FRA, PESA, Health, Sanitation and Education, Conservation of Forest & Wild life). This fund is transferred directly to GPs (Gram Sabha Kosh) from Secretariat based on population of the GP. Rest 95% of the TSP funds are spent for tribal development only through various schemes. For projects up to Rs. 3 lakh, no technical sanction is required. GS can decide on estimates and modalities of project implementation. Guidelines for selection of works has been issued. Sectoral allocations for utilization of fund is done with equal 25% each of the four sectors. Social audit of fund utilisation has been made compulsory. Web based work monitoring module has also been developed to track progress of works. Capacity building is done with support from YASHADA, Pune. Training modules have been developed. 220 Master Trainers were also identified including trainers under RGPSA and NGO representatives. 15000 stakeholders (Sarpanch/ Deputy Sarpanch-1, Members of Gram Sabha Kosh Samiti -3,

Member of Forest Right Committee -1) have been trained in 300 clusters (1 cluster-10 villages) across 60 blocks (MoPR, 2016).

In Jharkhand, State Mines Department has devolved funds (80% of the revenue from mining) to Panchayats to the tune of Rs.166 crore for both PESA and non PESA areas. The amount for PESA areas only is Rs.78 crore. State Government has taken initiative of Yojana Banao Abhiyan by converging resources under FFC and MGNREGS available at the GP level. Gram Sabha will suggest and approve schemes to be implemented utilising these resources. Five Departments out of 10 departments concerned have so far amended their rules in consonance with PESA. These are namely, Excise, Forest & Environment, RD & PR, Mines and Minerals, Agriculture. Powers related to control of village markets have been given to Gram Sabha. Minor Minerals Rule 2014 (Section 11,12,13,24, 34 have also been amended. (*e g.* Rule 11and GS approval has been made mandatory before the mining lease of minor minerals. With respect to capacity building, 80 Master Trainers have been identified and they would go to the districts and provide training to newly elected members of PRIs. 526 State resource trainers will do training at the Block level and facilitate Gram Sabha driven preparation of GPDP and implementation of schemes. Seven training modules for PRIs and Gram Sabhas have also been developed with support from UNDP and UNICEF. Jharkhand Panchayati Raj Act has been amended in consonance with Provisions of PESA. Fifth Schedule Areas will also be given importance while identifying and developing Beacon Panchayats (MoPR, 2016).

Rajasthan Government has framed and notified State PESA rules in line with PESA in 2011. A Committee under the Chairmanship of Chief Secretary looks after the amendments. Two amendments have been done so far and work is in progress for four other amendments. Several training programmes were organised in 2012 for activating Gram Sabhas and the State is committed to continue them. In Rajasthan, 20% more Gram Panchayats and 50% Panchayat Samitis have been added to Fifth Schedule Areas for which approval is awaited from Union Cabinet.

Subordinate Services Rules were introduced in 2014 to strengthen governance in Fifth Schedule Areas under which Scheduled Tribes already recruited in Grade-3 would not be transferred to other areas. Special recruitment drives have also been going on and Recruitment Service Commission has also been set up. Under FRA, 35000 people have been given land titles. State Government has also taken special initiatives to ensure financial inclusion along with activating Common Service Centres in all Gram Panchayats in Fifth Schedule Areas. Since human development indicators are comparatively poor in fifth Schedule Areas, the Tribal development department is doing their part to ensure holistic development of these areas. The issue of adverse condition of tribal population and bonded labour in some of the districts and pockets was raised by the house and it was suggested that even isolated tribal villages can be notified as fifth schedule area (MoPR, 2016).

In Andhra Pradesh, Panchayati Raj Acts were amended in 1998 to make it PESA compliant and a comprehensive PESA Rules were issued in March 2011. With regard to subject laws, concerned Departments have made amendments in their respective Rules but laws have not been amended. Girijan Cooperative Corporation (GCC) has got exclusive rights over MFPs and works under the Tribal Welfare Department. In fact, Tribal Welfare Department works as nodal department for implementation of PESA. For the conduct of Gram Sabha a comprehensive guidelines have been issued in 2013 and the guidelines covers Fifth Schedule Areas also. Notification of Gram Sabha is done by the Tribal Welfare Department and active SHG members are being used as Gram Sabha Mobilisers after necessary training. Role of different departments have been clarified through a Government Order issued in 2011.

In Chattisgarh, Section 129 A to F of the Chhattisgarh Panchayat Raj Act, 1993 contain the special provisions for Panchayats in the Scheduled Areas. With regard to compliance of provisions under clauses of Section 4 of the PESA, the Chhattisgarh Panchayat Act, 1993 is PESA compliant except 4(m) (ii) on ownership of MFP. Amendments have been made in subject laws such as Land Revenue Code, Chhattisgarh Excise Act, to make them PESA compliant and initiative on Minor Forest Produce need to be taken up at the Centre level. However the State is facing three issues, first facilitating alternative arrangements for micro-credit, easy loans, bank linkages on money lending; second politics of vested interests (outlets owned by locals, leading to locals *vs.* locals conflict) on toxicants; and third issue of inter-village shared resources (upstream-downstream) on minor water bodies. State has shared the draft with all concerned Departments and sought their opinion. Initial draft of the State PESA Rules has been prepared and is under legal consultation. A State level workshop cum training was organized in April 2016. Another State level workshop on PESA was held in October 2014 with participation of elected representatives from Panchayats, officials from line Depts., NGOs, activists. The State has translated PESA Act in local dialects/languages Chhattisgarhi and Further translation to be done in Halbi, Gondi, and Sargujia. There is a plan to script PESA Act in Braille/ audio version for better access. IEC programmes such as Hamar Gram Sabha have also been conducted. In addition, the State Government has taken following initiatives in Fifth Schedule Areas: (i) Relaxed Departmental Service Recruitment rules for all the vacancies of Class III and Class IV posts, of direct recruitment of the district cadres so that these posts are filled up from amongst the local residents of the respective reservation roster; (ii) Orders issued to cover up 20% of vacancies arising in each recruitment year among the posts reserved for Scheduled Tribes in Scheduled Area of the State, for being filled up from applications of candidates belonging to Particularly Vulnerable Tribal Group (PVTGs) like Pahadi Korba, Baiga, Kamar, Abujmadia and Bhujia and Panda Tribes, without following procedures prescribed for concerned Service Recruitment Rules, (iii) Relaxation of the condition of passing Teachers' Eligibility Test (TET) has been provided to candidates belonging to Particularly Vulnerable Tribal Groups (PVTGs), (iv) 20% of total seats reserved for PVTGs in Teachers Eligibility Test (TET), (v) Section 6(2) of Forest Rights Act 2006 has been amended to consider rejected applications for *suo-moto* revision under which rejected applications have been considered as appeals and title deeds have been distributed (vi) Section 4 of the Mines and Minerals (Development and Regulation) Act, 1957 amended - "Tin Ore" has been replaced with 'Tin Ore, Niobium Ore and Tantalum Ore' and "Co-operative Society which is under Scheduled Tribes" has been replaced with "Co-operative Society in which only persons of local Scheduled Tribes are members"; (vii) A sub-section added under section 16 of the Chhattisgarh Excise Act, 1915 to allow transportation of local drinks like "Landa" and "Handiya" on the occasion of religious festivals to a maximum quantity of five litres for house hold consumption in Scheduled Area by the members of the Scheduled Tribes. Another sub-section was added under Section 59-A of this act to make the offences relating to these drinks bailable if committed by a member of ST (MoPR, 2016).

## KEY ISSUES IN IMPLEMENTATION OF PESA

Although PESA is very important for governance in Fifth Schedule Areas and the Government of India and various State Governments is making all efforts in this direction, there are some issues in its implementation. Important among them are as follows:

(i) Villages are yet to be notified in States as per the spirit of PESA Act.

(ii) Panchayati Raj Acts and Subject Laws in States are still not fully compliant to the provisions of PESA.

(iii) Some Central Acts have provisions that are contradictory to provisions of PESA.

(iv) Only half of the States have notified PESA Rules.

(v) There are inadequate infrastructure and staff in Gram Panchayats.

(vi) Members of Gram Sabha in Fifth Schedule areas are not aware of their powers and duties as per PESA.

(vi) Follow up action on resolutions of Gram Sabha is inadequate and delayed.

(vi) PESA like Act may be formulated for urban areas too as there is suspicion that some rural areas in Fifth Schedule areas are being converted to urban areas with malicious intent.

## SOME GOOD PRACTICES IN PESA IMPLEMENTATION

Many villages in Fifth Schedule Areas of Rajasthan declared themselves "village republics" as part of "*Gaon Ganrajya*" movement and started asserting their rights over community resources like water, land and forest *(jal, jungle and jameen)*. Manathgaon village in Dungarpur district is one of the earliest villages which has declared itself as a village republic in the late 1990s. After declaration of their village as village republic, community was mobilized by forming Forest Protection Committee consisting of the members of the Gram Sabha (GS) to protect the adjacent forests which were considered as their traditional community forests until State Forest Department (SFD) took over. To institutionalize forest protection and sustainable use, rules and regulations were framed by the community. After almost more than ten years of its control and effective access and sustainable use, the traditional forest species are coming up naturally which is an indication of revival of healthy forest cover and hope for earning livelihoods by the communities depending on it. Ownership is still with the SFD, but people have limited access to forest resources and use them within the rules and regulations keeping in view of the needs of the community and sustainability of forests (NIRD&PR, 2011).

Pullangi Gram Panchayat in Maredumilli Mandal, East Godavari District, Andhra Pradesh has 11 habitations, with about 350 households of Kondaredd is a particularly Vulnerable Tribal Group, consisting of 1100 population. PESA Act empowers GS to take decisions on consumption of liquor in its area. Invoking the powers under PESA Act, the GS of Gumpenagandi in Pullangi GP area decided to stop the brewing of country liquor and consumption of liquor in the village. The GS discussed about the consumption and preparation of country liquor, and its adverse impact on the people in a meeting and passed a resolution banning the sale or consumption of liquor, or transport from other villages to the village. The GS passed the resolution noting that if any person violates this resolution, he/she will be liable to pay of fine of Rs. 50/- and in case of repeated violation, no villager will attend any function or ceremony in his or her house. There has been no event of liquor sale or consumption reported in the village since then (Rao, 2013)

Mendha Lekha, Gadhchiroli, Maharashtra is a small village consisting of *Gond* tribe. The village practises a unique system of local governance. It has its own laws, rules and regulations. All decisions regarding the village and its development are taken, with consensus, at the Gram Sabha. The village created a history on $26^{th}$ April 2011 when it's GS was accorded the rights for collection and disposal of bamboos at the hands of the then Union Minister of State for Environment, Forests and Climate Change. The Forest Rights Act, 2006, grants community forest rights to manage, protect, and revive the forest and to own and dispose of MFPs from forests where they had traditional access. This includes the right to sell. But the residents have not been allowed to sell bamboos to outsiders, as the State Forest Department did not issue transit passes. The village had been managing 2 $km^2$ of forest for more than 15 years. They applied for community rights over the entire village forest area of 18 $km^2$ under the Scheduled Tribes and Other Traditional Forest Dwellers (Recognition of Forest Rights) Act, 2006 and obtained the same (Singh n.d.).

Government of Maharashtra has provided of 5% of the Tribal-Sub-Plan funds (Rs. 258.5 crore) directly to tribal communities for informed decision making on local issues *(infrastructure, health, sanitation & education, conservation of forests & wild life).* This fund is transferred directly to GPs based on population of the GP and GP transfers it to Gram Sabha Kosh.

Under Yojana Banao Abhiyan in Jharkhand, a three-day planning exercise, facilitated by the Panchayat Planning Team (PPT) was organized for every 100 households by the GP, roughly coinciding with its Wards. It culminated in "Tola Sabhas" *(community meetings at hamlet level)* for prioritizing and approving the selected schemes. Institutioalisation of Tola Sabha followed by Gram Sabha will strengthen implementation of PESA in Jharkhand.

Inadequate staff at GP level in FSA has been a challenge in the implementation of PESA. Government of Rajasthan has introduced Subordinate Services Rules in 2014 to strengthen governance in FSA under which ST staff recruited in Grade-3 would not be transferred to other areas.

To create awareness on PESA, the Government of Chhattisgarh has translated PESA Act in Chhattisgarhi dialect and has a plan to translate in Halbi, Gondi, and Sargujia dialects in future. There is a plan to script PESA Act in Braille/ audio version for better access. A radio programme titled "Hamar Gram Sabha *(Our Gram Sabha)*" have also been broadcasted for this purpose.

## CONCLUSIONS

PESA Act intends to revitalize age old tradition of tribal self-governance. Effective implementation of PESA will not only bring development to tribal majority areas in ten States with Fifth Schedule areas but will also help curb discontent and extremism. While Government of India and State governments have taken several initiatives towards the implementation of PESA Act, lot more needs to be done. While various line departments of State governments are unwilling to let go their powers, there is also inadequate political will at the central and state level. Some good practices have emerged, particularly in Maharashtra with a push from the Governor office, which needs to be scaled up to other States.

## REFERENCES

Bijoy C.R. (2016), Policy brief on Panchayat Raj (Extension to Scheduled Areas) Act of 1996. UNDP India. New Delhi.

Bijoy C.R. and Kamodang M. (2014). Local Governance in Fifth Schedule Tribal Areas, A Study of Maharashtra and Odisha in the Light of PESA Act 1996. Working Paper Series Vol. III No. 01, IIDS, New Delhi.

ELDF. (2011). PESA IMPLEMENTATION – SOME ESSENTIAL PREREQUISITES AND SUGGESTIONS FOR THE STATE: Final Reports. New Delhi.

MoPR, GoI (2016), Report of the National Workshop on Implementation of PESA, New Delhi.

MoPR. (2015). Community Mobilisation in Fifth Schedule (PESA) Areas, New Delhi.

NIRD&PR. (2011). Extract from the study on "Gaon Ganrajya (Village Republic) Movement: A Case Study in Tribal Areas of Rajasthan" By Annamalai V, Hyderabad.

Rao P.T. (2013). Field Visit Reports, NIRD&PR.

Singh S. (*n.d.*). Participatory Forest Management in Mendha Lekha. Retrieved from http://www.ceecec.net/case-studies/mendha-lekha-using-self-governance-to-achieve-ecological-prosperity-and-livelihood-security/ on 05.03.2019

---

***Dr. Rajesh Kumar Sinha*** holds a Ph.D. from JNU and is currently working as Assistant Professor in NIRD&PR, Hyderabad. His research interests lie in rural local governance, rural development, social audit, and social accountability. He has worked with UNDP, Government of India, Society for Participatory Research in Asia, IDRF & Sewa International in past.

# 10

# Social Audit - Community Monitoring for Social Accountability in PRIs

Rajeev Bansal[12]

## INTRODUCTION

In a democratic country, the government has twin role – one, regulatory powers to implement rules and schemes, second-socio economic development with delivery of services to its citizens. This role casts upon the responsibility of accountability towards the governed as a fulcrum to make balance between rights and duties to avoid it to usurp authority of governance. This responsibility becomes more significant in the execution of local level governance where services are delivered by Panchayati Raj Institutions for community at the cutting edge level. The execution and implementation of programmes at front line are always on radar of local community for accountability. To ensure the accountability, participation of stakeholders and transparency in the working of the implementing agency is the mechanism required as an integral component of every scheme or programme. The participation of stakeholders is hardly ensured in implementation, monitoring and evaluation of development schemes. In a democratic country, people want to be a part of governance with participation in all affairs, activities and demand accountability,

[12] Himachal Institute of Public Administration.
*Corresponding author*: E-mail: rajeev.bansal14610@gmail.com

especially at the grassroot level. With the change in working of governments with democratic decentralisation, the downward accountability has become a need of time. Citizen centric administration, the space for common man, service guarantee acts brought in by different states, the governance with electronic tools; all have been the tested instruments of downward accountability. One such tool of accountability is "Social Audit". The word "Audit" attached to the term most of the time lead people to a wrong direction. People assume it to be a financial audit by the society, whereas, it is an audit by the stakeholders - the members of the society to monitor and evaluate the social results, benefits or outcomes incident upon them from the programmes or schemes implemented for their benefits.

## SHORT HISTORY OF SOCIAL AUDIT

In the mid 1970s in the UK and Europe, the term Social Audit emerged to describe evaluations that focused on the likely impact on jobs, the community and the environment if a particular enterprise or industry were to close or relocate. These evaluations used the term Social Audit to clearly make the point that they were concerned with the 'social' and not the 'economic' consequence of a particular action. Over the last few decades evaluations on the impact of particular actions have become ever more sophisticated and used by organisations to help them achieve improved performance.

The first recorded example of Social Audit was developed in 1978 at Beechwood College, an independent worker co-operative training centre in the England. In 1981, a manual called "Social Audit – A Management Tool for Co-operative Working" by "Freer Spreckley", was published. It contained an organisational method for democratic organisations to use in measuring their own social performance with four main elements Social Purpose, External View, Internal View and Social Accounting. One of the first recorded social reports was in Switzerland where the Migros Co-operative, a large multi-functional organization, first published a social report in 1978. Early on in the history of Social Audit was the Dunston Social Audit in 1982, which was published and widely distributed. In 1984, the Co-operative Retail Society started to look at the idea of Social Audit that larger organisations became interested in voluntarily undertaking a Social Audit. During the late 1980s, there was an explosion of interest in the ideas of Social Audit as a number of business schools started looking at social responsibility in industry. New Economic Foundation (NEF) in London, established in 1984, published the Social Audit Workbook in 1997. The NEF established the Institute of Social and Ethical Accountability that drafted a set of standards for monitoring the application of Social Audit. During the late 1990s, many organisations continued to develop and practice Social Audit. In 1997, Social Enterprise Partnership developed the first European Social Audit programme involving groups from Ireland, Spain, Finland, Sweden, Denmark and England. This programme used the Social Audit Toolkit model and it was translated in a number of European languages. Social Enterprise Partnership had run and been involved with three transnational Social Audit programmes that also included France, Belgium and Italy.

## CONCEPT OF SOCIAL AUDIT

People in different parts of the globe want to become part of the governance in their respective country and area. They want accountability in all service delivery systems and establishments made to deliver the services. Social audit is considered an important tool to ensure accountability and transparency in the system of governance.

The word 'Audit' came from the Latin word audire, which means "to hear". General definition of an audit is an evaluation of a person, organization, system, process, enterprise, project or product. The primary objective of an audit is to reveal defects or irregularities in any of the functions or activities examined and to indicate possible improvements so that organizational efficiency and effectiveness may improve.

Parthasarthy observed that social audit may be regarded as being at the extreme end of the spectrum of audit functions. Over the centuries, audit function have grown and evolved, starting from the most ancient kind which may be called vigilance audit as it was concerned mainly with the detection of frauds. Then came, in more or less chronological order, regularity audit, propriety audit, value for money audit, performance audit and lastly social audit (Parthasarthy, 1988).

A social audit is a process by which the people, the final beneficiaries of any scheme, programme, policy or law, are empowered to audit such schemes, programmes, policies and laws for evaluation of the benefits and objectives intended for them with the focus on social results instead of financial expenditure of progress. To sum up, it can be concluded that Social Audit is focused on broadening the base of 'viability' to include extra-financial factors that are imperative to long term sustainability. The Social Audit examines the procedure and performance of an organisation's social and commercial actions in relation to its stated objectives and its external and internal position.

## Objectives of Social Audit

The major objective of audit of social performance is to identify and measure the contribution of an individual entity or an institution to the aggregate social benefits and sacrifices. Ramanathan has rightly pointed out the following objectives of social audit:

- To identify and measure the periodic net social contribution at micro level of an individual institution, which includes costs and benefits arising from externalities affecting different social segments.
- To help in determine whether an individual institution strategies at micro level and practices which directly affect the relative resource and power status of individuals, communities, social segments and generations are consistent with widely shared social priorities on the one hand, and individual's legitimate aspirations on the other.

- To make available in an optimal manner to all social segments, relevant information on individual programmes, policies, methods of control, performance and contribution to social goals. Relevant information is that which provides for public accountability and also facilitates public decision making regarding social choices and resources allocation (Ramanathan, 1976).

A social audit is an ongoing process by which the potential beneficiaries and other stakeholders of an activity or project are involved from planning to the monitoring and evaluation of that activity or project. Social audit can be described as checking and verification of a programme/scheme implementation and its results by the community with the active involvement of the primary stakeholders. Social audit covers the quantity and quality of works in relation to the expenses incurred/disbursement made, number of works/materials used and also selection of works and location of works. The aim is effective implementation and control of irregularities. The administrative machinery is expected to extend full support without any interference in carrying out a social audit by the community.

## Purpose of Social Audit

Social audits can vary in terms of scope and purpose. A more specific and limited in scope social audit would be used by civil society and government agencies to manage a particular project in one village at a given time. The purpose of conducting Social Audit is NOT to find fault with the individual functionaries but to assess the performance in terms of social, environmental and community goals of the organisation. It provides an assessment of the impact of non financial objectives of an organisation through systematic and regular monitoring, based on the views of its stakeholders.

## Social *versus* Financial Audit

The comparison of financial and social audit elucidates the end objective of social audit which is quite different from financial audit.

***Financial audit:*** The financial audit undertaken by a departmental auditor or a chartered accountant is a financial tool where the area of concern is processed and procedure, rules and regulations etc. It deals whether the administrative approvals, technical and expenditure sanctions were taken at the appropriate levels, whether the funds were spent after observing all the formalities? Whether the procurements were made from the authorized dealers etc. Was the money spent correctly? The discrepancies on these accounts are reflected as audit para figured by Comptroller and Auditor General in government records. Such observations are further taken up in the house of legislative assembly in the estimates or public accounts committee. These deliberations come into the knowledge of a few elected representatives only who are nominated in these committees. There is hardly any focus on the results of expenditures and activities besides the beneficiaries have no role in this all process.

***Social audit:*** The practice of social audit is an outcome oriented approach. The performance appraisal is undertaken with active participation of the stakeholders *i.e.* the direct beneficiaries of programme. Its main focus is whether the spending has made a difference or not; whether the benefits envisaged by the scheme or programme have actually reached the people. The results and findings are shared with the stakeholders in a public hearing or gram sabha. The residents of the area, come to know the impact of the scheme which are put in the public domain. Social Audit assesses the performance, highlights the leakages and unpacks decisions; in this manner it complements the financial audit. The financial audit supplemented by the findings of the social audit presents an actual status not only of the programme implementation but also delivery of the services to the stakeholders.

Social Audit complements financial audit and presents a true picture. The government or institutional audit may remain the basic auditing practice, but would become far more transparent and inclusive of affected persons and intended beneficiaries by incorporating and integrating the practices of social audits. Social audits may be conducted in addition to government or institutional audits for a sample of activities, especially for those that involve distribution of disaggregated benefits at grassroots level or very large investments *e.g.* NREGS, ICDS, PDS. The findings of such social audits should be publicly compared to those of the government or institutional audits and correctives be identified and incorporated in both. There should also be a public rendering of action taken.

## People's Audit

People's audit is an example of an external social audit. People's Audit is based on the principle that people's participation can enhance systems of good governance. People's audit is therefore a process and not an end in itself. In any democratic system, public funds ultimately belong to the people and people should have a large role to play in evaluation of utilization in terms of results and outcomes. The government machinery must be held accountable for the manner in which it spends public money. People's audit provides a way to measure, understand, report and improve the social and ethical performance of the system. Social Audit is based upon this approach. There have been different approaches to conduct social audit in India *viz.*

***Campaign mode:*** This approach serves the dual purpose of raising awareness of the general public, which is then followed by sharing information at village, block or district level. For example, the mass social audit that took place in Dungarpur, Rajasthan in April 2006 is an example of this kind. This was used as a learning in Andhra Pradesh, where thirty-one NGOs and CSOs network came together with the Department of Rural Development, Government of Andhra Pradesh to conduct a mass social audit through a padayatra (street march) in Ananthapur district of the state in August 2006 (Centre for Environment Concern, 2006).

***Facilitated by Government Agencies:*** To collect information on the basis of a pre-designed format for all Gram Panchayats of the district. Reports are then read in the Gram Sabha and also consolidated at the block and district level to be transmitted to higher authorities. States like Jharkhand, adopted this approach in past. In Andhra Pradesh, Government constituted SSAAT, an independent society on the proximity of civil society organisations to undertake social audit, following this approach.

***Facilitated by CSOs:*** It is done in selective Gram Panchayat and Blocks and data is collected with the help of volunteers, largely outsiders, and presented at the block level and district level public hearings attended by government officials. This approach has been adopted by organisations like Astha, MKSS, and activist-academicians etc., during social audits in Uttar Pradesh, Jharkhand, Chhattisgarh, Rajasthan etc. Some groups have adopted an approach where the social audit is initiated by the Gram Panchayat, and facilitated by CSOs. Sikkim Government, has awarded NREGS social audit to Voluntary Health Association by adopting CSO facilitated approach (PRIA, 2013).

## Steps to Social Auditing

There are six key steps to conduct a social audit-

1. Preparatory activity includes understanding key principles of Social Audit, listing core values and social objectives of the department/programmes and matching activities with objectives, listing current practices and delivery systems, fixing the responsibility for doing Social Audit and budget for Social Audit.
2. Defining audit boundaries by identifying key issues and objectives and identifying stakeholders.
3. Selection of performance indicators for social accounting and social book keeping.
4. Preparing and using social accounts.
5. Presentation of social accounts to social auditor for the quality of the reports and further dissemination to stakeholders and civil society.
6. Feedback for fine tuning policy, legislation, administrative functioning and programming towards social objectives and institutionalization of the process

To put it concisely, social auditing is a process by which an organization accounts for its social performance to its stakeholders and seeks to improve its future social performance.

## SOCIAL AUDIT TO MEASURE SOCIAL PERFORMANCE

Charles Medawar pioneered the belief that Social Audit in principle is based on the fact that in a democracy the decision makers should account for the use of their powers and which should be used, as far as possible, with the consent and understanding of all concerned (Medawar, 1992). Spreckley defined "*Social auditing is a systematic and objective accounting procedure that enables organisations to measure a range of internal and external factors not covered by financial auditing*" (Spreckley, 1981). These definitions emphasize the key feature of social audit as being a tool which expands on financial audit to assess the broader impacts of an organisation's activities.

In other words, social audit may be defined as an in-depth scrutiny and analysis of working of any public utility *vis-à-vis* its social relevance. Garry Woller, in USAID Social Audit Tool Handbook described Social Audit as "an examination of the records, statements, internal processes, and procedures of an organization related to its social performance. It is undertaken with a view to providing assurance to the quality and meaningfulness of the organization's claimed social performance." On the basis of above, it is evident that social auditing is a process by which organizations can account for, report on, and improve their social performance. It indicates and quantifies the social impact and ethical behaviour of an organization in relation to its aims and those of its stakeholders (Woller, 2008).

Agrawal, N.P., explaining the meaning of Social Audit has mentioned, "Government non-commercial organisations termed as departments are operated with a view to provide facilities to public at large. Public concern for the ways in which organisations upheld their social responsibilities has created a tremendous pressure for social audits" (Agarwal, Mishra and Agarwal, 2008).

Blake, Frederick and Myers define the term Social Audit as "A systematic attempt to identify, analyze, measure (if possible), evaluate and monitor the effect of an organization's effect on society and on the public well-being" (Blake, Frederick and Myers, 1976).

World Bank Institute observed, "A social audit aims to make organizations more accountable for the social objectives they declare. Characterizing an audit as social does not mean that it does not examine costs and finances: its central concern is how resources are used to achieve social objectives, including how resources can be better mobilized to meet those objectives. Social audits involve more than just examining internal records, but include the experience of the people the organization or service is intended to serve. In addition, social audits strengthen a community's voice, not only by allowing people to express their views through surveys, but through formal mechanisms of participation in interpreting evidence and developing solutions. The entire process builds capacities at national and local levels, both in community organizations and among service providers (World Bank Institute, 2007).

MoRD's Social Audit Manual has clarified that the social audit process goes beyond accounting for money that has been spent to examine whether the money was spent properly and has made a difference to people's lives (MoRD, 2015).

A social audit verifies how programs and services are being carried out, with the goal of making them better and more reflective of social, environmental, and community objectives. A social audit is a process that collects information on an organization's resources. The information is then analyzed and shared publicly. Although the term "audit" may imply the mere examination of costs and finance, a social audit's central concern is how resources are used for social objectives. The term social audit refers to the audit of the social responsibility role performed by an entity. Social auditing provides an assessment of the impact of an organisation's non-financial objectives through systematically and regularly monitoring its performance and the views of its stakeholders.

## SOCIAL AUDIT IN INDIA

Social audit in India is part of international trend towards greater accountability in different development programmes. The concept of Social Audit is comparatively new in India which is globally known as People's Audit or Public Audit. In Indian context, social audit found mention in the recommendations of Ashok Mehta Committee (1977) constituted to give recommendations to revive panchayti raj institutions with new vigour and greater developmental role at the grass root level. The Committee recommended establishment of "Social Audit Cell" at the district level as a watch dog agency to monitor the utilization of funds earmarked for the socio-economic development of weaker sections. Later, 73rd Constitutional Amendment Act, 1993 provided constitutional status to Panchayati Raj Institutions. This new situation made Government of India to constitute Dilip Singh Bhuria Committee (1994) which recommended bestowing statutory status upon the Gram Sabha to conduct the Social Audit at the Panchayat level. Defining social audit, the committee said that the audit would not be in nature of financial audit or even of general programme discussions. Making it more specific, the committee emphasized that records would be subjected to close scrutiny and the criterion would be not financial disbursement but whether the intended benefits had reached the target groups. In context of Panchayati Raj, Vision Foundation defined, "Social Audit as a process in which, details of the resources, both financial and non-financial, used by public agencies for development initiatives are shared with the people, often through a public platform. Social Audit allows people to enforce accountability and transparency, providing the ultimate users an opportunity to scrutinize development initiatives" (Vision Foundation 2005). In India, civil society organisations (CSOs) like Mazdoor Kissan Shakti Sangthan (MKSS), Parivartan, etc. facilitated people's audit or public audit, particularly of some developmental schemes, in the last decade of the $20^{th}$ century. These audits played a crucial role in educating people and enabled them to put pressure on the political parties and the administrative system to take corrective measures. These early processes paved the way for the introduction and acceptance of social audit.

## EMPIRICAL EVIDENCES FROM INDIA

In 1993, with the enactment of the 73rd Constitutional Amendment by the government, it became compulsory to take a review of all the development programmes executed which it self is a social audit although the word social audit has not been used. Village communities were empowered to conduct such a review of all development work in their respective villages and the concerned authorities were duty bound to facilitate them. However, because of lack of clarity on how to conduct a social audit, most citizens in rural India were unable to effectively exercise their powers. Shah *et al.* in their study in 12 states across India, found that social audit by Gram Sabha was seriously carried out in only 10 of the 40 works; in ten more cases, it was done by the block administration, in four by NGOs and in two by the district administration. In case of more than a dozen works, no social audit was carried out by anyone (Shah *et al.*, 2010).

Despite of this quandary, there have been endeavours by fits and starts which paved the way for social audits, a few such empirical evidences from different states in different schemes and programmes are reproduced here:

**a) *Odisha*:** Action Aid India, a non governmental organization undertook a unique initiative called,"Samajik Samikhya" to evolve a model social audit process by the people and activists in Jharnipalli, a gram panchayat consisting of nine villages, located in Bolangir District, Odisha. Action Aid India discussed the idea of social audit, the records were studied. The team started collecting information related to various developmental works in the villages completed during the past three years, namely 1998–99, 1999–2000, and 2000–01. A team of volunteers from various organisations and villages stayed in each village for four days in order to verify the analysed the information. Access to information related to many development initiatives such as the public distribution system (PDS), non-timber forest produce (NTFP) such as Tendu leaves, Social Forestry and DPEP, was refused, and within the records made available, there were gaps. Measurement books were not available for engineering works, and utilisation certificates were missing for all the works, although two days before the social audit a few of these were made available. On the day of Public Hearing, around 2500 people mostly belonging to the villages under Jharnipalli GP, gathered to participate in the first opportunity of holding people in power accountable for their actions. People were then given time to read the visual presentations, seek clarifications and to check the records. It was discovered that all the ghost works had something in common – they had all claimed to have used the same tractor (and its driver) for transporting materials into various villages, with the same vehicle number, the same village, the same driver who signed on receipts. One of the gram sabha members informed everyone that this was the Secretary's own tractor! Subsequently, it was also revealed that the tractor had not been with the Secretary over the three years, though it appeared consistently on the records. There were instances of violation of norms and guidelines for minimum and equal wages, execution of works by contractors, breaching of estimates, and converted technical data into information that could be easily triangulated with the villagers. There were many muster rolls with false names, migrated and elderly people who had not worked at all. The wages in muster rolls were recorded higher than the amounts actually paid to the labourers. The failure of the local bureaucracy to monitor and check the possibilities of corruption was also brought out. There were many instances when they were in collusion.

***Learning:*** It became clear to the rural folk that social audit is indeed a powerful tool in the hands of the people, but the pilot also indicated the challenges in implementing it. It became clear that social audit is indeed a powerful tool in the hands of the people, but the pilot also indicated the challenges in implementing the processes. It has to be preceded by people's capacity building, both to carry forward this intensive process, and to protect the vulnerable from the wrath of the powerful. The relative lack of participation in the meeting of people from the poor and marginalised sections can only be speculated on. Lack of political awareness and marginalisation of specific groups were issues that need to be addressed to make such processes successful (Action Aid India, 2002).

**b) *Rajasthan*:** In April 2006 in Dungarpur District of Rajasthan, Mazdoor Kisan Shakti Sangathan (MKSS), an NGO, joined with other non-governmental organizations to conduct a social audit. The audit focused on program funds spent in Dungarpur under National Rural Employment Guarantee Act (NREGA). Over the seven days, participants visited every village and worksite where NREGA programs were operational. They met with 1,40,000 workers approximately helping to build roads, dams, wellsetc. Under the NREGA, discussed the operation of the program with them, and checked whether the program was being run according to NREGA standards. The social audit in Dungarpur identified many infringements, such as non-payment of minimum wages, late wage payments, and poor work site facilities. The pattern of wage payments also raised serious concern: in most of the work sites, laborers were paid much less than the statutory state minimum wage rate per day. All of these issues were raised in a public forum with the district administration, which promised corrective action.

***Learning*:** While a social audit may benefit from the involvement of a non-governmental organization, such third-party participation is not always necessary; an empowered community can undertake social audits by itself. However, non-governmental organizations can provide important assistance to a community undertaking a social audit by (1) training community members on the social audit process, (2) accessing information required to conduct the social audit, (3) helping collate and disseminate information to the community, and (4) documenting the social audit findings and following up with public officials to demand action.

c) ***Andhra Pradesh*:** The study, "Standing under the Arch", commissioned by the World Bank with support from the Government of Andhra Pradesh, and carried out by Intellecap, endeavoured to understand the effects of the process of social audits on the awareness levels of stakeholders, changes in programme implementation and developments in grievance redressal. Social Audits in Andhra Pradesh had been evolving since they began. In order to arrive at the most appropriate process for conducting these audits, inputs were taken from agencies that had conducted similar audits in other parts of the country, and adapted to suit the context of the state of Andhra Pradesh. Social Audits were being conducted in all the districts where NREGA in Andhra Pradesh was being implemented. The SPIU was responsible for taking all policy and management decisions related to the conduct of Social Audits on NREGA. The Social audit team conducts the social audit in the village through a process of door to door visits, screening of a film on social audits, and a Grama Sabha meeting for discussing issues related to implementation of NREGS. During this period, they queried the villagers on all aspects of the programme. The team also ensures that any wage seekers who would want to represent their grievances in the Social Audit Forum are appropriately informed of the date and encouraged to travel to the venue. The Social Audit forum also provides space for all stakeholders to interact at a neutral venue. The findings of the study indicate substantial changes in the level of awareness among wage seekers that social audits brought about a better awareness amongst the wage seekers regarding the programme, increasing from 39% in the first round to 98% in the third round; the Social Audit team gave them information regarding their entitlements and procedures under the programme. A part from wage payment delays and general village problems, not many specific problems were reported.

***Learning*:** The Social audit forum was thought as a good mechanism for bringing corrupt functionaries to book; most of the groups had knowledge of the payments, equal wages, muster rolls, and to a certain extent payment slips and accounts. Many groups mentioned that the Social audit was undertaken to catch corrupt people within the programme; Many groups reported that the Panchayat and Gram Sabha had met and resolved some of their common problems. Social audits under NREGA in Andhra emerged as the source for the people to know how the money was utilized. The experience of Andhra proved social audit a success.

**d) *Himachal Pradesh*:** In Himachal Pradesh, an initiative was undertaken for preparation of participatory Gram Panchayat Development Plan (GPDP) in Gram Panchayat Basha, Kandaghat Development Block in Distt. Solan by HP State Institute of Rural Development, Shimla in 2011 as a pilot project. Gram Panchayat Basha with five wards was comparatively an underdeveloped area since poor road connectivity, concentration of scheduled caste population, low health and educational indicators and challenges of sustainable livelihoods, crop protection from wild animals were the factors hindering its development. A well conceived methodology was adopted for this ambitious project which directly aimed at achieving the targets in a limited period of time. The first step involved imparting formal knowledge through training intervention and the second was imparting skills by actually working in the field. The capacity building initiative included training on development programmes, micro planning, participatory rural appraisal, preparation development plan and group exercise for the field work. The participants were organized into five homogenous groups with equal distribution of different stakeholders. Each group was assigned the task to cover one ward by transact walk and to organize cluster meetings to assess infrastructure available and the requirements of people in the pre designed formats. The complete process was undertaken with development ownership by the youth and other enthusiastic dwellers of the village. A first draft of Gram Panchayat Development Plan was prepared at each ward which was shared at Ward Gram Sabha for the suggestions and observations of residents. The Ward Plans were consolidates into Gram Panchayat Development Plan presented in the Gram Sabha for social audit for further claims and objections of the people. It was first time in the history of GP Basha that Deputy Commissioner, Solan and all the District Level Head of the Departments attended the Gram Sabha. All the District Level Head of the Departments gave their commitments to the schemes included in the plan for time bound implementation in the Gram Sabha itself. The GPDP was converted into Action Plan. To institutionalize the implementation of plan, it was approved by the Gram Sabha to constitute five sectoral committees at Gram Panchayat level. The 29 subjects entrusted to PRIs under Development Planning on matters in Eleventh Schedule (Article 243G) of Constitution formed the basis for allocation of subjects to these committees. The Action Plan was put to social audit by the members of Gram Sabha themselves after a quarter when no representative from District Administration or SIRD attended the meeting but the villagers found that their smaller issues had resolved, work on other issues had started and they were hopeful that development was not far away from their village. Each committee was headed by Elected PRI Representative and the Line Departments officials, members of CBOs, SHGs, and Volunteers were the members of these committees. The same youth and other enthusiastic dwellers of the GP Basha helped all the 24 Gram Panchayats of Kandaghat Block to prepare their development plans, later.

***Learning***: The participatory model for preparation and social auditing of GPDP was evolved by taking along all the direct and indirect stakeholders within a time period. Local volunteers with knowledge of inherent needs of their native area played a dynamic role in preparation of a development plan over a short duration of time. The initiative and effort proved that grassroot planning is possible and the local volunteers can play a dynamic role. The capacity development of all the stakeholders is an important aspect and suitable prescription administered through participatory training; the community and PRIs can do justice with their role and responsibility. The determination, commitment and sincerity in the endeavour with the support of administration were the key to success. All the stakeholders can play their role effectively in a convergent manner which ultimately leads to empowerment of people and strengthening of Panchayati Raj Institutions for decentralized planning.

## SOCIAL AUDIT IN MGNREGA

In the year 2005, the Government of India has taken a strategic initiative to implement Mahatma Gandhi National Rural Employment Guarantee Act (Govt. of India 2005) with statutory provisions through a specifically designed scheme. Section 3 of Mahatma Gandhi National Rural Employment Guarantee Act provided a legal guarantee of 100 days wage employment to every rural household whose adult family members volunteer to do unskilled manual work at the wage rate notified for the purpose in the respective states in a financial year. Apropos of it, the MGNREG Scheme in all the states of India has been envisioned to be implemented through participation of community in a transparent manner through the public accountability of the implementing agencies. Section 17 of the Mahatma Gandhi National Rural Employment Guarantee Act (2005) mentioned the concept of social audit as means of continuous public vigilance. Different changes in the provisions for social audit through rules, guidelines and instructions have been brought in by the GoI but these efforts failed to deliver the envisioned results as reports of scams, embezzlement, irregularities in MGNREGA have kept pouring in. The desired social audit could not take place since the structures described in rules, guidelines and instructions were deficient of administrative and political support in most of the states although Government of India notified Social Audit Rules in 2011 which provided a homogeneous structure and framework for undertaking social audit in all the states.

### Institutionalization of Social Audit in MGNREGS

Though provision of social audit has been made compulsory in different programmes of development sector *e.g.* National Rural Health Mission, Sarv Shiksha Abhiyan, Integrated Watershed Management Programme, Indira Awas Yojna, Backward Regions Grants Fund, Rajiv Gandhi Vidyutikaran Mission and National Drinking Water Mission etc. but it has hardly taken place there. Social audit is taking place in MGNREGA mostly on paper since it is a statutory compulsion under Section 17 of MGNREG Act.

Gram Sabha has to monitor execution of works within Gram Panchayat besides conducting regular social audits of all the schemes. In this respect, Gram Panchayat is under obligation to make available all relevant documents including the muster rolls, bills, vouchers, measurement books, copies of sanction orders and other connected books of account and papers to the Gram Sabha. But as observed in NREGA Reforms, (2009) that there is no real social audit process taking place in any location nor is there any system in place to do so. Social audits have been done to complete a formality. Monitoring and vigilance systems are either not present or inactive. Panchayat Secretaries have floated vigilance committees by entering a few names from the GP in their records. These names are also used for "ratification" by gram sabhas of various decisions. However, these members do not themselves know either of their membership of these committees or about their duties or powers. The worst thing that could have happened to social audit is the process of inviting tenders for conducting them. Taking cognizance of such ground realities, Ministry of Rural Development, Govt. of India notified Social Audit Rules. 2011 for all the states. The rules provided that audit of schemes shall include social audit and Director Local Fund audit to carry out audit of the accounts of a scheme under the Act. It has been further clarified that state governments to facilitate conduct of social audit in every GP at least once in six months and summary of findings shall be submitted by the state government to the Comptroller and Auditor General of India. With a view to institutionalize the system, state governments have been entrusted the responsibility to indentify or establish, under the act, an independent organisation called as Social Audit Unit. The said Social Audit Unit shall be responsible for building capacities of Gram Sabha for conducting social audit; towards this, identify, train and deploy suitable resource persons at village, block, district and state level drawing from primary stakeholders and civil society organisations with grass roots experience; prepare social audit reporting formats, resource material, guidelines and manuals for social audit process; awareness creation among NREGS workers; facilitation of verification of records; facilitating smooth conduct of social audit and putting social audit reports in public domain. The rules ensured providing all details of programme implementation with independence from NREGS implementing agency without its any interference in the process of social audit. Though Social Audit Units have been constituted in most of the states or in the process of constitution but less is heard about social audits conducted by them. The independence of Social Audit Units working under infrastructural, administrative, financial and functional control of government hardly have the liberty to do the justice with the assigned responsibility as their own sustainability will be in peril since the governing body of SAU is overpowered by NREGS implementing agency. In contrast to it, Social audit is being used on a massive scale in MGNREGS in Andhra Pradesh and Sikkim. In both the states, the social audits, as a common factor, are being conducted by the civil society organizations.

## MODEL FOR EFFECTIVE FOR SOCIAL AUDIT

On the basis of the discussions narrated in the preceding paragraphs, a co-relational model for social audit of any scheme or programme has been illustrated in the chart given below to ensure social accountability through the fulfillment of social objectives from social audit.

**Chart:** Social Audit Co-relational Model

1. ***Social Audit Practices*:** The prevailing practices of conducting social audit in the area provide an insight into the modus operandi of implementation of a scheme or programme. The analysis will reveal a picture of practical aspects related to coverage of social objectives of scheme while undertaking social audit in the gram panchayats. The knowledge of officials on rules, guidelines and provisions of scheme strengthen the base of scheme on one hand and provide the evidence of delivery of services to the people on the other. In addition to this, institutionalization of procedures of conducting social audit in the gram panchayat can indicate exact status. The social audit practices can be triangulated with the perceptions of the community which will present an actual status of delivery of benefits to them.
2. ***Social Audit Methodologies*:** The methodologies being followed for undertaking social audit show its direction towards achievement of objectives. The most important factor in this regard is the process followed for conducting social audit in the area under study as well as holding the public hearing or gram sabha meeting. These three factors joined with transparency followed in the process of social audit divulge the methodologies followed by officials and panchayati raj institutions.
3. ***Knowledge on Social Objectives*:** The social objectives referred to the deliverables from the implementation of scheme or programme will include knowledge to both demand and supply sides including the benefits from the scheme to all the stakeholders, especially to the direct stakeholders. The rights available to community, entitlements, protection of rights and understanding of stakeholders on the social objectives to be analyzed to draw conclusionsin this dimension.
4. ***Performance on Social Objectives*:** The social objectives, as discussed in the preceding dimension, are to be reviewed in terms of performance *i.e.* to which extent the expectations of direct stakeholders had been met. To ascertain the performance, the viewpoint of direct and indirect beneficiaries is to be monitored and presented to gauze the status on account of right based entitlements, exercising the

rights under the programme, access to officials for rights or relief and nurturing rights and entitlements.

5. ***Social Accountability***: Social accountability means answerability and responsiveness towards the society, the direct and indirect stakeholders. The social accountability involves the responsiveness of executing agencies *i.e.* officials, members of Gram Panchayat and others involved in execution/implementation of programme at Gram Panchayat level. The accountability meant responsiveness towards beneficiaries in particular and rural community at large. The information from stakeholders on four dimensions *viz.* monitoring and review of services to people, verification of activities/works executed, public hearing in gram sabha and impact of social audit are to be collected and analyzed to ascertain the social accountability, the end objective of social audit. The frequency of organizing gram sabha and conducive environment for the people to present their stakes in gram sabha, affording opportunity to raise voice and giving reasonable responses; all are the indicators of social accountability. In such a scenario, the dream of social accountability will turn into reality.

## SOCIAL AUDIT IN PRIs

A remarkable change in the democratic structure of governance has taken place in India following the 73rd Constitutional Amendment Act. The Act was the culmination of a historic political move towards deepening democracy and advancing development through decentralization by making Panchayati Raj Institutions (PRIs). The Act aimed at building up PRIs as institutions of self governance. Panchayati Raj has the capacity to bring governance processes closer to the people and to create both representative and participatory forms of governance.

Democratic decentralisation in Panchayati Raj System entails a system of governance in which citizens possess the right to hold local public officials accountable through the use of elections, grievance meetings and other democratic means such as social audit or citizen surveys etc. Decentralisation is purported to be democratic in that the key word is accountability of officials to the local public. Accountability of local institutions is a precondition for creating trust in the minds of the people. The expectations of the people from the PRIs do not remain confined only to the prevention of abuse of power or dishonesty in the use of public resources; but expect government to be responsive to their needs, wishes, and preferences. As such, the local government institutions must remain accountable for being responsive to the needs of the citizens they serve. In this context, Gram Sabhas where development initiatives are discussed with details of the income and expenditures, have resulted in greater involvement of people besides facilitating transparency and accountability at the village level as well as propelling the process of consultation and participation. These provisions have a direct impact on the citizens in the sense that now they can keep a check on the functioning of the local bodies. The experience gained from the experiment of Jan Sunvais (Public Hearings) in Rajasthan, Andhra Pradesh and Odisha is a proof that the citizens demand accountability on the floor and the funds cannot be misutilized for the fear of public shame. The villagers demand for all documents related to works undertaken with public funds under the social audit public hearing meetings. The Panchayat Pradhans in several villages have paid up the recoveries demanded by the people and Jan Sunvais have been highly effective in mobilizing villages on the issues of transparency and accountability. It is hoped that in the times to come, the local institutions will reconcile the ethical values of fair play and integrity, democratic values of rule of law, participation, responsiveness, transparency, and corporate values of providing services in an efficient and effective manner and will ultimately achieve the goal of decentralization besides holistic development of gram panchyats. Social audit to be made an integral part in the enshrined objectives of the Gram Panchayat Development Plan as an order of the day.

## CONCLUSIONS

The practice of Social Audit results into monitoring of social and ethical impact and performance of the organization and its impact on stakeholders; it further helps to ascertain that quantum of the mission and values of the organization it is living up. A participatory social audit provides a basis for shaping management strategy in a socially responsible and accountable way and to identify opportunities and potential problems. The findings of social audit facilitates improvement in social performance and social impact on communities, increase in the accountability to the groups it serves. In a retrospective effect, social audit may be fault finding process but it has trickled down the message of transparency and accountability in the functioning of PRIs for the prospective effect. This impact further percolates as potential benefits such as credibility among the villagers about the transparent and accountable functioning of panchayati raj institutions, increased confidence in social areas; and improves financial performance for the establishment of Gram Swaraj.

## REFERENCES

Action Aid India. (2002). Samajik Samikhya: A Social Audit Process in a Panchayat in Orissa. PLA Notes 43.

Agarwal N.P., Mishra B.K. and Agarwal S. (2008). Human and Social Audit. RBSA Publisher. Jaipur.

Blake D.H., Frederick W.C. and Myers M.S. (1976). Social Auditing. Praeger Publishers. New York.

Centre for Environment Concern. (2006). Report of Social Audit in Ananthpur District of Andhra Pradesh. Unpublished. Hyderabad.

GoI. (2005). Section 17, "Mahatma Gandhi National Rural Employment Guarantee Act, 2005. New Delhi.

Medawar C. (1992). Power and Dependence: Social Audit on the Safety of Medicines. Better World Books Ltd Dunfermline FIF. United Kingdom.

MoRD. (2015). Social Audit Manual. New Delhi.

Parthasarthy M. (1988). Social Audit and Audit of Public Utilities. Auditing Public Utilities. Ashish Publishing House. New Delhi.

PRIA. (2013). Participatory Social Audit: A Tool for Social Accountability-Module – I. New Delhi.

Ramanathan K. Y. (1976). Towards a Theory of an Individual Firm. Accounting Review.

Shah T. *et al.* (2010). Asset Creation through Employment Guarantee? Synthesis of Student Case Studies in Nine states of India. International Water Management Institute (IWMI). New Delhi.

Spreckley F. (1981). Social Audit: A Management Tool for Co-operative Working, Beechwood College. UK.

Vision Foundation. (2005). Social Audit: Gram Sabha and Panchayati Raj. Planning Commission. New Delhi.
Woller G. (2008). USAID Social Audit Tool Handbook. Chemonics International Inc.
World Bank Institute. (2007). Empowering the Marginalized: Case Studies of Social Accountability Initiatives in Asia. Washington D.C.
World Bank. (2007). Standing Under the Arch: Understanding Social Audits in the context of the Andhra Pradesh Rural Employment Guarantee Scheme. Intellecap. The World Bank and SPIU (GoAP).

---

***Dr. Rajeev Bansal*** is currently working as Research Officer in Himachal Institute of Public Administration and has served as the Director, Social Audit Unit of Himachal Pradesh. He has written several research papers and has conduted numerous trainings for officials and elected representatives.

# 11

# Capacity Building for Strengthening Panchayats: A Review

SHABEEN ARA[13]

## INTRODUCTION

With the implementation of welfare Schemes such as National Rural Employment Guarantee Scheme which is extended all over the country, the duties and responsibilities of the elected representatives of Panchayats is increasing manifold. In order to understand the complexities of these responsibilities and to fulfill the aspirations of their constituencies, the elected representatives need strong support in the form of Training and Capacity Building.

To address the challenges of rural unemployment, food security and regenerate the village economy in India and in order to realize the goals that set out for it, PRI plays an important role. There need to be first and foremost human capacities. The capabilities of these human capacities need to be developed so that they are able to undertake the responsibility mandated to them. Human capacities and capabilities further need to be backed by proper supporting institutions, which act as decision support systems, assisting in concurrent monitoring of outcomes and better management of the schemes initiated. Capacity building is not an ordinary shortage of staff and lack of training facilities but the

[13] Dr. Shabeen Ara is Editor in DY Patil Vidyapeeth (Deemed University), Pune.
**Corresponding author*: E-mail: drshabeenara@gmail.com

dynamic process of developing, strengthening and institutionalizing the 'rules of game', norms, standard operating procedures, skills, abilities, and resources that organizations, communities and individuals need to survive, adapt, and thrive in the fast-changing world of policy implementation.

## CAPACITY BUILDING

Capacity building, broadly speaking, has two major aspects; for organizations, it relates to whole gamut of governance, administration (including human resources, financial management, and legal matters), business processes, program development, evaluation, and policy changes for innovation. For individuals, capacity building refers to excellence in individual performance, leadership development, socializing managerial values, technical skills, training opportunities, organizing abilities, and other areas of personal and professional development that includes sensitivity to values of equity, participation and inclusion. Thus, individual empowerment eventually needs to result in the 'communitization of capacities' especially marginalized and socially excluded groups in the society.

The $7^{3rd}$ Constitutional Amendment Act 1993 gave Constitutional Status to Panchayats at the District, Intermediate and Village levels. During the first fourteen years following the enactment of the Amendment has resulted in substantially achieving the objective of broad basing political empowerment of people. However, the spirit of Part IX of the Constitution is essentially that elected Panchayats function as institutions of self-government in rural areas. The emphasis is to empower them with certain functional mandates, give them a significant degree of autonomy and impart to them an element of self-reliance and self-sufficiency.

The Implementation of Part IX of the Constitution and empowering Panchayats as institutions of local self-government, in the letter and spirit of Part IX of the Constitution. Hand-in-hand with the re-orientation of Central Schemes and Programmes, it has now the immediate responsibility to assist and support States in strengthening Panchayats to more effectively perform the functions devolved to them.

## ADMINISTRATIVE STRENGTHENING AND CAPACITY BUILDING OF PANCHAYATS

Ministry of Panchayati Raj has urged States and union Territories to devolve powers to the Panchayats in accordance with the Constitutional stipulation. The Ministry has provided assistance to States for capacity building of Panchayats through the Rashtriya Gram Swaraj Yojna (RGSY), Capacity Building grant of the Backward Regions Grant Fund (BRGF) and Panchayat Mahila Evam Yuva Shakti Abhiyan (PMEYSA) and promoted e-enablement of Panchayats through the e-Panchayat scheme. An untied grant is provided to Panchayats through States for bridging critical gaps in local infrastructure in 250 backward districts on the basis of decentralized planning under BRGF.

## RASHTRIYA GRAM SWARAJ YOJNA (RGSY)

The objective of the Rashtriya Gram Swaraj Yojana is to assist States for Training and Capacity Building of elected representatives of Panchayati Raj Institutions so that they can effectively perform the functions devolved and the schemes entrusted to them. The need for Training and Capacity Building of elected representatives and officials of Panchayati Raj Institutions at all the three levels of Zilla Parishad, Block Panchayat and Gram Panchayat cannot be underscored. The main purpose of the scheme is upgradation of knowledge and skills and attitude of Panchayat elected representatives to better perform their responsibilities towards the Panchayat.

Orientation of the key officials associated with the functions devolved to Panchayats for effectively serving and facilitating the Panchayats in the performance of devolved functions. On the one hand these officials represent a vast pool of detailed technical knowledge pertaining to the departments they serve and therefore, can play an important facilitatory role in advising Panchayat elected representatives and imparting to them their wisdom. On the other, these officials also would greatly benefit from imbibing lessons drawn from the grass-root level experiences of elected representatives, who will bring to mutual interactions their significant local knowledge of ground level nuances (MoRD, 2001).

## THE BACKWARD REGIONS GRANT FUND (BRGF)

BRGF is a program designed to "address regional imbalances in development." Strengthen Panchayat and Municipality-level governance with more appropriate capacity building, to facilitate participatory planning, decision making, implementation and monitoring, to reflect local felt needs. Provide professional support to local bodies for planning, implementation and monitoring their plans, Improve the performance and delivery of critical functions assigned to Panchayats, and counter possible efficiency and equity losses on account of inadequate local capacity (PIB, 2012).

## PANCHAYAT MAHILA EVAM YUVA SHAKTI ABHIYAN

The entrance of elected women representatives (EWRs) and elected youth representatives (EYRs) into the grassroots polity through elections to the PRIs in massive numbers is a relatively new political phenomenon in India.

Through the provision in the 73rd Constitutional Amendment for the reservation of one-third of total elective seats for women in all three tiers of the Panchayati Raj Institutions, the number of grassroots women, who have come to positions of elective responsibility is around 10 lakhs. While this is a revolutionary change, the actual fact is that the majority of these women continue to be hampered by capacity and knowledge shortfalls and institutional, political and societal constraints. Most elected women representatives (EWRs) being first-timers, lack technical knowledge and administrative skills. Their own lack of self-confidence makes it difficult for the EWRs to maneuver an unfriendly bureaucratic and administrative landscape leading them to exercise their powers only tentatively.

The need to positively address the special needs of EWRs assumes an increasing urgency in the face of the mounting demands placed on them in view of increasing financial allocations and work responsibilities of the PRIs.

## BEDEVILING ISSUES OF CAPACITY BUILDING FOR MGNREGA

Capacity Building for MGNREGA with its rights-based framework and focus on creation of 'durable assets', has the potential Issues. The Working group found the following issues bedeviling the implementation of MGNREGA with special reference to the capacity building aspects.

1. Inadequate Coordination among horizontal and vertical tiers of the government at various levels.
2. Poorly Crafted Administrative Systems. Some governments, for example, Bihar, Odishaand Chhattisgarh, continue to suffer from 'deficits' of poorly crafted and inadequate administrative and management systems at all levels.
3. Shortage of Professionals and Training Facilities.
4. Ad Hoc Appointments of Professional Staff, Inadequate Compensation and Turnover.
5. Dissatisfaction among Contract Staff. We find evidence of growing dissatisfaction of the staff especially those 'contract staff' with regard to poor working conditions and arbitrary contract appointment policies of various state governments
6. Failed experiments of social mobilization such as "Gaon Sathi" in Odishaand the idea of providing 'uniform' for mates and Rozgar Sevaks in Jharkhand, a state battling against 'uniformed and un-uniformed' Maoist rebels. At the same time there is acceptance in some states that SHGs be mobilized.
7. Lack of Strong Governance System at the National and State Level.

8. Lack of Dedicated Pro-active Teams of professionals at the Cutting Edge (CEGC, 2010).

## BEST PRACTICES OF CAPACITY BUILDING FOR STRENGTHENING PANCHAYATS

Under Article 243 G of the Constitution of India as well as the Panchayat Act of the State all the three tiers of Panchayats require to prepare plans for their areas. Some States conducted various experiments on planning from below by the Panchayat bodies and a simplified procedure for preparation of people-centered and participatory plan has been evolved in terms of its format for data collection and analysis in respect of different sectors.

Experience shows that it requires tremendous amount of sustained facilitation by dedicated experts for being able to prepare GP plans and therefore, takes time to replicate. The external facilitation also leads to acquisition of local capacities for replicating such exercises in future. The Panchayat plans will be duly integrated into the District Plans.

- Ensuring role clarity between different levels of Governments and Panchayats through 'Activity Mapping'.
- Ensuring that financial allocations to Panchayats match the functional assignments and are separately and clearly indicated in the State budgets through a separate Panchayat sector window.
- Ensuring that participative plans are prepared at each Panchayat level, which are then consolidated at the block level and finally at the district level into the district plan.
- Strengthening the capabilities of local governments in core areas of public financial management such as planning, collection of own revenues, budgeting, procurement, financial management, reporting and auditing; and
- Deepening accountability of local governments to citizens through strengthening opportunities for citizen participation and review through gram sabhas, particularly historically marginalized groups.

Most states have taken actions though in differing degrees to empower the Panchayats and are in different stages of progress.

**Bihar: "Aapki Sarkar Aapke Dwar"**

India has a PRI system as legitimate as any other body for governance in this country. The system gets its life and blood from the 73rd amendment of the Indian Constitution. Many Indian states have adopted the spirit of the 73rd amendment to an exhilarating state. The initiative in Bihar with the support of World Bank is a genuine step of the state government to help the state achieve the aspiration of the local self governance through the Panchayati Raj Institutions with Panchayat elections in 2001 and 2006 and the enactment of the Bihar Panchayat Raj Act, 2006.

Bihar aspires to achieve far more through strengthening the institutions under Panchayati Raj. The intention of the state government is to ensure the concept of local self governance at the doorsteps of the people. The concept of ***"Aapki Sarkar Aapke Dwar"*** is just the reflection of the state government's commitment to decentralization of power to the Panchayats.

In order to strengthen and accelerate the process of rural decentralization and to make PRIs effective institutions and tools for socio-economic development of the rural people and visioning them as strong Institutions of good governance and self-governance, the series of reforms were initiated which are being consistently pursued by Government of Bihar with strong commitment. It was realized that the actual benefit of PRI system is unachievable without strengthening the units of governance under the Gram Panchayat. It is, hence, proposed to ensure that with the Bihar Panchayat Strengthening Project that the state shall make adequate investments in the institution development under the PRI system at the level of Gram Panchayat. Capacity building of PRI involves various interventions which lead to better functioning in terms of governance, improved delivery of services to the citizens and utilization of available resources more efficiently. In order to strengthen PRIs as strong institutions of self and good governance, capacity building programmes have to be designed accordingly which define the functional domain of PRIs more specifically to enable them to focus their activities, in improving the quality of services delivered by them and respond to citizens' demand for diversifying the areas of service.

Planning process at the GP level cannot be sustained and quality of service delivery cannot be improved without strengthening the GPs as institutions. The other two tiers of PRI namely Zila Parishad and Panchayat Samiti also need to be strengthened to provide a wider institutional context, coordination and leadership to ensure that all three tiers of PRI institutions work in synergy to optimize benefits of the decentralized rural governance to the people at large. So interventions for institutional strengthening and installation of planning process will need to go together. Institutional strengthening in this regard will need a two-pronged support from top in terms of policy decisions, mandates, resources, manpower and capacity and a push from below. It transpires that translating all the reforms in rural local governance into reality and institutionalization of participatory planning process will require huge support for capacity building of PRIs and their support institutions.

Capacity building interventions for PRIs are multi-dimensional, which can be classified into the following categories:

- Decentralised and participatory planning process , implementation and monitoring
- Organizational dynamics and strengthening intra-tier, inter-tier, inter-institutional and inter-sector linkages and inter-personal relationships
- Manpower management with clear responsibility mapping in respect of various tasks and programmes
- More effective service delivery
- Management of various programmes/schemes with enhanced skills
- Active participation of vulnerable(women/SC/ST) in decentralized planning and decision making process

Institutional capacity implies procedures, systems, structure, roles and responsibilities, decision- making, transparency and accountability, planning, implementation and monitoring, and also mechanisms for building linkages with others. Capacity building activities for PRIs would include a totality of inputs needed by the functionaries of PRIs and their support institutions to perform their assigned responsibilities more effectively and efficiently and to improve the quality of services expected from them. Capacity building interventions for them would address attainment of adequate knowledge, overall awareness, appropriate attitude, adequate skills and self-confidence following adult learning principles and would include themes like motivation, commitment, values, self-confidence etc. (BGSYS, 2019).

## KERALA - COMMUNICATION AND AWARENESS GENERATION

Communication is one of the critical areas for effective and efficient implementation of the Development Progeammes. The Information Educational and Communication (IEC) strategies include newspapers, TV and radio spots, pamphlets and brochures to create awareness. States organised Gram Sabha to communicate key features of the Act. This helps another critical element for the strengthening of administrative systems pertains to training of different stakeholders - Village level Rural Development Functionaries, Representatives of Community Based Organisations, Grama Sabha Facilitators, SC/ST Promoters, Vana Samrakshana Samithi members and members of SHGs & NHGs (Govt. of Kerala, 2019).

## ODISHA - TO SATISFY THE LOCAL NEEDS AND ASPIRATIONS OF THE RURAL PEOPLE

Rural local Government has been in operation in Odisha, since the early years of independence with greater responsibility to satisfy the local needs and aspiration of the rural people. It is a system of direct and active involvement of the people of a local area into the administration of local affairs, for the satisfaction of local needs with the help of the local resources and through organized local efforts.The success of a democratic system largely depends upon the existence and efficient operation of such a system of local government at the grassroot level.

The 73rd Constitutional Amendment Act, 1992 transfers the representative democracy into participatory democracy with devolution of power to PRIs in the Country. The Act came into force on 24th April, 1993 and ensures the right of the states to take local factors of geographical, politico-administrative and others into consideration while adopting the new system.Odisha Panchayat laws were amended in consistent with the provision of the Act and provision of Panchayat Extension to Scheduled Area Act, 1996 (PESA). Odisha is the first State to conduct PRI election in 2002 according to PESA Act, thereby ensuring social justice to scheduled tribe communities.

However even before the 73rd Amendment of the Constitution, Odisha had taken the lead in providing reservation in favour of SCs, STs and women in 3-tier PRIs. A distinguishing feature of the Panchayati Raj System in Odisha is that either the Chairperson or the Vice-Chairperson of all the 3-tiers of PRIs is women. Despite these important roles, PSs and GPs could not emerge as institution of self Government. But factionalism, casteism, communalism and groupism and the nasty game of Politics that has been carried to the doorsteps of innocent villagers. In fact, the PR began to totter and even crumble, under the heavy weight of political factionalism, scramble for control over patronage among politician and bureaucrats, scarcity of economic resources and not the least of all, the general apathy of the people.

The entire contour (outline) of the democratic decentralization has completely changed by the 73rd Amendment Act. It is considered now as a very important department not only for the quantum of funds it handles, but also for the fact that its activities have a direct bearing on rural development and poverty alleviation. Political education and training to the representatives of the PRIs, thus required, without which they cannot become well functioning and active participants in the democratic system. The PR Department has got a state level institute at Bhubaneswar namely the State Institute for Rural Development for training and capacity building of PRI elected representatives and field functionaries. Originally it was established in 1964 by the Government of India as one of the core distinguished institutions of the country for conducting training and research programmes in Tribal and Community Development. In 1967 it was named as Tribal Orientation and Study Centre (TO&SC) under Government of Odisha. In 1975 its name was changed to State Training Institute of Community Development (STICD). From 1984 onwards as the State Institute for Rural Development (SIRD) it acts as a nodal institute of the state for training, research, evaluation and consultancy in the field PRD, Government of Odisha (Dash, 2015).

## RAJIV GANDHI PANCHAYAT SASHAKTIKARAN ABHIYAN (RGPSA) & UNDP

The role of Panchayati Raj Institutions (PRIs), the constitutionally mandated local authorities in planning economic development and imparting social justice, is critical for ensuring social inclusion. However, one of the concerns of the Government of India is the lack of capacity of panchayats to deliver their mandate. In addition, a large number of elected representatives of PRIs are unaware of their roles and responsibilities, programmes, procedures or systems. In fact, past experience has shown that mere creation of structures of elected local governments does not necessarily guarantee effective local governance. For devolution to be real and meaningful, local governments should be effectively empowered to frame regulations, take decisions and enforce their will.

It is against this background that the Rajiv Gandhi Panchayat Sashaktikaran Abhiyan (RGPSA) was launched in 2013. It is a holistic scheme of the Government of India to strengthen panchayats in the country. RGPSA aims to enhance the capacities of panchayats and gram sabhas; enable democratic decision making in panchayats; strengthen institutional structures for knowledge creation; promote devolution of powers and responsibilities to panchayats and gram sabhas; and strengthen the constitutionally mandated framework on which panchayats are founded.

UNDP with a Budget: US$ 1.25 million, along with Implementing Partner: Ministry of Panchayati Raj and Other Partner(s): Departments of Panchayati Raj in select states, Panchayat Resource Centres of select states, District level Panchayats and officials, District-level training centres, PRI elected leaders and civil society organizations is strengthening panchayats in the country since 2013 and continuing still in 2017.

## MAINTENANCE POLICY AND MANAGING MAINTENANCE OF RURAL ROADS - ILO, WORLD BANK

Rural roads are recognized as an infrastructure that provides access to social and economic services. They are an entry point for poverty alleviation and act as facilitators to create agricultural surplus, improve basic health and provide access to schools and employment opportunities. Allied agricultural activities such as animal husbandry, dairy development and fisheries, etc. are closely linked to availability of rural road network. Therefore, rural roads need to remain as we build them.

For building rural roads, the implementation of Pradhan Mantri Gram Sadak Yojana (PMGSY) launched since December 2000 has revolutionised the system of planning of road network for each District in due consultation with the Panchayati Raj Institutions (PRIs), Members of Legislative Assembly (MLAs) and Members of Parliament (MPs) and creating well engineered assets. The states are following similar standards for their own non-PMGSY rural roads. However, maintenance of these roads on a timely and regular basis continues to be an area of concern.

To address the maintenance challenge, the Ministry of Rural Development with support from the International Labour Organization and the World Bank prepared Guidance Notes for Maintenance Policy and Managing Maintenance of Rural Roads and circulated the same to all the states. Several states have formulated their maintenance policy and notified the same. This has helped in four-pronged strategy for improved maintenance namely government commitment, adequate funding, institutional reforms and implementation efficiency. This is essential so that these roads continue to help in generating agricultural surplus and provide benefits of access to our people on a sustainable basis. Maintenance of rural roads has witnessed increasing commitment from state governments in the recent past.

## COURSES AND DIPLOMA FOR CAPACITY BUILDING

As such, traditionally, various training institutions, *i.e.*, State Institute for Rural Development, Panchayati Raj Training Institutions (PRTIs), Extension Training Centres (Etc are involved in delivering schemes specific training programmes, including those aimed at improving capacities of elected representatives and officials of PRIs. Universities and research centers are also providing professional Diplomas so that government functionaries can perform well. A number of NGOs too have been working in this area either directly or in partnership with the training institutions. The Ministry of Panchayati Raj (MoPR) has also provided funds and other support under Rajiv Gandhi Panchayat Sashaktikarana Abhiyan (RGPSA) to strengthen the state and district level training institutions to enhance their CB & T delivery capabilities in partnership with the state Panchayati Raj Departments.

## THE NATIONAL INSTITUTE OF RURAL DEVELOPMENT AND PANCHAYATI RAJ (NIRD&PR)

An autonomous organisation under the Union Ministry of Rural Development, is a premier national centre of excellence in rural development and Panchayati Raj. Recognized internationally as one of the UN-ESCAP Centres of Excellence, it builds capacities of rural development functionaries, elected representatives of PRIs, bankers, NGOs and other stakeholders through inter-related activities of training, research and consultancy. In view of rapid changes in communication and technology and increasing need of massive trained manpower in rural development, NIRD has established a Distance Education Cell. The Cell is mandated to initiate a number of programmes for capacity building of development personnel of Governmental Organisations, elected representatives and educated youth to function as change managers. It offers Post Graduate Diploma in Rural Development (PGDRDM), Post Graduate Diploma in Sustainable Rural Development (PGDSRD), Post Graduate Diploma in Tribal Development Management (PGDTDM), Post Graduate Diploma in Geospatial Technology Applications in Rural Development (PGDGARD). NIRDPR from this year has started offering an online Diploma Course in Panchayati Raj (NIRDPR, 2019).

## INDIRA GANDHI NATIONAL OPEN UNIVERSITY (IGNOU)

IGNOU offers Diploma in Panchayat Level Administration & Development (DPLAD). As a result of this historic legislation and passing of Conformity Acts by various states and holding of elections in the country in mid 1990s, there were more than 3 million people elected at various levels of Panchayati Raj Institutions. While as a number of steps are being taken by various organizations to develop awareness programmes, for these elected members, there are more than million development functionaries across the country serving these institutions and working shoulder to shoulder with elected representatives. There are exercise/ activities entrusted to the Panchayats that need expertise and coordinated action by various development functionaries. This diploma programme in Panchayat Level Development and Administration through distance mode of learning is addressed towards fulfilling this task.

The major objectives of this programme are to:

a) Equip panchayat level functionaries with the necessary knowledge, skills and talents needed for strengthening local democracy and the process of decentralized planning.
b) Help them to work with elected representatives in a cooperative and coordinated fashion, and

c) Facilitate people's participation through a *denovo* approach, attitude and action by the panchayat level functionaries (IGNOU, 2019).

## THE GANDHIGRAM RURAL INSTITUTE - DEEMED UNIVERSITY

The Rajiv Gandhi Chair for Panchayati Raj Studies in the Gandhigram Rural Institute is committed to developing Panchayati Raj as an inter-disciplinary academic subject at graduate and postgraduate levels in universities and colleges. It organizes Refresher Courses on Panchayati Raj for university and college teachers to take up Panchayati Raj as a subject for teaching, research and extension. The Chair has designed a course on Panchayati Raj at postgraduate and underegraduate levels and circulated it among the universities of Tamilnadu with a request to introduce them in their universities. The publications of the Chair on different aspects of Panchayati Raj have been used as textbooks and reference books by students and research scholars working on rural development, rural economics, political science and sociology. In addition, the Department of Political Science and Development Administration, Gandhigram Rural Institute, is offering core and optional courses on Panchayati Raj to different Faculties of the Gandhigram Rural Institute and Research Scholars in the Department are encouraged to take up research problems related to Panchayats like common property resource management, empowerment of women, food security and grassroots level planning. In order to enhance the capacity of the researchers to pursue research on Panchayati Raj System with more theoretical rigour, a methodology course was conducted for the researchers who are pursuing research programmes in Panchayati Raj and Rural Development. This was supported by ICSSR, New Delhi. Gandhigram Rural University also offers Diploma in Panchayati Raj Administration (DPRA) (Gandhigram Rural University, 2019).

Shivaji University in Kolhapur offers Certificate Course in Panchayati Raj and Kuvempu University offers Diploma in Panchayati Raj (Distance)

## CHALLENGE OF SENSITISING THE YOUTH, WOMEN, SC, ST IN PANCHAYATI RAJ

The important stakeholders of the Indian population 'the youth' are still in the periphery and there is a need to bring them to the centre stage. The challenge is of sensitizing the youth in Panchayati Raj to involve them in decision making, to ensure social justice and youth representation in local bodies, and build civil society and accountability. There has also been no concerted or coordinated effort for building a movement for involving youth in Panchayat functioning. Across the country, with successive elections, panchayats are getting progressively younger leadership and representatives. The number of youth in the age group of 13-35 years, as per the 2001 census, was estimated at about 41 crore, which is anticipated to increase to about 51 crore by the year 2016. The availability of human resources of such magnitude for achieving socio economic change needs commensurate infrastructure and suitable priorities to maximize contribution to national development.

These vibrant and valuable youth partners are already included in the process of national planning and development. The remaining youth of the country similarly need to be empowered to effectively participate in the process of decision making at all levels. Having an emphasis on youth in panchayats is an immeasurable advantage. Youth can make a clean break from the past, to adopt the values of equality and secularism to create a society that is just and fair. This is an area where one needs to take a lead and create a movement aimed at greater linkage between Youth and the Panchayats.

A study for the Assessment of Knowledge, Attitude and Practice of young elected members of PRIs and young citizens comes up with the following findings (RGNIYD, 2012). In the assessment of knowledge of young citizens, it is noted that their knowledge in the aspects like Panchayat functioning, Poverty Alleviation Programmes, functions of PRIs and public redressal mechanisms, they could be rated as 'Above Average'. It is suggested that the young citizens need to be given more knowledge on some of the critical areas like service delivery system of GP, finance of PRIs and Grama Sabha. This will enable them to make necessary interventions and will equip them to contribute towards strengthening the system.

It is noted that in the service delivery system of GP, the assessment of attitude of young citizens could be rated as 'Excellent'. In the assessment of aspects like PR system and structure, functions of PRIs, finance of PRIs, Grama Sabha, Poverty alleviation programmes and Right to Information, their attitude could be graded as 'Above Average'. However, in the aspects like public redressal mechanisms, elections to PRIs and youth association in panchayat functioning, the rating could be viewed as 'Average' only.

While taking up the assessment of practice of young citizens, it is noted that no single aspect could be rated as 'Excellent'. However, in various aspects like functions of GP, service delivery system of GP and Grama Sabha, the assessment of practice of young citizens could be rated as 'Above Average'. It is noted there is a need to enhance practice of young citizens in certain critical areas like public redressal mechanisms, right to information act, poverty alleviation programmes, etc.

A composite grading of the assessment of knowledge, attitude and practice of young citizens in Panchayati Raj indicates the rating as 5.82 points, 6.50 points and 5.32 points respectively on a scale of 10 points. It is noted that assessment of attitude of young citizens is 'Above Average' whereas in terms of knowledge and practice, they could be rated as 'Average' only. Comparison between the assessment of knowledge, attitude and practice indicate that the knowledge and practice of the young citizens in Panchayati Raj stands low. There is a need to translate the positive attitude of young persons towards the panchayati raj system by providing necessary knowledge inputs to them in those aspects where their performance has been rated less and to empower them to practice effectively.

## CONCLUSIONS

The enactment of the 73rd Constitutional Amendment made it mandatory that all Panchayati Raj Acts of the states of the country should follow a uniform system, where reservations were made for women and the Scheduled Castes for the ordinary seats as well as the post of president. While the reservation of seats for women has been accepted to some extent, the same has not been the case with the reservation of president's posts for the Scheduled Castes. Reservation of seats has been provided for ordinary seats and that of office bearers for Scheduled Castes, Scheduled Tribes, women, and Backward Castes. All this makes for a large proportion of the panchayat seats being reserved for one group or the other.

However, the intensity with which people see the presence of members of Scheduled Castes occupying seats of the panchayats, which have been reserved, or even that of the office bearers, *i.e.*, presidents and vice presidents appears to be much lower. This area needs attention on the part of the Capacity Building for Strengthening Panchayats.

## REFERENCES

BGSYS. (2019). Apki Sarkar Apke Dwar. Retrived from http://bgsys.gov.in/content/project-components/capacity-building-gps on 18.03.2019.

CEGC. (2010). Final Report of the Working Group on Capacity Building: Volume I Main Report. MGNREGA, MoRD. Retrieved from http://nrega.nic.in/CEGC/CAPACITY_BUILDING.pdf on 15.03.2019.

Dash H. (2015), Odisha Review, February-March – 2015. Retrieved from http://odisha.gov.in/e-magazine/Orissareview/2015/feb-mar/engpdf/8-11.pdf

Gandhigram Rural University. (2019). Rajiv Gandhi Chair on Panchayati Raj. Retrieved from http://rajivgandhichairgri.org/ on 20.03.2019.

Govt. of Kerala. (2019). MGNREGS Capacity Building. Retrieved from http://www.nregs.kerala.gov.in/index.php/mgnregs-kerala/capacity-building on 18.03.2019

IGNOU. (2019). Diploma in Panchayat Level Administration & Development. Retrieved from http://www.ignou.ac.in/ignou/aboutignou/school/soce/programmes/detail/529/2 on 20.03.2019

MoRD. (2001). Rashtriya Gram Sawarj Yojana. Retrieved from *https://en.wikipedia.org/wiki/Swarnajayanti_Gram_Swarozgar_Yojana on 12.03.2019*

NIRD&PR. (2019). Post Graduate Diploma in Rural Development. Retrieved from http://www.nird.org.in/index.aspx on 15.03.2019.

PIB. (2012). Backward Region Grant Fund. Retrived from http://pib.nic.in/newsite/efeatures.aspx?relid=79312,%20,%20https://en.wikipedia.org/wiki/Backward_Regions_Grant_Fund on 12.03.2019

RGNIYD. (2012). Knowledge, Attitude and Practice of Youth in Panchayati Raj- A Study of Kerala. Retrieved from https://www.researchgate.net/publication/287491460_Knowledge_Attitude_and_Practice_of_Youth_in_Panchayati_Raj_-_A_Study_of_Kerala on 25.03.2019.

---

***Dr. Shabeen Ara*** is working as Editor in the DY Patil Vidyapeeth (Deemed University), Pune. She holds Ph.D. degree in Sociology from Karnataka University. She also holds a Post Graduate Diploma in Distance Education. Since 1992 she is involved in research, course development in education administration. Dr. Ara has published various papers and book reviews and has been Editor of various journals in her 25 years of service.

# 12

# Whatever Happened to Panchayati Raj?

M.A. Oommen[14]

## INTRODUCTION

Twenty-five years have gone by since India passed the 73rd/74th Constitutional Amendments (CAs) heralding decentralised governance, and 23 years since all the States passed the conformity legislations ushering in the third tier of government in Indian federal polity. Looking back, this was a momentous event, a paradigm shift in democratic governance and fiscal federalism.

While the fiscal federalism literature of the West treats citizens as customers or consumers, the CAs envisage citizens as political entities engaged in the transformation of their environment. The pattern of decentralisation in India since the Government of India Act 1935 and even after the inauguration of the Republic in 1950 was at best only a deconcentration exercise which happens when a superior assigns duties and responsibilities to a subordinate agent to carry out specific tasks. But CAs envisages a devolution package which implies autonomy in regard to assigned functions backed up by funds and functionaries.

Devolution as provided for in parts IX and IXA of the Constitution is a process towards ushering in participatory democracy. This process is set in a framework with several standardised features

[14] Centre for Development Studies, Thiruvananthapuram.
**Corresponding author*: E-mail: maoommen09@gmail.com

such as quinquennial elections, reservations for historically marginalised communities and women, the introduction of participatory institutions for governance, the creation of a State finance commission to rationalise State-sub State level fiscal relations, the establishment of a district planning committee to evaluate resource endowments, to do spatial planning, and manage the conservation of resources with a mandate to draw up a draft development plan for the district as a whole, and soon.

Besides, State legislatures have to endow local governments (LGs) with powers, authority and responsibilities to function as institutions of self-government tasked to prepare and implement schemes "for economic development and social justice". But looking back, the central tendency of local democracy in India tells a story of indifference if not neglect. After a quarter century of decentralisation, local expenditure as a percentage of GDP is only 2 percent compared with the OECD (14 per cent), China (11 per cent), and Brazil (7 per cent).

## SOME AUTONOMY

To be sure, while the CAs provided all the necessary conditions, other conditions were left to be designed by the State legislatures and governments. With no champions to keep afloat the much-needed social demand for deepening democracy, an agenda for economic reforms, demonetisation, JAM and the like took precedence over this foundational reform. For example, as the CAs do not provide a separate list for local governments, the Eleventh Schedule that lists 29 subjects for PRIs, and the Twelfth Schedule with 18 subjects for urban local governments, carry no operational meaning because almost all local functions are State-Concurrent. The need for clear functional assignments broken up into activities and sub-activities to ensure clarity in roles and responsibilities was loud and clear.

Kerala showed the way in activity mapping and amended the Panchayat and Municipality Acts as early as 1998. The Ministry of Panchayati Raj since its inception in 2004 made a drive to encourage activity mapping in the States but it slowed down and reached nowhere. Several States that took to activity mapping (Chhattisgarh, Madhya Pradesh) put them in cold storage for years. Core functions like water supply, sanitation, link roads, street lighting, maintenance of community assets etc., continue to be in the hands of State governments. The MPLAD and MLALAD (local area development) continue to bypass local governments. The mission-based administration of schemes by some States (Gujarat, Kerala) dampen the smooth growth of democratic decentralisation. State Finance Commissions, a counterpart of the Union Finance Commission, are not independent bodies in most States.

## FLOUTING THE CONSTITUTION

It has become clear that States can flout the Constitution with impunity. The mandate to establish a district planning committee to prepare a draft development plan has been violated and distorted in most States. In all States, parallel bodies encroach on the functional domain of LGs and continue to grow unchecked. States like Punjab, Haryana and Rajasthan abolished local taxes. Haryana created a rural development agency under the chief minister. ThroughoutIndia there is a swing towards centralisation. To crown everything, the judiciary seems to be ignorant about or indifferent to sustaining decentralisation as an integral task of deepening democracy.

The Prime Minister should not be a silent spectator to the erosion of democracy at the local level. We live in a time when we celebrate ceremonial values and neglect instrumental values. The outcome of the 73$^{rd}$/74$^{th}$ CAs has been a classic case of upholding ceremonial process rather than instrumental process. The political scientist Alexis de Tocqueville famously said that for democracy to succeed it should take roots in the "habits and hearts" of the people.

What happened to reservation for women and historically marginalised communities? The stark reality is that the empowerment of women and inclusion with dignity of the excluded (inclusion on the terms of the excluded) is a distant dream despite a quarter century of decentralised governance. Women, adivasis and dalits remain largely excluded. Certainly this is to be treated as a social failure. Women's agency is as important as their well-being. Women have to be made agents of social change. Instead, they continue to suffer iniquities and inequalities.

Amartya Sen in *The Argumentative Indian* mentions six prevailing inequalities: (1) survival inequality as seen in the adverse female-male ratio against the biological reality; (2) (natality inequality (sex-specific abortion)) (3) ownership inequality; (4) unequal facilities in education, healthcare; (5) unequal sharing of household benefits and division of labour within the household; and (6) domestic violence and victimisation. All these show no signs of abating. Is growth more important than improving this situation?

## HOLES IN THE BUDGET

The financial reporting system is in disarray. Despite repeated efforts by the Eleventh, Twelfth and Thirteenth Finance Commissions, the continued absence of a reliable and consistent database calls for corrective reforms. Surely India lacks a credible financial reporting system when it comes to local governments. The Union and State budgets are vital instruments of financial control and management. Can we say this with reference to the panchayats and municipalities?

Democracy, which is a government of people, by the people, for the people, must ultimately win for it is not only an intrinsic value but is instrumental to ushering in an inclusive and just society. This cannot happen without developing democratic local governance with a sense of urgency.

(Note: Reproduced with due acknowledgement to the Hindu Buisiness Line)

---

***Prof. M.A.Oommen*** is currently associated with Centre for Development Studies, Thiruvananthapuram as Honorary Fellow and is Patron of Kerala Economic Association. He has served as Professor, Institute of Management in Government, Trivandrum, (1985-92); Professor & Head of the Department University of Calicut (1984-85); Professor & Head of the Department University of Botswana (1980-84) and Professor & Head of the Department University of Calicut (1976-80).

# 13

# Participatory Local Planning/Budgeting: An Experiment with Direct Democracy

VINAY SAHASRABUDDHE[15]

## INTRODUCTION

Democratic countries of the world, including India, have a common goal of making democracy deliver goods and services to its people in most effective manner. There is a shared vision of empowering people through good governance. And the relationship between empowerment of the people and good governance is that of chicken and egg. Good governance is the mother of popular empowerment and empowered people alone can bring about true good governance. To influence the democratic discourse world over, it is necessary that we deliberate upon ways and means of making democracy deliver and in that sense ensuring that people continue to repose their confidence in the idea of democracy.

## DEMOCRACY AND PARTICIPATION

Human beings are considered as social animals and hence collective activity is something inherent to the concept of society. Democracy also is a social process. Democracy is all about participation. If people refuse to come for voting, no matter how many candidates are contesting, true election cannot happen.

[15] Indian Council of Cultural Relations.
**Corresponding author*: E-mail: vinays57@gmail.com

Similarly, if candidates decline to stand for elections, thumping voting will be rendered meaningless. Hence, participation is inherent to the idea of democracy. Every democracy has to be participatory democracy. Democracy without participation is like a temple without worship, church without a prayer or a mosque without Namaz. Participation is the soul of democracy.

But over the years, the idea of representative democracy has been facing serious challenges. The toughest of all the challenges is the challenge of trust-deficit. People do have huge hopes from their own elected representatives but more often than not, elected representatives fail to meet the expectations of the electorate. This happens because of the two main reasons. Firstly, because of the abysmal performance of the elected representative who many a times performs poorly as their eyes are more set on perpetuating their positions mainly to overcome instability in politics. Overall, the behaviour of the elected representative makes electors lose their confidence in him or her and the representational value of the representative erodes. Secondly, oblivious of the systemic limitations; electors continue to have unreasonable expectations from their representative. With almost complete lack of serious efforts to educate and inform electorate on the part of political parties as well as Governments, these unreasonable expectations add to the growing disconnect between the electors and the elected.

## DIRECT DEMOCRACY

In response to this situation, in regions like the State of California in USA and also at several other democracies what was experimented with was the idea of Direct Democracy. As against representative democracy, Direct Democracy is more attractive and perhaps more risky as well. It is attractive because unlike in Representative Democracy, every citizen or every voter has not only just some say, but also a pro-active role in decision making. Direct Democracy offers various opportunities to the electors, offers them more leverages and in that sense empowers them in multiple ways. But at the same time, Direct Democracy also presupposes an enlightened, conscious and responsible voter-community. Here, participating voters cannot wash off their hands by putting the blame at the door of the elected representative.

## PARTICIPATORY LOCAL PLANNING

The idea of Participatory Local Planning or Budgeting has its origin in the concept of Direct Democracy. It's undoubtedly very attractive but essentially very difficult especially when one has to deal with rural people. This is because of significant differences in social and community climates in cities and in villages. Effective engagement of citizens require awareness and public education. In a way, this is more plausible in cities than in villages due to greater access to information.

So far, as the currently available literature on Participatory Planning/ Budgeting points out, Porto Alegre in Brazil, few cities in Ghana, cities like Pune and states like Kerala in India have fairly successfully experimented the idea of people's participation in budgeting. It is obvious that participatory budgeting leaves elected representatives with less amount of political power and hence reduction in available leverages. Hence, without strong political will and huge resoluteness on the part of elected representatives, this idea cannot be taken further. And yet, it is very heartening to note that several Latin American countries, countries in Europe and also cities like New York are continuing with their experiments for Participatory Budgeting.

## CITIZENSHIP ENGAGEMENT

Although Participatory Planning/ Budgeting is a process, but more than that, it is an approach, a psychological tenet, a mind-set and also a philosophy. In today's world, there cannot be any theoretical opposition to the idea of Participatory Budgeting. In fact, bureaucracy should be happy if people decide about the budget and later take responsibility of their own decisions as well. However, participatory governance in general and budgeting in particular is easier said than done. We have to remember that Participatory citizenship engagement is the prerequisite of

Participatory Planning/Budgeting. For Participatory citizenship engagement to succeed, several issues will have to be taken into consideration. These issues are as follows:-

### a. Sense of belonging and the phenomenon of non-resident villagers (NRVs)

Unlike cities, villages have a more vibrant, close knit and open social life. In cities, people very easily become faceless and hence anonymous. This normally doesn't happen in villages. But due to a new and now established phenomenon of Non Resident Villagers (NRVs), villages are in to face same kind of challenge that cities have been facing all along. If a school teacher teaching in village school, Government record keeper, a physician attached to the Primary Health Centre or for that matter even elected Head of Village Body decide to stay in a nearby town and be a visiting functionary of the village, his relationship with the villagers weakens seriously. That makes his sense of belonging to the village very superficial as to put it crudely, his stakes in the well-being of the villagers become very superficial and only matter of factly. Sadly, the number of such non-resident villagers is increasing as cities are seen as more alluring in many ways. This kind of villagers may not take the task of Local Planning/Budgeting with due seriousness and yet wield a huge influence because of their pseudo status. Should this happen, the limitations of Representative Democracy will continue to impact on village governance.

### b. Sense of Ownership of the entire village

Villager community, as pointed out by none other than Dr Babasaheb Bhim Rao Ambedkar is often a divided lot. Social divisions in villages are very sharp and difficult to evaporate. Overcoming them and creating a more assimilative milieu is not at all easy. In addition to this, it is a fact that nuclear and disjointed families are no more confined to cities. Even in villages we have independent, separate families and hence the culture of collectivism, sharing and participation is on the decline here too. In a situation like this, making villager's think of the entire village with a holistic approach and collective ownership of the whole is extremely difficult. To that end, without massive public education and cultivation of minds, the idea of common good and an approach of give-and-take for a larger and loftier cause cannot be evolved.

**c. Sense of continuity of governance: sense of past and future, longer term vision and freedom from myopia**

Governance is a continuing process. While planning/budgeting, if majoritarian thinking allows a short-term and myopic thinking to have the last laugh, due to sheer burden of numbers, longer term vision will be at great loss. In areas like Natural Resource Management (NRM), one has to think in a futuristic manner. Today's budget also have to invest in tomorrow and plan for the day after. If collective decision making inhibits such futuristic thinking for an understandable burden of urgent and important, future of present generations will also be in peril.

**d. Holistic and social integrationist approach. Rising above compartmentalism**

Participatory Planning/Budgeting process has to address concerns, aspirations and agonies of even numerically smaller sections and geographically tiny areas. To that end, majority of participants will have to rise above sectarian and narrow considerations. If this doesn't happen, Governance will cause further fragmentation of our village communities instead of uniting them. Democratic Governance framework often ends up with continued political dominance of those who are socially well established. When decision making is *via* Elected Representatives, at least for the sake of appearing to be inclusive; representatives may ensure that concerns of marginal sections are duly taken care of. But now, in a direct democracy mechanism, when people themselves are out to shape the contents of the budget, one cannot rule out the possibility that marginal actions bring left unattended. This may invite the danger of further accentuating social division as marginal section may carry a deep sense of deprivation in a situation where the doors of participation are apparently wide open.

## e. From Outsourcing to Insourcing

Before I close, there is yet another very serious challenge that I must flag here. It is the challenge of outsourcing mentality. With faster pace of life, urban people are outsourcing most of the things which normally they would do on their own. They often outsource parenting, old-age care and even relationship management. In an era of greater outsourcing, expecting people to insource something they are not accustomed to is a tall order. Let's be aware of this.

Learnings so far from the experiments in Participatory Local Planning/Budgeting in urban areas are very encouraging. There is evidence to suggest that in Brazil, after Participatory Budgeting was adopted, municipal bodies have spent more on education, sanitation and that has also seen reduction in infant mortality by some 20% which is really very remarkable. But closer home, in cities like Pune in India it has also been pointed out that low participation of poor and marginalised sections often make the process lopsided and biased.

After all, one has to remember that Direct Democracy is a tool with double-edges. What is required is adroit handling, dextrous planning and pure, unadulterated commitment. All the three commodities are unfortunately in short supply and hence the challenge is manifold. But when Democracy itself is a challenge and we all have to meet the same through Citizenship Training. Enlightened Citizens or villagers are more likely to make Participatory Local Planning/Budgeting a success. If Participatory Local Planning/Budgeting is to become a movement, building capacities of the participating individuals is a MUST.

*[Note: Paper is based on author's key note address delivered at BRICS Conference on Participatory Local Budgeting at Kochi, Kerala on 3 November, 2016]*

---

***Dr. Vinay Sahasrabuddhe*** is a Member of Parliament (Rajya Sabha) and Chairperson of Indian Council of Cultural Relations. He also heads Public Policy Research Centre, New Delhi. He has served as the Diretor General of Rambhau Mhalgi Prabodhini, Mumbai. A prolific thinker, he has been contributing to formulation, monitoring and evaluation policies for ushering in good governance in India.

# Subject Index

## F



## G



## H



## I



## K



## L



## M



## N



## O



## P